Renaissance of Classical Allusions in Contemporary Russian Media

Renaissance of Classical Allusions in Contemporary Russian Media

Svitlana Malykhina

LEXINGTON BOOKS
Lanham • Boulder • New York • Toronto • Plymouth, UK

Published by Lexington Books
A wholly owned subsidiary of Rowman & Littlefield
4501 Forbes Boulevard, Suite 200, Lanham, Maryland 20706
www.rowman.com

10 Thornbury Road, Plymouth PL6 7PP, United Kingdom

British Library Cataloguing in Publication Information Available

Library of Congress Cataloging-in-Publication Data

Malykhina, Svitlana, 1963– author.
Renaissance of classical allusions in contemporary Russian media / Svitlana Malykhina.
pages ; cm
Includes index.
ISBN 978-0-7391-7844-7 (cloth : alk. paper)—ISBN 978-0-7391-7845-4 (electronic) 1. Allusions in mass media. 2. Mass media and literature—Russia (Federation) 3. Mass media and language—Russia (Federation) 4. Russian language—Discourse analysis. I. Title.
P96.A4342R853 2014
302.230947—dc23
2013044304

∞™ The paper used in this publication meets the minimum requirements of American National Standard for Information Sciences Permanence of Paper for Printed Library Materials, ANSI/NISO Z39.48-1992.

Printed in the United States of America

Contents

A Note on Transliteration and Translation

I have used the Library of Congress system of transliteration throughout this book, with the exception of certain well-known terms and names that have been Anglicized.

Translations are my own, except where otherwise noted.

Acknowledgments

I am truly and deeply indebted to so many people that there is no way to acknowledge them all or even any of them properly. Still, I want to mention a few people here. It is important for me to recognize those professors who directly and indirectly influenced my career trajectory. In Ukraine, at Karazin Kharkiv University I was fortunate to have been taught by Dr. Neonila Boiko and Professor Viktor Marinchak. The late Dr. Rita Poddubnaia is the one of the professors who truly made a difference in my life. It was under her tutelage that I developed a focus and became interested in the social functions of literature. A very special thanks goes out to Dr. Ludmila Savchenko (my doctoral supervisor), who provided me with direction and became more than just a professor, but also a mentor and friend. I also benefited from working with the late Professor Gennady Melnikov, formerly of the Peoples' Friendship University of Russia. His intelligence and deeply critical and analytical way of looking at ideas made him a fantastic mentor. I would like to thank Prof. Doctor Habilitus Eleonora Lassan (Vilnius University, Lithuania) for taking time out from her busy schedule to serve as my external reader and for making my move to media studies possible.

Henryk Baran (my MA supervisor), Rodney L. Patterson, Sophie Lubensky, Charles Rougle, Nadia Kizenko, Robert E. Sanders, and my intellectual mentors at SUNY Albany planted seeds that they may find bearing fruit in this work. I have particular fondness for Dr. Danielle Jones, formerly of SUNY Albany, who has been not just an inspirational writer, but also a wonderful teacher, one who can do excellent work and still provide a warm, friendly, and convivial atmosphere. Especial thanks to Michael S. Gorham of the University of Florida for his deep and thorough review and invaluable critique of the manuscript. I was very lucky to have crossed paths with Professor Jeffry Brooks of John Hopkins University and Professor John

Dunn of the School of Modern Languages and Cultures, University of Glasgow, to whom I am particularly grateful. I would like to thank these scholars for their careful reading of earlier drafts of this book. They should not, however, be thought to endorse the views expressed herein.

During the writing of this book, I traveled to Pittsburgh as a part of the Summer Language Institute and to Moscow as a part of the Study Abroad Program at the University of Pittsburgh; I had to depend on the kindness and support of many. I have and still continue to learn many valuable lessons from Christine Metil of the University of Pittsburgh. My deepest affection and most profound gratitude go to Professor Bruce McConachie, Dr. Stephanie McConachie , Professor Oscar Swan, Dr. Gerald McCausland, Dr. Dawn Seckler, and Dr. Julie Draskoczy—all of the University of Pittsburgh—who helped me in a hundred different ways, but most of all I cherish our conversations, through which different cultural aspects of media became meaningful for me.

During the long years I have been working on this project, many colleagues of mine have shared with me their observations on media reception and media a udiences. Above all I am grateful to Professor Alla Nedashkivska of the University of Alberta, who read a chapter on Ukrainian media from this manuscript, providing helpful suggestions and alerting me to a number of specialized studies. Also I thank sociologist Natalya Ryabinska from the Institute of Philosophy and Sociology, Polish Academy of Sciences, for her many stimulating thoughts as well as her interest in my work.

Special thanks also go to the Slavic Library of the University of Illinois at Urbana-Champaign and the New York Public Library for opportunities to work there. I am happy to acknowledge the expert help of Helen Sullivan (Slavic Library, UIUC) and Edward Kasinec (New York Public Library's Slavic & Baltic Division, Bakhmeteff Archive of Columbia University). Members of the Summer Research Lab at the University of Illinois at Urbana-Champaign organized and sponsored by the Russian, East European, and Eurasian Center and the Summer Institute, "Visual Resources for Teaching and Research in Early East Slavic Cultures," sponsored by the National Endowment for the Humanities, provided valuable guidance and were instrumental in getting me into the field.

I would also like to thank AATSEEL, ASEEES, and the Association for Women in Slavic Studies conferences' participants, particularly Anna Pleshakova of Oxford University, for insightful discussions about my study that helped enrich my research and shaped the initial project. I am grateful to Dina Odnopozova of Yale University, whose response was particularly helpful; Yuri Shevchuk of Columbia University, who gave excellent comments on an earlier draft of my work; and Professor Alexei Shmelev of the Institute of Russian Language, Russian Academy of Sciences, for his criticism and suggestions. As usual I wish I knew how to better incorporate more of the participants' ideas into my book. I am most grateful to the journalist and writer Nadezhda Azhgikhina and the founding editor of *Russia Profile*, Andrei Zolotov, who encouraged me to consider a number of key media issues. I would also like to thank my friends in the *Novaya Gazeta* and the *New Times* for our many conversations both in Moscow as well as on the phone, our many interesting and good-spirited philosophical debates relating to this research , and my venting of frustration during my research, which enriched the experience.

I owe a special thanks to the anonymous reviewers who made numerous suggestions that led to great improvements in this book and saved me from many embarrassments. And again, any remaining errors are my responsibility. I thank my editors at Lexington Books for their invaluable encouragement and advice on every aspect of the book. I would like especially to thank Erin E. Walpole, acquisitions editor for history and Slavic studies at Lexington Books, who got me into this and has provided advice and sympathy along the way.

The Department of Languages , Literatures, and Cultures (LLC) at the University at Albany supported me during the early stages of my writing with teaching assistantships. The members of the Modern Languages at the College of the Holy Cross have been unfailingly generous and welcoming, giving me class time to present my research to students. The chairman and my colleagues in the Department of Modern Languages, Literatures, and Cultures, University of Massachusetts, provided crucial help in navigating a range of difficulties. I am also indebted to the students I had the pleasure to work with. Special thanks to Grant Bauer, John Dunn, Jacob C. Barr, and translator Viacheslav Boitchenko for their very interesting insights and solutions to difficult translation puzzles. For the careful proofreading of the early version of my manuscript, I am indebted to Catherine Burgess.

I want to express my love and special thanks to my mom, my husband, and my son, who commented on the manuscript and offered advice on every aspect. They provided encouragement and support when I needed it the most.

Although I have been influenced by many scholars, all mistakes, omissions, and errors are mine. Some of you may not agree with my interpretation and conclusions, but I do hope you all recognize my sincere attempts to acknowledge the help of those without whom this book would ever have been completed.

Introduction

The idea for this book sprang from my study focused on the rhetoric of contemporary Russian media discourse. My fascination with Russian classical literature and its implicit and explicit repercussions made through all kinds of public discourse resulted in this book. I am particularly interested in journalistic narrative about current events interpreted through the plots and larger-than-life characters from the Russian classics. Here, too, I focus on a tendency in the news media to give fresh life to old clichés while adopting what might be seen as traditional Russian values.

From a twenty-first-century perspective, the influence of classics is related to national authorities, to the mass media, to the educational system, to the literary establishment. To the journalists, Renaissance of the "old-fashioned" framework of classical literature makes it possible to create the illusion that it depicts life "as it really is," while laying bare its very "quintessence." After all, not many people have a clear recollection of life and legacy of the Russian writers, but are familiar with the names of Pushkin, Dostoevsky, Tolstoy, Chekov. At the same time, one cannot help but feel that the poetry of Pushkin, the humor of Gogol, the depth of Dostoevsky, the imaginative scope of Tolstoy, or the lyricism of Chekhov are distinctive in their own connotations and carry their own peculiar aura. After all, names impose themselves. To the media readers, it is an ability to see the rich, varied world of Russian literature that has a reputation for psychological depth, spiritual insight, and political allegory as an interpretative framework for "explaining" current events. In this book I present a broad picture of this phenomenon and the discussions surrounding it in Russia today.

This book is about media. In the last two decades, there has been a miniboom of publications on issues with regard to Russian media. Traditionally, discussions of recent mass media have dwelt on their administration and content more than rhetoric and reception, but in the end of the twentieth and the beginning of the twenty-first century, another source of attention to Russian media has been the centrality of mass media as a vehicle of culture. The organization of narrative through text and interpretation is clearly something media and literature have in common. One much-debated point, however, is whether the literary allusions enhance or obfuscate the message constructed in media discourse; are alluring allusions efficient in allowing dispersed and fragmented pieces of the literary discourse to coexist with the reflection of current events and political reality in news media? There may be several explanations as to why the Russian media question has received this attention: contemporary media studies have been highly sensitive both to developments concerning the nature of media power and to constructing a national culture and identity that reflect the collective memory.

This book is about memory. One of the functions of media discourse is to understand communication, memory, and identity. I argue that allusion is a mnemonic unit of a kind, a ready-made block for storing information, as well as symbolic representation. The allusion has a strong tendency to replace reality with its ready-made mnemonic blocks and constitute the major part of identity with a combinative, sometimes even manipulative history or a nostalgic idealization. The obliteration of the contextual use of allusions and references in media discourse leads to their misinterpretation or ironic manifestation sometimes apparently, sometimes implicitly.

This book is about identity. My interests include the role of language in reflecting the cultural identity, as well as the role of literary and cultural allusions in shaping public discourse. Although research has been done in how media language shapes communication and forms social identity and group membership, the role of media production in reflecting cultural beliefs and heritage is yet to be explored.

This book is about culture. As Lotman points out,

> Мы живем в мире культуры. Более того, мы находимся в её толще, внутри неё, и только так мы можем продолжать своё существование.
>
> [We live in a world of culture. Moreover, we are in the thick of it, inside of it, and that is the only way we are able to continue our existence.] [1]

This argument resonates strongly with Anderson's notion of the "imagined community"[2] as a mass mediated collectivity where members may not all know each other but share the idea of a common belonging. Quintessentially, the textual analysis for establishing "media message" is incomplete without an analysis of the culture of the various practices of media production and consumption that exist in Russian society.

This book is about contemporary Russian media. The transformation of the media discourse has, in general, attracted very little attention from recent scholars. While the Soviet media presented a single Communist Party–approved version of events, it would be an exaggeration to say that post-Soviet journalists were completely free from the Soviet legacy, from the requirement to be serious and to avoid irony. I remember the 1990s when journalists who had been freed from the rigid Soviet style often were criticized for showing off, but this may have been because readers were unfamiliar with this particular style of writing. Russian media modernization has been, in many aspects, incomplete; traditional elements have been preserved. Of course, while some of the discursive practices and norms of journalism are linked with the Soviet media, others are not. The convergence and competition of various discourses emerged as typical of the contemporary media situation in Russia. That does not mean, however, that these competing discourses are impermeable and could not influence each other or interact to create new types of narrative and identities. As Jeffrey Brooks has pointed out, the Western view according to which the Soviet press functioned as "a voice of central authority or a vehicle of interest groups and factions among the leaders" tallies "with Lenin's idea of the press as a propaganda tool and organizer, but it fails to include the reluctance of elite party members to go into journalistic work or the medium's complexity. All newspapers are inherently pluralistic and open to hostile counter-reading."[3]

This is a book about framing. Particular habits and media of communication frame our collective sense of time, place, and space; they define our understanding of the public and the private. Though the particulars of each media are not yet fully defined, they are valuable to our larger understanding of how media help to shape and reshape culture. My interest in the presentational manner of the Russian media is rooted in the assumption that the media's impact comes not only from the information brought to the audience but also (and more likely) from the way the media organize and package this information. It is important to note that frame theory in media studies has had a broad social orientation, whereas here I focus my interests specifically on frames of reference, their message, and the basic orientation of those "winged words" that were called upon to provide a "usable past."[4] In the case of my analyses, they provide a utilization of the purportedly universal appeal of classical literature for contemporary purposes.

This book is about allusion. I offer a map for understanding allusion in Russian media. I show how allusions can be approached, in the hope that readers' curiosity will be piqued to read further so that they will also be more prepared to interpret what they find with each classical allusion. This book proposes that literary allusions should be included in studies of modern Russian media discourse: the phenomenon of literary allusions appears to have been mainly reviewed in the past in such fields as literary criticism and linguistics, but literary allusion in media is only marginally included in the analysis of the discourses in media, anthropology, and cultural studies. Careful consideration suggests that inclusion of allusions into media discourse is not only a feature of journalism creativity, but also an element of discourse, dialogue of authors, ideas, and cultures. It is through the lens, through the prism of Russian classical literature (in some sense, archetypes), that journalists quite often examine current affairs. The classic wit and wisdom mirror the ideas and reflections of contemporary journalists. Apparently, their interpretation helps sustain the cultural orientations and symbolic codes, and has a power to reflect absurdities and paradoxes of the social life. This book seeks to examine the most significant and enduring archetypes of the Russian classical literature that the post-Soviet Russian culture calls upon and uses in current media.

Finally, this book is about Russian classical literature. While researching this book, I came across a large body of media articles with quotes, aphorisms, witty sayings, and the like taken from the greatest Russian novelists and philosophers of the nineteenth century being reused and recycled in news coverage. Many of the quotes and allusions to Russian classics have been told many times, in many settings, and can be used as a means by which to study society. My main motive in writing this book has been to uncover the surprisingly powerful impact of the classical literary tradition, and offer an original account of the continuity of the cultural revelations made by the intellectual voices of that age on the absurdities and paradoxes of the social life readers found, and continue to find, themselves. More specifically, I aim to address the role of literary classical allusions in media as a means of reconstructing the national identity.

Today, to ignore or to make no attempt in understanding the underpinnings and contours of allusive rhetoric of media is, I believe, to misconstruct the message of the fourth estate in Russia. To do so means to limit our ability to realize a linguistic realm of Russian media that generates its own empire of signs.

NOTES

1. Yuri Lotman, *Izbrannye stat' i v trekh tomakh. Tom I. Stat' i po semiotike i topologii kultury* (Tallin: "Aleksandra," 1992), 3.

2. Benedict Anderson, *Imagined Communities: Reflections on the Origin and Spread of Nationalism*, rev. and expanded ed. (London: Verso, 1991), 224. Anderson focuses on certain ways the media create imagined communities, through targeting a mass audience or generalizing and addressing citizens as the public.

3. Jeffrey Brooks, "Official Xenophobia and Popular Cosmopolitanism in Early Soviet Russia," *American Historical Review* 97 (December 1992): 5, 1435.

4. Lois Prakinson Zamora, *The Usable Past: The Imagination of History in Recent Fiction of the Americas* (Cambridge: Cambridge University Press, 1997). In her look at the reconstruction of the past, Zamora finds that the anxiety of origins "impels American writers to search for precursors (in the name of community) rather than escape from them (in the name of individuation), to connect to traditions and histories (in the name of usable past) rather than dissociate from them (in the name of originality)" (p. 5).

Chapter One

Review

The purpose of this chapter is to consider emergent research on media and scholarship on allusions in media within their historical contexts. The main goal is to analyze many different approaches that exist at one moment, place my own pragmatic research in the context, and make it rather flexible and effective in principle.

Until recently, most studies of post-socialist media have taken a non-comparative perspective to focus primarily on the media's ideological message and the freedom of the media from government control. Studies have also considered the impact of media ownership on media independence and pluralism, as well as the crucial role of economic reforms and new legislation in media transformation. Few studies have examined the actual reporting carried out by the media.[1] Media experts acknowledge that in nearly every country of Eastern and Central Europe, the process of media reforms remains far from complete, and the prospective scenarios for the creation of effective and democracy-promoting media are blurred.[2] In addition, most studies put the emphasis on television,[3] thereby neglecting the much more active role of the Internet media in the process of change.

On the opposite side of the spectrum, many researchers have been keen to focus on a specialized issue concerning "the anthropological approach" to mass media, which has been rendered mainly by British cultural studies.[4] In this vein, there have been major insights in contemporary linguistics (and semiotics) drawn on Voloshinov's[5] views of the sociohistorical dimensions of textual production and reception. Mainstream Western media theories of the 1990s adopted his assumptions, which state that competencies to interpret particular media genres are distributed differentially in various cultures, and have shifted toward the ethnographic and anthropological methods in analysis of empirical material.

This tradition in the West has been developed on the material of French and British media (Hall, Bourdieu). According to Bourdieu, class distinctions in France are partly constructed in differentiated media use. The aged, still relevant concept habitus, associated with Pierre Bourdieu's legacy,[6] brings new insights into the floating concept of individual and collective identity. This approach moves analysis of context and contextualization beyond the individual communication act, and positions it in the scope of media communication. Although Bourdieu's analysis is enlightening, I can see some shortcomings if we try to implement his approach to the analysis of Russian media.

In the Russian context, due to the past Soviet policies that explicitly intended to minimize differences among classes, social and economic relations have evolved beyond stratification as a result of market reforms. There is an important point to be made here. While the disparity between urban and rural and rich and poor is likely to be topical, the attitudes and values shared by a social group should be taken into account with regard to the dynamics of the society.[7] The question of class development is particularly interesting in terms of the role of readership for current media (for more on this, see chapter 4).

At the same time, the "interpretive" audience has not been made up of passive recipients, and it is particularly important in encoding the message of media. I emphasize the modifier "interpretive" as I realize that readers or viewers have no direct influence on media production. Later research borrowed the views from literary critics (Wolfgang Iser,[8] Stanely Fish[9]) manifests "audience is a myth" rather than a real player in media discourse that "a journalist invents for himself,"[10] while journalists widely consider readers as agents who mediate social reality and the appeal to be made to the audience because of this.

In Hall's model, audiences are those who accept, reject, or resist what is conveyed based on their own class position within society. The British culturologist argues that "[the mass media] have progressively colonized the cultural and ideological sphere. As social groups and classes live . . . increasingly fragmented and sectionally differentiated life, the mass media are more and more responsible a) for providing the basis on which groups construct an 'image' of the life, meanings, practices, and values of other groups and classes; b) for providing the images, representations and ideas around which the social totality, composed of all these separate and fragmented pieces, can be coherently grasped as a 'whole.'"[11]

This resonates with Anderson's[12] notion of the imagined community as a mass-mediated collectivity where members may not all know each other, but where each shares the idea of a common belonging. Unfortunately, Anderson's conceptualization of mass media as vehicles of culture, and as a mode of imagining and imaging communities, has had limited empirical application to the Russian data. Without the implication of the result of scholarship in the global community, an analysis of the culture of media production, the political reasons and social history of the Russian media market, and the various practices of media consumption that exist in contemporary Russian society would be incomplete.

In line with the recent developments in media studies, some of the new work provides a new direction into the culturally based, innovative production styles, and the linkage with other forms of cultural knowledge and linguistic expression. It is not surprising that sociolinguists have begun to consider some implications of globalization for media discourse. The issues of linguistic variation and change[13]—the central role of language in the construction of social relationships[14]—recently have received much attention. A few recent monographs treat the post-Soviet media culture, including the printing press, television, and the new media, and discuss how media changed in Russia since the end of communism.[15]

One of the most recent books, *Globalisation, Freedom and the Media after Communism: The Past as Future*[16]—which attempts to remap the relationship between political and cultural studies approaches, between textual analysis and audience research, and between practitioner-led and scholarly approaches to the post-Soviet media—is a good example of a discussion of a widely debated, multidimensional concept of globalization. Regardless of the side taken by the contributors in the debate on the global media, as they reflect on the pervasive feature of politics in its contemporary "mediatized" forms they agree that media language and style have drastically changed.

As Norman Fairclough[17] demonstrates in his extensive study on critical discourse analysis, politics is getting increasingly promotional and quite often entertaining. He investigates how and why alternative reporting provides for an informed, active, and meaningful citizenship. He takes account of many changes that have occurred in media culture demonstrating how the audience becomes more like consumers than citizens. Closely related to the public discourse about politics is the risk of trivialization of politics, a loss of seriousness, and a lack of nuanced, engaging, and detailed analysis of changing media discourse. Admittedly, media discourse manifests itself in personal narratives with blurred boundaries between written and spoken discourse practices that are tied up in part with an increasing prestige and status for spoken languages and informal style of speech.[18] There are many linguistic features that mark the new trend in "mediatized" political discourse. Among those discursive features "conversationalization" described by Fairclough is one of the ubiquitous element of media discourse. Peters[19] notes that "we [now] live in the age of conversation," and media makers specifically design the discourse to communicate intimacy. This includes the use of informal styles of speech, colloquial vocabulary, and colloquial spoken language that simulate intimate, face-to-face interaction. Fairclough is certainly skeptical of this form of "pseudoindividualization." Indeed, questions regarding the legitimacy of this "fake intimacy" achieved by means of "fake" personal address are worthy of discussion, but such issues are beyond the scope of this study. What this book addresses is the complexity behind such traditional polarities as "information" and "entertainment," everything that gives personal style to the media and appeal to the readership and sheds new light on key concepts such as "rhetoric" and "engagement." That in turn requires close analysis of discursive practice that underscores important intersections of political communication and cultural studies, and highlights with insights and clarity the inexorable links between two functions of media language—to depict and shape public opinion. Moreover, a diachronic perspective can contribute to the understanding of how media discourse changes to reflect the reality.

In line with the recent developments in the new media network, quite an old concept of the parallel public sphere seems to provide a new direction into the culturally based, innovative media studies. Habermas's concept of the public sphere stemmed from the political debate that organized mediation between the bourgeois civil society and elective authorities through different public channels, such as the periodical press (and especially mass press), debate clubs, and saloons.[20] Oscar Negt,[21] using Habermas's framework, developed the ideas of the significance of oppositional and non-bourgeois public spheres and proposed studying forms of "resistance and the auto-organization of alternative debates facing the dominant bourgeois public sphere" (e.g., the proletarian public sphere).[22] Examples of such parallel media that generated a political debate with the official public sphere were the anti-Soviet political activity (i.e., dissident activity) and samizdat, which contributed to destruction of the official public sphere in the Soviet Union. In the same vein, new media that serves the informational needs of a very narrow group of socially active people, whose needs are catered to by Internet use, may be considered as counter-public or alternative. These media are the television channel Rain, the Echo Moskvy radio broadcast, and *Novaya Gazeta* print newspaper.[23] Online media also play a role in this field.[24]

At the moment, the material means and the conceptual modes of new media have not become fixed, and such media cannot yet be accepted as natural when their own meanings are in flux. What is important for us is that media consumption cannot be perceived only as a passive activity of absorbing symbolic forms, but also as a kind of possible resistance to dominant symbolic forms or specific cultural forms. Thus, by consuming official or alternative media, readers affirm their cultural identities, which are partly connected with their political orientation, and which contribute to organizing them according to different social groups with particular forms of debate.[25]

Such discourses are not only polyphonic and multi-voiced, but also often dissonant and antagonizing. As outlined above, the intention to inflate current media with historical and literary voices, make use of intertextual connections, allusions, and references often drawn from conflicting sources, combine facts with imaginaries and emotions, mix trauma and pathos, cynicism and humor, and blend the social and the linguistic elements of discourse and counter-discourses. In analyzing allusions I draw on various aspects of the theories mentioned above.

Compiled to support my own study, the following scholarship on use of allusion in media is not comprehensive. The initial meaning of "allusion" in English was equal to "illusion." My etymological digression is somewhat supported by Bloom.[26] In the early Renaissance the words were used as pun or wordplay. Another meaning involves any implied, indirect, or hidden reference. Since allusion and intertexuality are two interrelated concepts, we would not think of isolating them in our analyses. "Intertextuality" as a term was coined by Julia Kristeva in 1969[27] and has been much expanded by other academics since then. It is used in literary criticism to describe the variety of ways in which texts interact with other texts, largely through verbal echoes between texts. Since it is not easy to establish a list of functions of allusions, much of the relevant literature treats the nature of the background cultural and intertextual knowledge allusions demand of readers by setting out the stages involved in understanding an allusion. Allan Pasco comments, "Although the term 'allusion' is a commonplace. . . very little attention has been paid to the way it works—to what it does for those who recognize and interpret it."[28] Pasco's monograph *Allusion: A Literary Graft* clarifies and integrates the most viable elements of past research on allusion. His book also raises important issues about method of study, particularly the applicability of references to the context from which writers are drawn to their allusions. He studies the limitless potential of allusion and demonstrates how the covert allusion requires a literate reader who can both identify the source and make something of the connection, but the overt allusion is hardly as simple as it appears. His excellent literary examples of allusion are insightful and thought provoking. One could say that this book provides valuable data set in the context of the classical Western literature.

With respect to Kristeva's notion of intertextuality, I support the concept that the meaning of a text does not reside in the text, but is produced by the reader in relation not only to the text in question, but also to the complex network of texts invoked in the reading process. Allusion is a form of intertextuality that works largely through verbal echoes between texts. One of the most comprehensive studies on allusions is Paul Lennon's *Allusions in the Press: An Applied Linguistic Study*,[29] which is a corpus-based study of allusions in the British press that shows the range of targets journalists allude to—from Shakespeare to TV soaps, from Jane Austen to Hillary Clinton, from hymns to nursery. For the purpose of his study Lennon defines "allusion" as "an instance of text-based indirection . . . which [the reader] understands as intended implicature on the writer's part, and which is signaled by foregrounded elements of the text."[30] In contrast to several previous studies of allusions, Lennon offers stimulating insights into functional domains of allusions. He distinguishes five functions of allusions and illustrates each one by numerous examples. The five domains are (1) to attract reader attention; (2) to borrow stylistic effects, such as ironic effects of ridicule or criticism, or humorously grotesque effects and to exploit the productive ambiguity of words and phrasal units; (3) to establish common ground with the reader and convince the reader by appealing to cultural values shared with him; (4) to challenge the reader cognitively and encourage him to continue reading; and (5) to display the writer's world knowledge, beliefs, values, and wit.

Generally speaking, Lennon takes up various theories of "indirect language comprehension" and argues that the intratextual domain is associated with stylistic foregrounding, the contextual domain with implicatures, the metatextual domain with evaluation, the processing domain with easing the understanding, or conversely making it more puzzle like, and the interpersonal domain is concerned with phatic bounding between writer and reader.[31] Lennon's ways of conceiving and analyzing allusions owe much to his broad samples drawn from every British daily from September 1995 through August 1996. He explores how allusion is integrated into existing theories of indirect language and is linked to idioms, wordplay, and metaphor. His particularly acute awareness of both the theoretical aims and the practical knowledge makes the book suitable in practical sense for exploring allusions in Russian media production.

Josef Pucci introduces the study of allusion to the concept of "the fully-knowing reader,"[32] who is noticing and interpreting an allusion. Joseph Pucci's book introduces the study of allusion and its greater terminological and conceptual clarity. Pucci's study of allusion offers generous historical sweep ranging from Sappho to Ezra Pound, and specifically provides an interesting study of allegorical practices concerned with allusion to ancient authors. Pucci provided a survey of modern reflection on allusion from the New Criticism to post-structuralism, and manifests his own approach, which presents allusion as a form of reading: the "full-knowing reader" creates an allusive space where the contexts of the allusive text and the text alluded to are allowed to interact. His major thesis states that previous theories of allusion have ignored the role of the reader and instead have either focused on the alluding author or treated allusion as a kind of sign, despite the fact that "the connection of the two phrases that compose the allusion can only occur in the mind of the reader, who is reminded by virtue of shared language of a connection between a later set of words and an earlier set, and who configures on his own terms the interpretive outcomes of this connection."[33] As Pucci points out, the concept of the empowered reader is a provision for allusion. In a theoretical chapter Pucci is careful to indicate that "full knowledge . . . does not correspond to a complete knowledge of all that the allusion can mean."[34] The scope and lucidity of Pucci's theoretical survey make it, by itself, a significant contribution to the study of textual interrelationships, the most clear and comprehensive such overview available. Pucci also includes a set of focused readings on particular allusions, and reads the two texts side-by-side, moving from a particular allusion to a wider engagement with a whole classical text in the allusive space. But in the chapters in which he offers interpretations of particular allusions, Pucci presents his readings as belonging not to him but to the "full-knowing reader." When we investigate how scholars consider allusion in literary texts, however, we find that more emphasis is placed on covert allusion—that is, allusion that does not announce its referent, but awaits discovery by the reader—and less on overt allusion, which presumably is so clear-cut in its function that it makes explication superfluous.[35]

My goal is to look at the problem of allusions in media at the social, cultural, and linguistic dimensions and locate media power and value in a more diffused, rather than direct and casual, sense. Although linguists and literary critics have addressed the question of allusion and its functions, this device has not been properly contextualized synchronically, that is, within the post-Soviet media sphere.

This review focuses whenever possible on articles and books that identify specific problems of intertext in Russian media rather than on the theory and history of use of allusions in Western media in general. While the subsequent years have seen considerable improvement in the scholarly rigor of media language and linguistic usage, there remains a wealth of material for interpretation. Scholars essentially bypass the issues of intertext and allusions in media and its role in nation-building and the projection of a national identity. The vast scholarship emanated mainly from linguistics and literary criticism and is an invaluable source of information on language change and new stylistic trends, but it does not provide much commentary, interpretation, or strategy for Western analysts, interpreters, and historians that are apt to solve the puzzles of allusions in the media texts.[36]

Some scholars propose that post-Soviet irreverence toward the national literary heritage is a reaction to the "centuries of logocentrism."[37] Slavic scholars have offered important insights about the media language of the first years of perestroika and glasnost. Most Russian scholarship done in the field of mass media focused primarily on media text, reflecting the essence of changes undergone by mass media and its. As an immediate consequence of perestroika and glasnost, the language and public rhetoric changed dramatically. As A. N. Baranov discusses in detail, "ritualistic language"[38] of a totalitarian state acknowledging dogmas and tiresome rhetoric of ideological propaganda was gradually superseded by the genuine living language when media was allowed to express pluralistic attitudes and presented Soviet past as devalued.

Within the functionalist approach, the dominant issue in media language studies has been the general ironic tone of modern Russian press, the use of intertexts contributing to an emerging ironic tone, as well as the use of clichés, quotations, allusions, puns, and wordplay in media text.[39] Critical discussion of the phenomenon of allusion (in the sense of a brief, identifiable verbal reminiscence of an earlier literary work in a later one) is beset by Fateeva.[40] For the theoretical introduction to Russian wordplay and on the often negative evaluation of wordplay in Soviet literary criticism, see Sannikov.[41]

Oleg Lekmanov used Moscow newspaper headlines to compile what he believes is the most commonly quoted lines from Russian modernists, or poets of Russia's Silver Age (1890–1917).[42] His method involved surveying newspapers chosen for the project, covering the period from 1985 to 1995. It seems the decision as to which newspapers to examine followed a rough geographic approach. In order to limit the scope of the project, he chose the Moscow area, perhaps because of the ease of access to the resources. The reader should keep one thing in mind with regard to the dates. The culture of the Silver Age was forbidden under the Soviet regime. However, during the initial post-perestroika years, many of the forbidden names were revived and their works became available, and even widely published. Lekmanov collected 234 headlines that alluded to twelve Russian classics. The list is topped by Mayakovsky, followed by Boris Pasternak and Alexander Blok. Evidently, as a rough guide to those of the Modernists who garnered the particular interest for modern Russian society, the list makes for interesting reading. While providing a clear statistical claim, Lekmanov aims to reflect the trend of the public interest to that period of Russian literature, and to emphasize that what used to be elite culture has become mass culture. What is not clear in this study design is whether the chosen newspapers are most readily opinion forming, whether there are any excluded topics of the news stories, whether the chosen newspapers are of a quality sector or of tabloids. It also remains unclear how the culture of the Silver Age can address the problems of today's extremely politicized Russia. Although the author realizes that allusion is not a simple set of words just waiting to pop out, he grants the classical allusions an active propagandistic value. He left behind the stories the articles told, as well as the messages ingrained in those lines.

This review, while detailing the current landscape of scholarship on allusions in media, also shows the specific issues that go beyond the scope of the scholars. Meanwhile, in my book I focus on allusions in media that recount collective memories and "history," and provide data for historical parallels that function and become an essential medium for self-expression and identification. In demonstrating further, however, they also serve commemorative purposes.

NOTES

1. E. Mickiewicz, "The Conundrum of Memory," in *The Post-Soviet Russian Media: Change and Conflicting Messages*, ed. Birgit Beumers, Stephen Hutcheson, and Natalya Ryulova (New York: Routledge, 2008); Olessia Koltsova, *News Production and Power in Post-Soviet Russia* (London and New York: Routledge Curzon, 2006).
2. P. Gross, *Entangled Evolutions: The Media and Democratization in Eastern Europe* (Washington, DC: Woodrow Wilson Center Press/Johns Hopkins University Press, 2002); I. Zassursky, *Mass-media i politika v 90-e gody* (Moscow: Moscow State University Press, 2001).
3. Floriana Fossato, "The Russian Media: From Popularity to Distrust," *Current History* 100, no. 648 (2001): 343–48.
4. S. Hall, "Cultural Studies and Its Theoretical Legacies," in *Cultural Studies*, ed. L. Grossberg, C. Nelson, and P. Treichler (New York and London: Routledge, 1992), 277–94. D. Morley, "The Nationwide Audience—a Critical Postscript," *Screen Educ.* 39 (1981): 3–14.
5. There is perhaps an irresoluble debate regarding Bakhtin's authorship of publications attributed to Pavel Nikolaevich Medvedev and Valentin Nikolaevich Voloshinov, members of the Bakhtin's circle during the 1920s. As such, I will interpret the works as the product of "like-minded intellectuals" and include both names in the references. V. N. Voloshinov, *Marksizm i philosophia iazyka* (Leningrad: Priboy, 1930).
6. Pierre Bourdieu, *Outline of a Theory of Practice* (Cambridge: Cambridge University Press, 1977); Pierre Bourdieu, *Language and Symbolic Power* (Cambridge: Cambridge University Press, 1991), 131–32.
7. Jeffrey Klugman, *The New Soviet Elite: How They Think and What They Want* (New York: Praeger, 1989).
8. W. Iser, *The Act of Reading: A Theory of Aesthetic Response* (Baltimore: Johns Hopkins University Press, 1978).
9. S. Fish, "Literature in the Reader," in *Reader Response Criticism*, ed. Jane P. Tompkins (Baltimore: Johns Hopkins University Press, 1980).
10. P. J. Shoemaker and S. D. Reese, *Mediating the Message: Theories of Influences on Mass Media Content*, 2nd ed. (White Plains, NY: Longman, 1996), 96.
11. S. Hall, "Culture, the Media and the 'Ideological Effect,'" in *Mass Communication and Society*, ed. J. Curran, M. Gurevitch, and J. Woollacott (London: Edward Arnold, 1977), 340.
12. Benedict Anderson, *Imagined Communities: Reflections on the Origin and Spread of Nationalism*, rev. and expanded ed. (London: Verso, 1991), 224.
13. Norman Fairclough, *Norman Language and Globalization* (London and New York: Routledge, 2006), 186.
14. P. Bourdieu, "Structures, Habitus, Practices," in *The Logic of Practice* (Stanford, CA: Stanford University Press, 1990), 54.
15. *Post-Soviet Russian Media Conflicting Signals* exemplifies such treatment.
16. Birgit Beumers, Stephen Hutchings, and Natalia Rulyova, eds., *Globalisation, Freedom and the Media after Communism: The Past as Future* (New York: Routledge, 2012).
17. Norman Fairclough, *Critical Discourse Analysis* (Boston: Addison Wesley, 1995), 19.
18. Norman Fairclough, "Conversationalization of Public Discourse and the Authority of the Consumer," in *The Authority of the Consumer*, ed. Nicholas Abercrombie, Russel Keat, and Nigel Whiteley (New York: Routledge, 1994), 253–68.
19. John Durham Peters, "Media as Conversation, Conversation as Media," on *Media and Cultural Theory*, ed. James Curran and David Morley (London: Routledge, 2006), 115–26.
20. J. Habermas, *The Structural Transformation of the Public Sphere: An Inquiry into a Category of Bourgeois Society* (Cambridge, MA: MIT Press, 1991).
21. O. Negt, *L'espace public oppositionnel* [Oppositional public space] (Paris: Payot, 2007).

22. Ilya Kiriya, "The Culture of Subversion and Russian Media Landscape," *International Journal of Communication* 6 (2012): 447, http://ijoc.org/ojs/index.php/ijoc/article/viewFile/1196/713.

23. However, even though independent radio stations, such as Ekho Moskvy (Echo of Moscow), which has a listening audience of about nine hundred thousand, enjoy more freedom than television, they are pressured by the government when coverage is critical of the Kremlin. See David Remnick, "Echo in the Dark," *New Yorker*, September 22, 2008, www.newyorker.com/reporting/2008/09/22/080922fa_fact_remnick.

24. See B. Etling, K. Alexanyan, J. Kelly, R. Faris, J. Palfrey, and U. Gasser, *Public Discourse in the Russian Blogosphere: Mapping RuNet Politics and Mobilization* (Cambridge, MA: Berkman Center for Internet and Society, Harvard University, 2010), http://cyber.law.harvard.edu/sites/cyber.law.harvard.edu/files/Public_Discourse_in_the_Russian_Blogosphere_2010.pdf.

25. R. Hoggart, *The Uses of Literacy* (Piscataway, NJ: Transaction Publishers, 1998); D. Morley and C. Brunsdon, *The Nationwide Television Studies* (London: Routledge, 1999).

26. M. Wheeler, *The Art of Allusion in Victorian Fiction* (London: Macmillan, 1979), 3.

27. Julia Kristeva, *Desire in Language: A Semiotic Approach to Literature and Art* (New York: Columbia University Press, 1980), 69.

28. Allan H. Pasco, *Allusion: A Literary Graft (Theory/Culture)* (Toronto: University of Toronto Press, 1994), 8.

29. Paul Lennon, *Allusions in the Press: An Applied Linguistic Study* (New York: Mouton de Gruyter, 2004).

30. Lennon, *Allusions in the Press*, 14–15.

31. Lennon, *Allusions in the Press*, 235–38.

32. Joseph Michael Pucci, *The Full-Knowing Reader: Allusion and the Power of the Reader in the Western Literary Tradition* (New Haven, CT: Yale University Press, 1998), 263.

33. Pucci, *The Full-Knowing Reader*, 36.

34. Pucci, *The Full-Knowing Reader*, 38.

35. Pucci, *The Full-Knowing Reader*, 39.

36. Ludmila Ferm, "Osobennosti razvitiia russkoi leksiki v noveishii period (na materiale gazet): Uppsala, Acta Universitatis Upsaliensis," *Studia Slavica Upsaliensia* 33 (1994); V. G. Kostomarov, *Iazykovoi vkus epokhi: Iz nabliudenii nad rechevoi praktikoi mass-media* (Moscow: Pedagogika, 1994); A. Dulicenko and W. Lehfeldt, *Russkii iazyk kontsa XX stoletiia* (Munich: Otto Sagner, 1994); E. V. Kakorina, *Transformatsiia leksicheskoi semantiki i sochetaemosti (na materiale iazyka gazet): Russkii iazyk kontsa XX stoletiia (1985–1995)* (Moscow: Iazyki russkoi kul'tury, 1996), 67–88; E. V. Kakorina, *Stilisticheskii oblik oppozitsionnoi pressy: Russkii iazyk kontsa XX stoletiia (1985–1995)* (Moscow: Iazyki russkoi kul'tury, 1996), 409–25.

37. For a detailed discussion of cultural and philosophical implications of logocentrism, see the conclusion to Mikhail Epstein, *After the Future: The Paradoxes of Postmodernism and Contemporary Russian* (Amherst: University of Massachusetts Press, 1995), 328–39.

38. A. N. Baranov and Yu. N. Karaulov, *Slovar' russkikh politicheskikh metafor* (Moscow: Pomovskii i partnery, 1994).

39. Y. A. Zemskaya, "Klishe novoiaza i tsitatsiia v iazike postsovetskogo obchshestva," *Voprosy iazikoznaniia* 3 (1996): 23–31. Yuri Stepanov, *Intertext, Internet, Intersub"ekt: (k osnovaniiam sravnitel'noi konsteptologii)* (St. Petersburg: Neva, 1999).

40. N. A. Fateyeva, *Kontrapunkt intertekstual' nosti, ili intertekst v mire tekstov* (Moscow: AGAR, 2000).

41. V. Z. Sannikov, *Russkii iazyk v zerkale iazykovoi igry* (Moscow: Iazyki russkoi kul'tury, 1999), 490, 513, 515.

42. Oleg Lekmanov, "Russkie modernisty—'soavtory' zagolovkov moskovskikh gazet (1985–1995)," *Novoe Literaturnoe Obozrenie* 71 (2005), http://magazines.russ.ru/nlo/2005/71/lek35-pr.html.

Chapter Two

Method

This chapter examines how media discourse uses quotations, allusions, and paraphrases from classical literature but, most importantly, how the quoted and alluded texts are framed in the official and alternative media discourse. The analysis of data is informed by a complex theoretical framework combining concepts from frame analysis as a type of critical discourse analysis (Fairclough's model),[1] reader-oriented theories of interpretation (Iser's framework), and theories of sarcasm and irony (Attardo, and Wilson and Sperber). I have briefly surveyed some approaches for definitions and terminology. Thus my framework, one that is rather analytical and pragmatic, does not coincide with a theory, though stemming from several with a goal to find a conceptual mapping tool that is also operational for empirical research.

Specifically, I propose to view the literary allusion in media discourse not only in its function of metaphor and metonymy, but also as a mnemonic unit and a building block in the construction of creating a stylized, ritualistic discourse, as well as a rhetorical strategy. This strategy provides tools and terms from rich and diverse historical-cultural contexts for the author to choose: modus operandi, for example, is a means to approach various political, social, and metaphysical issues within the sphere that supplanted other forms of public reflection and explanation.

One of the clearest definitions of the seemingly paradoxical concept of discourse is given by Van Dijk, who defines 'discourse' in a broad sense as a complex unit of language form, meaning, and action that might best be captured under the notion of a communicative event or communicative act.[2] In Van Dijk's framework, ideologies are actively involved in the process of discourse interpretation and construction, which can be defined as "basic systems of fundamental social cognitions and organizing the attitudes and other social representations shared by members of groups."[3] A discourse perspective, or "a linguistic turn,"[4] on media discourse has raised issues of interest to linguists: the impact of the modes of presenting texts; the intertextual relevance of the alluded or quoted texts; the themes of allusions; and the display of identity through referring quotes. Allusion is one of the types of discursive strategies, that is, "a more or less accurate and more or less intentional plan of practices (including discursive practices) adopted to achieve a particular social, political, psychological or linguistic aim."[5]

In history as well as in journalism, a text involves listening to a "chorus of different voices sounding through the text."[6] Based on Fairclough,[7] textually oriented critical discourse analysis brings together three levels: textual, interpersonal, and situated in a wider societal context. In other words, Fairclough's analytical framework[8] includes the text, the discursive practice, and the sociocultural practice. Not yet fully applied to the analysis of post-Soviet media discourse in Russia, this theoretical framework offers a rich potential for explicating the specifics of Russian discursive practices to construct any kind of nationally unified, shared meaning. In this book I concentrate on the discourse-historical approach, committed to critical discourse analysis in order to understand discourse as a part of social practice that involves the production and interpretation of texts. I focus on the study of the language structures produced in a discursive event, examine the consumption of the text, and finally, investigate what is happening in a particular socio-cultural framework. Significantly, in Fairclough's logic the language is both socially shaped and socially shaping. Thus an analysis of discourse can best be performed with the theoretical assumption that texts and discourses are socially constitutive: "Language use is always simultaneously constitutive of (i) social identities, (ii) social relations and (iii) systems of knowledge and beliefs."[9]

To analyze the media discourse, I apply the framing approach as a type of critical discourse analysis. Linguistic frame analysis is carried out to reveal story structures as well as salience or backgrounding of particular features. The way the media chose to package the news stories fundamentally affects the reader's perception. Studies in communication[10] come to understand the framing effects as "changes in judgment engendered by subtle alterations in the definition of judgment or choice of the problems."[11] The original sociological notion of framing as used by Goffman refers to the principles of social organization of a situation, consciously or unconsciously invoked.[12] Frames appear in various guises and occur widely in different types of news. This study is mainly interested in the frames imposed by the historical and cultural context. If we accept such a wide interpretation, we can define frames as expectations and presuppositions about ways of understanding of current affairs, which are continually checked against experience and revised. The use of allusions as a rhetorical form is deeply and unavoidably involved in shaping the frame.

By assuming that media impact comes not only from the information brought to the audience but also (and more importantly) from the way the media rhetorically organizes or "frames" and packages this information, I understand a frame as a selection of some aspects of a perceived reality and making them more salient in a communicating text. According to Neuman, news frames are conceptual tools on which media and individuals rely to convey, interpret, and evaluate information.[13] In such a way framing promotes a particular problem definition, causal interpretation, moral evaluation, and/or treatment of the event described. Surprisingly, allusion is commonly manifested by a frame. I focus on the following components of the journalistic texts usually containing "rhetorical devices": headlines and kickers (small headlines over the main headlines); subheads; leads (the beginnings of news stories); selection of sources and affiliations; selection of quotes; pull quotes (quotes that are blown up in size for emphasis); and concluding statements or paragraphs of articles. In addition, I paid attention to several other tools commonly considered to be used for rhetorical purpose: metaphors, epithets, sentence structure (syntax), choice of language, and stylistic choices.[14]

I would like to call attention to one specific feature of my study. My study involves translation of allusions. The number of problems I encountered while translating allusions reveals the problematic nature of translation's ability to communicate "otherness" of the alluded text, keeping lucidity of expressions and receptiveness of the intention. Indeed, potential peculiarity of the journalist's intention can subdue the specificity of the allusion or precludes intertextual relations between primary and adoptive texts that are more or less explicitly linked. Moreover, being culture-bound, allusions taken outside of the original may inhibit the very possibility of translation due to semantic and syntactic interference effects. Following Leppihalme,[15] who makes a distinction between proper name allusions and key-phrase allusions, I claim that the two groups require slightly different lists of potential translation strategies. It is also important to pay attention to the word class or phrase type of the allusion, differentiating the range of syntactic varieties such as noun-phrase allusions, verb-phrase allusions, and adjective-phrase allusions, or marking out allusions based on syntactic functions with categories as premodifying allusions, subject compliment allusions, and so on.

The strategies I used for translating allusions are based on the following parameters: the length of the phrase, non-standard spelling and syntax, deviations in style, and rhythm and rhyme. After analyzing every allusion and its function in the micro and macro context, I decided which strategy to use: sensu stricto, or substitution or non-idiomatic paraphrasing for lack of the etymological and idiomatic correlates between the two languages. I took into consideration content analysis of headlines, pull quotes, and content analysis of the article and cultural implications of allusions. Although the forms allusions take in the journalistic discourse (e.g., alliteration or similar) are not as crucial as their functions, I try not to ignore them. Among my additional strategies are providing extra-allusive guidance and endnotes, marking wording or syntax, making the connotations explicit by explaining the tone of the allusion in the journalistic text, providing extended annotations explaining the hidden allusion, and suggesting adequate explanation of the articles' subject matters.

Within the space of a typical media article, readers are bombarded with a series of often contradictory allusions, which—according to linguists George Lakoff and Mark Johnson in their book *Metaphors We Live By*—is understanding and experiencing one kind of thing in terms of another.[16] In my study, I turn to the analysis of reception of the allusions that frequently provide metaphors and give rise to further analogical thinking.

Although allusion and reference fall into the category of textual exploitation of another text, it remains necessary to stress that they are also forms of indirect language, which readers understand as intended implicatures on the journalists' part, and which are signaled by foregrounded elements of the text. Grice[17] distinguishes between the literal meaning of the utterance and what the speaker really intends to say, for example innuendos or insinuations. A communicative approach in my study demonstrates violation of the Gricean Cooperative Principle.[18] On the one hand, both the speaker and the addressee should employ the conversational maxims in order to communicate effectively. On the other hand, deviation of the maxims manifests implicitness and is inherently associated with ambiguity, subjectivity, and irony.

Bakhtin[19] and the post-Bakhtinians have drawn attention to the dialogic construction of meaning and consequent recognition of audience as co-author.[20] The recent theoretical developments within the field of reader-oriented theories indicate a move toward the distinction between real audience and a hypothetical reader implied by the text. One of the reasons for this may be the complexity of the proper definition of the concept of "the reader." Wolfgang Iser, who has made an important contribution to the study of the reading process, defined "the reader" extremely broadly as "a textual structure anticipating the presence of a recipient without necessarily defining him."[21]

Specifically, Iser concentrates on the rhetorical reading as a process of evoking the meaning of the text by the reader.[22] Meanwhile a useful point of departure for analyzing this aspect is Iser's examination of "repertoire" or "framework," or a mold for the reader's personal interpretation: "The repertoire consists of all the familiar territory within the text. This may be in the form of references to earlier works, or to social and historical norms, or to the whole culture from which the text has emerged."[23] Whereas Iser concerns on "the repertoire of the text"[24] he concentrates on intertextual reminiscences and the rhetorical effect upon which the text draws. In a similar vein, Stanley

Fish captures the attitude of readers' interpretive activity, influenced by their historical, social, and theoretical contexts.[25] Fish also holds that linguistic competence is fundamental for text interpretation. It should be noted, however, that linguistic competency and the ability to recognize cultural allusions do not necessarily go hand in hand: a reader may be a native speaker of Russian, yet be unable to decode ambiguous allusions. Proceeding from a close reading of media texts, I concentrate on specific interpretive strategies. I depart from Iser's concept of the "implied reader" and the repertoire of the text used to explore how readers might make sense of allusions in media texts by tracing the rhetorical and discursive techniques employed in media texts. I do not aim to propose any new typology of "the reader," but will try rather to outline two types of "the reader": one with the competence to recognize the allusions, and the reader who fails to grasp them. I hold that hypothetical readers of both types are implied by the media text, that designs a dual rhetorical perspective. Thus these different starting points determine the potential allusive reply.

In some instances I propose two perspectives of analyses, the first of which posits an ideal hypothetical reader who is able to resolve an allusive puzzle, the second of which posits a hypothetical reader unfamiliar with the text source and cultural allusions that appear in the media text. Benedict Anderson emphasizes the role of the novel and the newspaper as "the technical means for 're-presenting' the *kind* of imagined community that is the nation."[26] Slightly modifying this statement, one can see the nation as "*the kind* of imagined community" with an "imagined past." According to Anderson, "Fiction seeps quietly and continuously into reality, creating that remarkable confidence of community in anonymity which is the hallmark of modern nations."[27]

While traditional media ultimately succeeded in the creation of their "imagined communities" with "imagined pasts" within the dominated Kremlin traditions, Russian Internet journalism is creating alternative discourses that undermine the rhetoric of unanimous consent and overcome the creation of official myths and information manipulation, functionally proving the diversity of the journalism network in Russia.

In a step to formalize such basic concepts of my analysis, it is useful to refer to the concept of "habitus" presented by the French sociologist Pierre Bourdieu.[28] I am not considering the sense of habitus, related to sociology and science in general, but rather use the potential in Bourdieu's theory to understand contemporary identities. This topic is discussed at greater length in chapter 4.

When trying to define the nature and extent of the readers' comprehension of allusions it is important, first of all, to keep in view the journalists' means of making the audience grasp the message or particular points. The turn to the reader-centered approach seems to have built up momentum for a focus on allusion as a rhetorical tool that is deployed in media contexts in ways that go well beyond the task of explaining its meaning and usage in literature per se. Allusion does not only function as a tool for naming: after being extensively used, an allusive expression that has originated as a product of successful naming may begin to lose its former descriptive content and becomes cliché. Consequently it can gradually accept its new descriptive content as well as the referential content it has when used interpretively. During interpretation, knowledge of the nineteenth- and the twentieth-century foundational works of Russian literature—including how texts from the same period treat similar themes or topics—is crucial, for it fosters an understanding of allusions and how they describe a character's motive, actions, or persona.

Allusion is related to presuppositions—that is, the inferences that can be made from the structure of language that provides a path from the words expressed to what are actually the person's thoughts, memories, beliefs, and values. The concept of presupposition is central to linguistic pragmatics. The analysis of presuppositions within speech act theory, which began with John Austin and John Serle,[29] makes it possible to make explicit the implicit assumptions and intertextual relations that underlie allusion usage and perception.[30] Allusions depend on shared knowledge, while a journalist who alludes to something counts on resonance. What is not pronounced in allusions creates a puzzle, or secrecy. Allusion, however, exists within a "repertoire of collective knowledge." Thus, familiarity suggests something like "we all know what is meant," linking living past to the present, and making the past "usable," to use Zamora's term. That is the mechanism of how cultural memory promotes inclusiveness.

Allusion is the source of practices and perception that reproduces cultural memory.[31] Some scholars have sought to understand why the past is usable, and what exactly the past does to shape identities and define cultural tradition in the present. Among those who employ a more functionalist vocabulary, I would like to mention two theories whose authors imbue them with a vocabulary enabling a more critical exploration, namely Bourdieu's theory of habitus and Mikhail Bakhtin's theory of genre. Both theories are promising in analyzing instances of "usable past" or collective tradition—what is communicated from one generation to the next. This line of inquiry was prompted by Jeffrey K. Olick's monograph *The Politics of Regret: On Collective Memory and Historical Responsibility*.[32]

It would certainly be folly to attempt to summarize Bakhtin's and Bourdieu's projects in the space of a few paragraphs. My purpose here in mentioning Bourdieu's concept "habitus" is merely to suggest that it provides some conceptual innovations in dissolving the distinction between the individual and the collective. By the same token, Bakhtin, though employing a very different vocabulary, provides tools for understanding this dichotomy.

The central idea in Bakhtin's work is that of dialogue. Genres, Bakhtin argues, are the central mechanisms of dialogue, "the drive belts from the history of society to the history of language."[33] Bakhtin develops a concept of genre to identify kinds of utterances, which are the results of "a continuous generative process implemented in the social-verbal interaction of speakers."[34] He writes: "A genre lives in the present, but always remembers its past, its beginning. Genre is a representative of creative memory in the process of literary development."[35] He argues that all utterances take place within unique historical situations, while at the same time contain memory traces of earlier usages, meaning not that any utterance can be decoded to reveal earlier usages, but that the specificity of every term is the product of a long historical development. In this way, genres reflexively mediate between past and present. Although Bakhtin and Bourdieu have different theories and practices, both study conditions under which cultural memory is preserved across generations.

The literary semantics view allusion as a form of deliberate yet implicit intertextuality.[36] In the purpose of our study, we assume that while the concept of intertextuality implies a cultural code—habitus in terms of the inseparability of culture, literary works, and authors—allusion is perceived as a reference to common experiences, a genre, a commemorative text, constituted by the source to which it refers, and carried forward to the present context where they are produced.

Whereas conversational irony may be accompanied by visual or articulatory clues, ironic message of the written text can be elusive (though instantly recognizable). Pragmatically speaking, the clash between the literal meaning of an utterance and the implicature serves the purpose of defining irony. Further, the various possible relations between irony and sarcasm can be catalogued and illustrated with corpus evidence. Stated in this way, it would seem that we are able to distinguish the various types of verbal irony, sarcasm, or humorous wordplay, or could at least separate them in practice. In fact, the clear distinction is neither possible nor sensible. However, discourse-based theories like Haiman's determine exactly what is being evaluated through irony on each occasion and include the perspective of the recipient, whose task is to recognize incongruity between expectations and actual interpretations. The great strengths of Haiman's proposal are its direct connection with a description of discourse and its potentially unified treatment of irony, put-ons, and sarcasm. Analyzing contexts in authentic discourse, he argues that "sarcasm is not a totally isolated speech act,"[37] and the sarcastic tone is provided entirely by the reader's inference, and of course, not all readers will "hear the snigger if there is no overt mark of insincerity."[38] Haiman claims that "situations may be ironic, but only people can be sarcastic."[39] Thus it is possible to go further and capture one significant feature of irony—while sarcasm is always intentionally combative, irony may enhance a feeling of rapport.

On the evidences given by Wilson and Sperber and Haiman, the notion of sarcasm is implied by derisory "mention,"[40] and more appropriate to negativity, while irony is characterized by linguistic markers of pretense, invokes evaluation, and may or may not be perceived as hostile rhetoric strategy, but rather is capable of articulating a wide range of subtle attitudes. In fact, it is implicit when one quotes not only another's actual words but also another's diction and syntax. There is no conflict between these theories, however: the mention theory does not support the relation between sarcasm and verbal aggression, and pretense theory pays less attention to the consideration of ideas of style, rhythm, exaggeration, norms, standards, variations, to name only a few fundamental speech features. Particularly, I explore ironic contexts where irony results from certain discrepancy, contrast, or inappropriateness between some semantic and/or pragmatic features of an utterance,[41] and ironic utterances that implicitly convey the speaker's subjective attitude toward the words of the Other.[42]

NOTES

1. N. Fairclough and R. Wodac, "Critical Discourse Analysis," in *Discourse as Social Interaction*, ed. T. Van Dijk (London: Sage, 1997), 258–84.
2. Teun A. Van Dijk, "Critical Discourse Analysis," in *Handbook of Discourse Analysis*, ed. D. Tannen, D. Schiffrin, and H. Hamilton (Oxford, UK: Blackwell, 2001), 352–71.
3. Teun A. Van Dijk, "Discourse Semantics and Ideology," *Discourse & Society* 6 (1995): 243.
4. Richard Rorty, *The Linguistic Turn* (Chicago: Chicago University Press, 1967).
5. Ruth Wodac, "Populist Discourses—the Rhetoric of Exclusion in Written Genres," *Document Design* 4, no. 2 (2003): 132–48.
6. Richard Evans, *In Defense of History* (New York: W. W. Norton, 1999), 92. Michel Foucault developed the idea of a field of discourse in *The Archaeology of Knowledge and the Discourse on Language* (New York: Pantheon, 1972).
7. N. Fairclough, *Discourse and Social Change* (Cambridge, UK: Polity Press, 1992).
8. Fairclough has developed a dialectical theory of discourse and an approach to explore to what extent and in what ways the social changes are reflected in discourse.
9. N. Fairclough, *Critical Discourse Analysis: The Critical Study of Language* (New York: Longman 1995), 134.
10. For example, W. A. Gamson and A. Modigliani, "Media Discourse and Public Opinion on Nuclear Power: A Constructivist Approach," *American Journal of Sociology* 1 (1989): 1–37; K. Callaghan and F. Schnell, "Assessing the Democratic Debate: How the News Media Frame Elite Policy Discourse," *Political Communication* 18 (2001): 183–212; M. Ferree et al., *Shaping Abortion Discourse Democracy and the Public Sphere in Germany and the United States* (Cambridge: Cambridge University Press, 2002).
11. S. Iyengar and D. R. Kinder, *News That Matters* (Chicago: University of Chicago Press, 1987), 816.
12. E. Goffman, *Framing Analysis: An Essay on the Organization of Experience* (New York: Harper & Row, 1974).
13. Russell Neuman, Marion Just, and Ann Crigler, *Common Knowledge: News and the Construction of Political Meaning* (Chicago: University of Chicago Press, 1992).

14. J. Tankard, "The Empirical Approach to the Study of Media Framing," in *Framing Public Life*, ed. S. Reese, O. Gandy, and A. Grant (London: Lawrence Erlbaum, 2001).

15. Ritva Leppihalme, *Culture Bumps: An Empirical Approach to the Translation of Allusions* (Clevedon, UK: Multilingual Matters, 1997), 56.

16. G. Lakoff and M. Johnson, *Metaphors We Live By* (Chicago: Chicago University Press, 1980).

17. H. P. Grice, "Logic and Conversation," in *Syntax and Semantics: Speech Acts*, ed. P. Cole and J. Morgan, vol. 3 (New York: Academic Press, 1975), 41–58.

18. The cooperative principle is a principle of conversation that was proposed by Grice (1975). The cooperative principle, along with the conversational maxims, states that any discourse, whether written or spoken, is a joint effort. Structurally, maxims are loose, and are subject to each individual's assessment.

19. M. Bakhtin, *The Dialogic Imagination*, trans. C. Emerson and M. Holquist (Austin: University of Texas Press, 1981); Bakhtin, *Speech Genres and Other Late Essays*, ed. C. Emerson and M. Holquist, trans. V. McGee (Austin: University of Texas Press, 1986); M. Bakhtin, *The Bakhtin Reader: Selected Writing of Bakhtin, Medvedev and Voloshinov*, ed. P. Morris (London: Arnold, 2001).

20. For example, S. Fish, "Literature in the Reader," in *Reader Response Criticism*, ed. Jane P. Tompkins (Baltimore: Johns Hopkins University Press, 1980), 70–100; W. Iser, *The Act of Reading: A Theory of Aesthetic Response* (Baltimore, MD: Johns Hopkins University Press, 1978).

21. Iser, *The Act of Reading*, 34.

22. Ibid., 24.

23. Ibid., 34.

24. Ibid., 69.

25. Fish, "Literature in the Reader," 86–87.

26. Benedict Anderson, *Imagined Communities: Reflections on the Origin and Spread of Nationalism* (London and New York: Verso, 1991), 25.

27. Ibid., 36

28. Pierre Bourdieu, *Outline of a Theory of Practice* (Harvard: Cambridge University Press, 1977).

29. J. Searle, "Metaphor," in *Pragmatics: A Reader*, ed. S. Davies (Oxford: Oxford University Press, 1991), 519–39.

30. Deborah Schiffrin, *Approach to Discourse: Language as Social Interaction* (New York: Wiley, 1994).

31. The concept of "cultural memory," a phrase coined in 1925 by the Durkheimian sociologist Maurice Halbwachs, remains very useful in approaching the issues of identity formation. See Maurice Halbwachs, *On Collective Memory*, trans. and ed. Lewis Coser (Chicago: University of Chicago Press, 1992).

32. Jeffrey K. Olick, *The Politics of Regret: On Collective Memory and Historical Responsibility* (London: Routledge, 2007).

33. Bakhtin, *Speech Genres and Other Late Essays*, 65.

34. V. N. Vološinov, *Marxism and the Philosophy of Language*, trans. Ladislav Matejka and I. R. Titunik (New York: Seminar, 1973), 98. There is a long-standing debate about the author of various texts in the so-called Bakhtin Circle, which included Bakhtin himself, Vološinov, P. N. Medvedev, and others.

35. Bakhtin, *Speech Genres and Other Late Essays*, 106.

36. Graham Allen, *Intertextuality* (London: Routledge, 2000). Allen provides the best overview of intertextuality from the perspective of literary theory, referring to such theorists as Vladimir Volosinov, Mikhail Bakhtin, Julia Kristeva, Roland Barthes, and Gerard Gennete, who largely focused on the effect of intertextuality and questions of the originality of texts.

37. John Haiman, *Talk Is Cheap: Sarcasm, Alienation, and the Evolution of Language* (Oxford: Oxford University Press, 1998), 18.

38. Ibid., 27.

39. Ibid., 20.

40. Cf. Wilson and Sperber, "On Verbal Irony."

41. V. Y. Propp, *Problemy komizma i smekha* (Moscow: Iskusstvo, 1976), 99–100; A. Attardo, *Humorous Texts: A Semantic and Pragmatic Analysis* (Berlin: Mouton de Gruyter, 2001), 114–17.

42. Attardo, *Humorous Texts*, 120–22.

Chapter Three

Media Landscape

Data for this book was drawn from various types of media. A great deal of the scholarship on media tends to make newspapers represent journalism as a whole; meanwhile the late twentieth- and early twenty-first-century media became more varied than ever before. To date, the most extensive attention has been given to mainstream journalism. Such interest reveals the general trends in the media and downplays the diversity that exists in the world of journalism.

Before we look at the present-day situation, however, it is necessary to say a few words about the background to this issue. Throughout the Soviet period, Russia had an incredibly high newspaper readership rate. In the late 1980s the Soviet Union published more than 8,000 daily newspapers, with a combined circulation of about 170 million. Between 1970 and 1990, practically every Russian household subscribed to several periodicals: one or two leading central newspapers, such as *Pravda*, *Izvestia*, or *Komsomolskaya Pravda*, and at least one local newspaper and several specific magazines (e.g., *Woman Worker, Peasant Worker*). The subscription rate of those publications was unreasonably low while the circulation was quite high. This was due to the state system of media financing, in which the idea of media profitability did not play a significant role. Polemical discussions in periodicals seemed to deal exclusively with cultural and literary issues, but in essence they dealt with the contemporary political situation in Russia. The authors of the Western-oriented magazines and newspapers such as *Yunost* and the *Literary Gazette*, the only national illustrated periodicals then whose ideological content at different periods of the country's development provided a sort of a barometer for the entire state of journalism in Russia, argued with the "nationalists" from *Our Contemporary* and *Ogonyok*, a pallid feature magazine that quoted Feliks F. Kuznetsov, head of the Moscow branch of the writers' union, as disparaging Vladimir Nabokov, the émigré author, as anti-Soviet.

In this sense, it is possible to say that Soviet print media, generously subsidized by the state, were drumming official myths into public consciousness, creating the Soviet mythology of incredibly happy life in the USSR behind the thick iron curtain. Only a small part of the population used to listen to their shortwave radio foreign broadcasts each time anything untoward seems to be taking place. The collapse of the Soviet Union has changed this system forever. The period of perestroika under Gorbachev was the most productive time for the Soviet media. State control and censorship were waning. Economic and financial pressures had not yet struck media outlets. Such independence brought a great deal of freedom of expression.

Newspapers and magazines such as *Literaturnaya Gazeta* and *Ogonyok* had become increasingly provocative and published articles that Soviet readers simply were not used to seeing. Readers were pointing out that investigative reporting on the war in Afghanistan or the chilling expose about Stalin's terror raised controversy and went farther than ever before in discussing difficult issues.

At the same time, the system of state subsidies that existed under communism vanished. Oligarchs acquired controlling interests in many of the leading titles, while less popular publications were left to struggle for survival. Media scholars acknowledged that "circulations seem to rise and fall along with political hopes."[1] By 2000, although the trend of media growth continued, the boom times of the 1980s and 1990s were gone. The campaign to control the media began almost as soon as Vladimir Putin took office in 2000. It introduced stiff penalties for disclosing anything not officially permitted but gave no indication what was permitted. A large proportion of the urban and rural dwellers experienced no immediate changes in their social position as a result of the downfall of the USSR. Since the reading public has never had much experience with independent news, most readers have gotten used to the pattern of official concealment that has become traditional. A long habit of withholding and soft-pedaling bad news came as no surprise to anyone in a country that has had censorship for four hundred years.

For much of the 1990s, the press has been comfortably overtaken by television, which was more popular, had far wider reach, and attracted more investments. Nevertheless, the Russian newspaper market offers its consumers a diverse range of views A well-established tradition of reading print media was revived in Russia. With declining newspaper circulation, online newspapering has been increasing dramatically, with the possibility to read digital versions of most newspapers. Now the Internet is providing a wide range of options for those keeping up with current events. There was one factor, however, that was completely new for most Russians: the wider selection of professional outlets devoted to the distribution of daily news. Readership has dramatically changed in Russia. However, in the majority of cases, online presence is not always effective, since websites are poorly considered and badly implemented. Little thought is given to the significant strategic advantage an online presence can provide.

Thus, Russia has a very wide range of print media.[2] There are over four hundred daily newspapers, covering every field and offering all kinds of perspectives. The print runs of most of the central newspapers fell from millions to tens of thousands, while the output of the local presses was still on the rise. Since the move toward "interpretive" audience has been recognized as beneficial, the variety of the media outlets in both language and content tends to be taken at face value. In this chapter I focus on brief profiles of media outlets I have drawn the data from and comment on the rank of their popularity. While there are papers that provide so-called civic-minded portrayal of politics, including liberal newspaper *Novaya Gazeta* and magazine *Novoe Vremya*, others—like *Vedemosti* and *Kommersant*—have focused on cultivating a reputation for taking critical views of the government when necessary. Nonetheless, maintaining an aura of respectability is a key factor for these media outlets, and they, on occasion, support initiatives put forward by the ruling party, as well as the ruling president. Finally, in today's Russia it is often difficult to differentiate between independent and opposition newspapers. Glossy lifestyle magazines to some degree have liberties as a second-class press, and their readership is mostly the Westernized upper class. For example, the Russian *Esquire* is a monthly anti-Putin tabloid with some fashion, or the liberal *Snob* magazine funded by oligarch Mikhail Prokhorov, the youth-oriented influential weekly magazine *Afisha*, whose former editor Ilya Krasilshchik played a prominent role in the New Decembrist movement and published *Bolshoi Gorod* paper in Moscow, openly liberal but far less antagonistic than *Novoe Vremya.*

One useful way to introduce the dynamics of Putin's and Medvedev's media is to juxtapose it to the media of Central Europe. Print press today is not a growing industry, so when it comes to finding financial backing for newspapers and magazines, an oligarch often stands behind a project, and for many of Russia's oligarchs, media outlets provide a useful mouthpiece for their political and business interests. One of the challenges to the unbiased performance of privately owned media arises from economic pressure. Few media outlets manage to remain both commercially viable and relatively independent. Against this backdrop, tabloidization effects are being seen across the media spectrum, meaning that quality press is being replaced by tabloid-like dailies that do not function as tools for trading influence and manipulating public opinion in the interests of power holders.[3] "Some broadsheets," argued Andrew Roth, "that have previously had a reputation for their candor have been slowly reined in over the years. The current reputation of

Nezavisimaya Gazeta is intertwined with one man: oligarch Konstantin Remchukov, who acquired the paper in 2007."[4]

Continued concentration of media market and ownership, along with the politicization of state-owned media in Russia, means that the media are most likely to give voice to those segments of society that currently hold economic or political power in order to deter some media outlets from exercising a watchdog function and encourage others to do so only when it serves their partisan interests. The development of the Russian press incorporates many trends of a global nature, and in many respects the Russian situation remains unique. Compared to other European countries, the Russian media system has some peculiarities. Scholars from East European countries have discussed the historical context of the post-Soviet states and have also focused on how the Russian journalists and the Russian media are affected by the omnipresent censorship experienced in the Soviet era.[5] Zassoursky,[6] Jakubowicz,[7] Koltsova,[8] Pasti[9] are important contributors to this discussion. Ultimately, in countries like Russia—which have weak rule of law at the local level—political bosses' crackdowns on critical media should have an even more chilling effect on watchdog journalism. Another reason, as journalist Andrew Roth from *Russia Profile* manifests, is that "Russia has plenty of editorially independent and opposition-minded media outlets, but they don't seem to be making much of a difference in the country's political life."[10] According to Lipman and McFaul,[11] Russia's national TV outlets compared to independent media are strikingly different in their choices of news priorities and newsmakers, as well as in general tone. The picture one gets of the situation in Russia from reading and listening to independent news sources is entirely different from that put forward by federal TV. These are just a few reasons that impact the independence and pluralism of the Russian media. Researchers claim that today's social media is increasingly personalized and may be a freer environment than traditional media. Readers trust bloggers and columnists that put bloggers on an equal footing with journalists.[12] At the same time the Russian government actually allows some critical press to continue to exist, as Masha Lipman pointed out. As is true elsewhere in the world, the Russian media industry is now faced with another challenge—the spread and popularization of the Internet. Internet brought new media and revolutionized not just the way Russians consume information, but the actual way that news is defined and delivered. The growth of Internet newspapers and blogs makes information so widespread that Russia's online media and blogs have almost become the only way of delivering socially important information to the public in Russia and abroad, including to Russian officials. And the Internet is believed to have remained wholly uncensored. As a result, even sites like LiveJournal and, later, Facebook and its local clone, VKontakte, began to function less as social networks in the Western sense than as alternative mass media.

Journalist Larisa Latynina notes, "Already earlier than asserting its monopoly on gas, the economy, the parliament and the powers that be, the regime of Vladimir Putin asserted its control of television." And to this day, "the seizure of television is considered by the regime as the first and chief stage of the seizure of everything else."[13] But of course, she continues, control over television "did not mean the complete destruction of freedom of information." "But it marked a monopoly on the generation of news." Six years ago, "news was only what was shown on television." If something wasn't on television, "it wasn't news."[14]

In 2012, the market research company TNS conducted a survey using participants between the ages of twelve and fifty-four, living in cities with a population of over one hundred thousand. According to this survey the Russian Internet search engine Yandex drew 19.1 million visitors a day in April compared to Channel One, which attracted 18.2 million viewers daily. What we can conclude from these results is that more people in Russia spent time on web portals than watching traditional TV.[15]

Undoubtedly, Runet has challenged the state's monopoly on information in Russia. The battle between those who argue that "either the Internet will destroy the [Russian] regime or the regime will destroy the Internet,"[16] and those who believe that it seems quite naive "to expect Internet civil society activities in Russia to have a significant impact on the offline world"[17] has been going on over the last couple of years. Meanwhile, an opposition rally against election fraud, which took place in Moscow's Bolotnaya Square, is a classic example of the increasing ability of the Internet to become a generator and a source of news. Internet became an alternative source of information, which is defined as a "source of information, provided by agents other than the government."[18]

After a long consideration I decided to analyze quality media outlets as well as nationwide printed outlets of a pronounced tabloid character. To do this, I sifted through the so-called central press: Moscow-based, nationally distributed newspapers and magazines. I selected newspapers that offer different political perspectives that looked interesting for several reasons. Considering that the Internet surpassed print newspapers as a source for national and international news, I searched the electronic versions of these outlets. I also focus on a new alternative media project that was created in a new media context and introduced additional layers of meaning through the use of visual culture. The following include brief profiles of the media outlets, which maintain an online presence, arranged alphabetically. Together, these media outlets dominate the market: that is, they have preferential access to the minds of the largest part of the population.

Argumenty i Fakty, the popular right-wing weekly, has a mix of political analysis and speculation, high-profile interviews, regional supplements, and consumer advice. It was founded in 1978 and has the highest circulation of any Russian newspaper—2,750,000. One of Russia's largest banks, Promsvyazbank, has controlling interest in the paper. It enjoys wide readership that is described as "working people, businessmen, intellectuals politicians and managers."

Ezhednevnyi Zhurnal, the tabloid with the highest circulation of all Russian periodicals, is an illustrated weekly and was founded by the Media-Most company in cooperation with *Newsweek* magazine in 1996. It is viewed in Russia as less influenced by self-censorship and more closely aligned with the opposition than mainstream Russian media. It has a reputation for belonging to the oppositional press in the pre-Putin era and for employing a highly professional and educated staff. It voices liberal intellectuals' critical attitude of government policy.

Gazeta.ru and Lenta.ru are two of Russia's largest, more successful, and independent online Russian news publications, covering politics and business. They are by far the leaders in this category and are often referenced in the *New York Times* and the *Washington Post*. They are set up in the format of a news blog and popular with educated readers and the international press. As of November 2011, Gazeta.ru was the third most popular news outlet in all of Runet. It belongs to Rambler, which was Russia's first search engine and which now also owns a cable TV network.

Izvestia, one of the largest national dailies, was established in March 1917. During the Soviet regime, *Izvestia* was on the left of the political spectrum with a clear pro-Kremlin line; and throughout much of the 1990s it was a relatively independent daily with a wide readership among the intelligentsia. It is one of Russia's leading business broadsheets, and widely regarded as one of Moscow's most Kremlin-friendly dailies. It describes itself as "one of the most authoritative and influential publications" that provides a variety of primary source documents such as press briefings and official speeches about Russia. This indicates the journalists' unwillingness to get engaged seriously in political debates that would have ramifications for their lives. In its modern incarnation, though, *Izvestia* has an average issue readership (AIR) of 371,000 (TNS Gallup Media, 2007) and has a circulation of 6.7 million. The paper has come to symbolize the failure of the Russian press and its co-option by the Kremlin, a kind of return to the Soviet model. In 2008, Gazprom Media sold its majority stake to the SOGAZ insurance company. The newspaper is currently owned by the National Media Group.

Kommersant is a liberal business-oriented broadsheet that originated in 1989. Originally a weekly publication, *Kommersant* now has a circulation of 87,000 (NCS, January 2008) and describes itself as "one of the most authoritative and influential publications for Russia's decision-makers." The exile oligarch Boris Berezovsky owned it in the late 1990s, but it is now owned by Alisher Usmanov—one of the richest men in Russia, according to *Forbes*

Magazine. *Kommersant* generally attracts readers who are not necessarily businessmen, but certainly are members of the privileged classes.

Moskovsky Komsomolets is the popular Moscow daily that combines tabloid content with broadsheet format. It is well known for its high-profile exposes of corruption among senior officials; it is sensationalist, gossipy, and not very reliable. Its reporting focuses on issues of interest to people living in Moscow. It often defends popular interest in such areas as human rights. But it criticizes only the lower levels of government—never the higher. It is liberal enough, but it is never punished, because its criticisms are not harsh. But it is always pushing the boundaries of what is allowed. Not surprisingly, its version of events is disputed, and the authorities counter it. It also publishes series of regional editions and supplements in the former Soviet republics. Its AIR is 1,215,000 (TNS Gallup Media, 2007). Its editor-in-chief, Pavel Gusev, is believed to own much of the newspaper's stock.

Neskuchny Sad is an Orthodox magazine covering the world's largest Orthodox Church, as well as the trends and attitudes toward Orthodox religion in a society that has increasingly embraced its Orthodox roots. The magazine discusses religious faith with both newly devout believers and those who are still finding their way in the church. *Neskuchny Sad* is considered a successful diocesan publication with a print run of about twenty thousand. While the magazine is most easily found in churches and religious literature stores, it can be found on many newsstands, next to secular papers. The Orthodox magazine is supported by advertising, mostly of icons and religious literature.

Nezavisimaya Gazeta, the centrist daily, occupies a prominent position among the Russian press. The newspaper offers a more independent, usually more critical look at Russian news. Its circulation—AIR (in Moscow only) seventy thousand (TNS Gallup Media, 2007)—is one of the smallest in Russia, but the paper is popular with liberal, educated, and politically active Russians, and is often quoted in international media. It is regarded as a prestigious platform for politicians, businessmen, academics, and political scientists. The paper was bought in August 2005 by Konstantin Remchukov, at the time an adviser for the Russian government. He appointed himself editor-in-chief in February 2007.

Novaya Gazeta is published twice a week, and is best known for its hard-hitting investigative critical reports on government corruption, human rights abuses in the North Caucasus, and abuses of power in Russia's armed forces. This is one of the few newspapers to report in detail on the liberal opposition. The newspaper—with a circulation of 171,000 (NCS, October 2007)—has come under intense government pressure in its two decades of existence. The former Soviet leader Mikhail Gorbachev and wealthy businessman Alexander Lebedev purchased a 49 percent stake; its staff is the majority shareholder.

Novoe Vremya, a liberal publication, is unusual in being fully independent of the state. The magazine contains articles on politics, economics, and social life, as well as investigative journalism. It specializes in long-form investigative stories, and spares little in its criticism of the Kremlin. Additionally, a number of columnists provide readers with their opinions regarding recent news and events.

Slon.ru is a popular Russian website launched in 2009 with an estimated 1.1 million visitors per month. It is modeled after Western online publications, such as Business Insider and TechCrunch. Not only does it report the news, but it also delivers unique takes on stories that differ significantly from traditional media and have much room for the kind of critical, intellectual commentary on politics, business, and economics. This website manages to distribute information before it gets picked up by traditional media. Its audience is intellectuals who are unhappy and dissatisfied with TV programming, and form their opinions based on blogs or columns that they trust more than conventional newspapers.

Sobesednik, started in 1984, is the supplement to *Komsomolskaya Pravda.* It is a weekly magazine with articles about Russian lifestyle issues. It presents up-to-date news, facts, and commentary on the state of events in Russia. Sobesednik.ru is ranked 18,409 in the world (among the 30 million domains); a low rank means that this website gets many visitors. This site is relatively popular among users in Russia. Dmitry Bykov is a weekly columnist for *Sobesednik.*

Trud was once the official paper of the Soviet trade union movement. Traditionally *Trud* devoted much of its coverage to social affairs. Since 2008 the paper changed its format and now places more emphasis on stories from the world of entertainment. The paper is financed by Promsvyazbank. Its AIR is 375,000 (TNS Gallup Media, 2007).

Zavtra is an ultra-nationalist newspaper that covers local news, sports, business, jobs, and community events. It is known for its strident anti-Semitic rhetoric in the political arena on both the national and local levels, as well as a number of highly public acts of anti-Semitic violence.

Although these outlets are far from Western quality newspapers, their publications are often quoted and referenced by other mass media, including local media in different regions. There are three reasons why I utilize data from a broad spectrum of media. First, due to the fact that the sector for quality media in Russia is poorly developed, there was a problem finding full-sense quality dailies among Russian newspapers like the *New York Times* or the *Washington Post.* Second, for the purpose of my study it is important to draw on the data from newspapers with different political content, specializing in different ideologies and satisfying readers with opposing views. Third, most of the Russian press today does not actively define itself as pro- or anti-Putin, or as pro- or anti-administration, but "the issue of reputation remains paramount for papers to keep a steady readership."[19]

NOTES

1. Adam Federman, "Moscow's New Rules," *Columbia Journalism Review*, January/February 2010.
2. Ivan Zassoursky, *Media and Power in Post-Soviet Russia* (Armonk, NY: M. E. Sharpe, 2004).
3. Boguslawa Dobek-Ostrowska and Michal Glowacki, *Comparing Media Systems in Central Europe* (Wroclaw, Poland: Wydawn, Uniwersytetu Wroclawskiego, 2008); Karol Jakubowicz, "Post-Communist Media Development in Perspective," 2005, http://library.fes.de/pdf-files/id/02841.pdf; A. Wyka, "On the Way to Dumbing Down . . . the Case of Central Europe," *Central European Journal of Communication* 1, no. 2 (2009): 133–47.
4. Andrew Roth, "Warriors of the Keyboard," *Russia Profile*, December 14, 2011, http://russiaprofile.org/culture_living/50997.html.
5. Sarah Oates and Gillian McCormack, "The Media and Political Communication," in *Developments in Russian Politics*, ed. Stephen White (Durham, NC: Duke University Press, 2010); Daniel Treisman, *The Return: Russia's Journey from Gorbachev to Medvedev* (New York: Free Press, 2011).
6. Zassoursky, *Media and Power in Post-Soviet Russia.*
7. K. Jakubowicz and M. Sükösd, *Finding the Right Place on the Map: Central and Eastern European Media Change in a Global Perspective* (Bristol, UK: Intellect, 2008).
8. Olessia Koltsova, "News Production in Contemporary Russia," *European Journal of Communication* 16, no. 3 (September 2001): 315–335.
9. S. Pasti, "Two Generations of Contemporary Russian Journalists," *European Journal of Communication* 3 (2005): 315.
10. Roth, "Warriors of the Keyboard."
11. Maria Lipman and Michael McFaul, "The Media and Political Developments," in *After Putin's Russia: Past Imperfect, Future Uncertain*, ed. Stephen K. Wegren and Dale R. Herspring (Lanham, MD: Rowman and Littlefield, 2010).
12. Alexei Navalny, one of Russia's leading opposition figures, who coined the phrase "the party of cooks and thieves," referencing United Russia, and established RosPil, a website that tracks state corruption, owes much of his success and popularity to his personal blog; his readership is estimated at over 1 million. His activity creates a separated news flow in social media. He is undoubtedly at present the driving force behind the opposition, however inchoate and drifting it currently may be. He has brought the issue of the corruption elite into the center of Russian politics, and has done more than anyone else to connect that the United Russia bloc, that bastion of the cynical, the careerist, and the corrupt. At present, there is no one else who can assume his mantle, no one else who has a chance—no more than a chance—of being able to turn the middle-class metropolitan opposition into a credible political force. Highly professional economist blogger Maxim Averbukh launched a special blog where he discloses the deeds associated with Gazprom. During the 2012 election, campaign-election-monitoring association Golos was effective in capturing the attention of large social media audiences. The TV channel Dozhd began televising alternative news and commentary in Moscow, and became the first network for national distribution of independent video production. It openly covers the 2011 Russian protests against the alleged rigging of the parliamentary elections.
13. Yulia Latynina, "Libo internet unichtozhit rezhim, libo rezhim unichtozhit internet," *Ezhednevnyi Zhurnal*, September 13, 2010, www.ej.ru/?a=note&id=10384.
14. Ibid.
15. "Internet More Popular Than TV in Russia," Z News, May 26, 2012, http://zeenews.india.com/news/net-news/internet-more-popular-than-tv-in-russia_777734.html.
16. Latynina, "Libo internet unichtozhit rezhim, libo rezhim unichtozhit internet."

17. Boris Dubin, cited from Floriana Fossato, "Discussion: Is Runet the Last Adaptation Tool?," *The Russian Cyberspace Journal* 1, no. 1 (2009), www.russian-cyberspace.com.

18. R. A. Dahl, "What Political Institutions Does Large-Scale Democracy Require?," *Political Science Quarterly* 120, no. 2 (2005): 187–97.

19. Roth, "Warriors of the Keyboard."

Chapter Four

Habitus and Identity

This chapter focuses on the discourses of the last decade as performed among newsmakers of the official and alternative media. While I address the question of how references to Russian classics shape the public discourse, I also want to look at how allusions can mislead the readers and how the dominant and marginal discourses are impacted by the allusive references. In short, blending of references with shared values across various types of public discourses is accounted for in part by the attractiveness of the wide array of allusions to different readerships and communities. From this perspective, journalists' particular strategies and textual choices can only be understood through establishing a setting and community in which particular values are recognized by the readers.

For a cohesive framework for my analyses, which is rather analytical and pragmatic, I use the concepts of "habitus" and "identity" in order to interpret the complexity of identities in contemporary society and underscore the different, even competing individuals and collective perspectives on public discourse.

Pierre Bourdieu's concept of "habitus" was selected for its key connections to the personal and social dimensions of identity.[1] This concept refers to the enduring outlooks (perceptions, appreciations, behaviors) that are internalized by particular social groups. The habitus that was related to the positions that individuals occupy in the social space (class, in the first instance), and originally attached to the notion of class differentiation can be defined as a performative system of dispositions, values, and expectations of particular social groups, related in turn to the complexity of cultural knowledge that can be interpreted through the lens of an individual, as well as presented as the perspective of a group.[2] When removed from sociology and thanks to the broad definition of the "system of disposition," the current uses of Bourdieu's concept undertake the conceptual transformation. In my framework, habitus and identity are conflated to project the duality of identity in the intimate sphere and public life with its objective and subjective determinants. This opens up a whole new outlook of personalized individuals that are modeled by media. In my view, habitus is indexed to the important questions of identities, converging the outcomes of both individual and collective patterns and highlighting engagement/empowerment and readership. In media discourse linguistic identity is fluid and highly variable and unspecified in the multifaceted public sphere. This model of the discursive space based on the fusion of intertwined and superimposed streamlining thoughts with different combination of democratic tendencies in discursive practices allows a number of interpretations at once.

Not surprisingly, this model permits all kinds of misinterpretation that can be discarded as discursive distortions. In this sense the revised understanding of the habitus concept can also generate predictions regarding individual and group behavior in the discursive space. A revised conceptualization of the habitus is less a label but rather an umbrella term for different, even competing perspectives of individuals, collective bodies, ties, and processes. Thus, with regard to the important question of identities, it represents, rather than defines, social groups and communities. In relation to the media, we may find other kinds of new dimensions in dispositions, mainly concerned with contemporary forms of urban cultures, legacy, visual and informational references, cultural and civic commitment.

The following discussion views these discourses within the conceptual framework of habitus theory. A habitus concept, modified as I have suggested above, predicts if we view the habitus as a forum for discussions for a group of interested individuals or institutions like publishing enterprises and newspapers who engage in vernacular discourse about specific issues. It would be more valuable to understand habitus as a "discursive space." Then the audience for whom the competing discourses become available as a "commodity" can determine meanings on their own, verbalize their opinions, and state them explicitly. In this way readership is engaged in vernacular discourse about specific issues on discussion forums, where meanings and opinions are articulated, distributed, and negotiated. Public forums for discussions not only are formed around the dialogue surrounding issues, but also reflect identities of all private people—as readers, listeners, and spectators—who could avail themselves and get engaged in the discussions of public opinions. The habitus incorporates people's assumptions, beliefs, and attitudes on the public discourse, but also can constrain many of their responses to the established order and the established meanings in the public discourse. It is important to note the significance of an individual's habitus that develops as a response to realities of the social environment in which he or she was raised. True, it would not be an overstatement to say that these realities leave their imprint across the interwoven cognitive and bodily dimensions of the habitus. Therefore the revised concept leads us to expect that habitus incorporates notions of embodied cognition, or more accurately depicts the relations between the individual and the cultures and subcultures in which and through which an individual lives. We encounter the same use of the term as representative of some self-expressions in response to social experiences of everyday life. Among cultural interdiscursive and mediatized assets,[3] in which these expressions of identity are presented, are public debates, books, letters, photographs, sites, blogs, YouTube, and so on.

Considering the context of my study, the notion Bourdieu applied is suitable in defining both the dominant mainstream public discourse of the official sphere (doxa or orthodox discourse) and the subversive and oppositional discourse of alternative media (heretical or heterodox). Any established tradition or symbolic order perceived as truth, as the law, or as political consensus can be described as "orthodoxy," and any discourse diverging from it as "heterodox" or "heretic."[4] In a similar manner, a departure from the existing language dispositions is called a *heretic break* with the established order.[5] Apparently, these content-oriented concepts originally coined in the religious discourse are a shrewd "shorthand" expression for much of the socialization that individuals of particular groups have undergone. When we turn to contemporary use of the term "habitus," with regard to media text, there is still a frequent focus on addressing the orthodox and the heterodox discourses within separate specific historic periods. Take, for instance, Lara Ryazanova-Clarke, who applies Bourdieu's model to juxtapose four discursive stages covering the period from 1992 to 2007, and examines the different combination and interrelation between the heretical and orthodox language.[6] As she has put it, the standard critical narrative attributes the influx of heterodoxy in the period of Boris Yeltsin's presidency and domination of orthodox discourse in the period of Vladimir Putin's presidency. Perhaps the "linguistic tools" are then reflected in a linguistic distinction prevalent in various discursive stages, though the distinction is never truly clear. I argue for a different reading of this shift. It appears that it makes no difference what particular political leader is in place; the defining alternative media will operate and will convert to the new situation, whenever a major political or cultural change of manifold occurs. Namely, we should in no way be surprised by the appearance of the alternative discourse of liberal opposition and those excluded from the area of politics in December 2011 and during the first half of the election year. While it could be argued that it is natural for alternative, yet lacking integrity discourse to take place in the face of newly found intellectual freedom, this does not necessarily signal the new discursive stage.

If we look back at the Soviet-era media landscape, we see that samizdat as the unofficial dissemination of secretly published and distributed literature within "totalitarian" political systems occurred first in the Soviet Union as early as the 1920s, before the term was used, and then emerged in the 1950s, following Stalin's death in 1953, largely as the dissident political movement against official restrictions on the freedom of expression.[7] In his essay "The Terrifying Mimicry of Samizdat," Serguei Oushakine establishes a tradition which appears to be productive for the rhetorical analysis of alternative discourse. He argues that "the oppositional discourse of the Culture dissident movement in the Soviet Union manifested itself as very much a 'surface' phenomenon,"[8] or in other words, "it echoed and amplified the rhetoric of the regime, rather than positioning itself outside of or underneath it."[9] Characteristically, samizdat discourse is defined by Oushakine mainly through negation, while the dominant orthodox discourse of mainstream media serves as a background against which the specific qualities of samizdat can be defined. When we turn to the contemporary media landscape we see that with regard to the dominant-marginal dichotomy, it does not differ substantially from its predecessors. On the current media landscape we can thus speak of coexistence of mainstream and alternative media. Both types of discourse are endowed by communicative dynamics, and amplify examples of interpretation of classical allusions and references, mostly ironic and sarcastic.[10]

It should be noted that new media outlets have been implicitly rhetorical and have played an increasingly important role in recent years, organizing protest events, and publicizing corruption scandals and human rights abuses. Because it most frequently appeared in the new format of digital media that introduce concepts and ideas that challenged the status quo, Bourdieu's term "heretic" can be applied to discuss and describe linguistic tools of current media discourse. Several reasons are repeatedly given to explain the marginal status of alternative media. The most common of these claim current turbulent political situation as a retarding factor in the development of new media. While there is truth in this reasoning, I would add an additional explanation, namely, members of these media tend not to assert themselves as a community in any substantial way. However, rather than dismissing the marginalization of alternative media as a sad side effect of the contemporary political situation, maybe we're better off seeing this form of media for how it is at its best. The popularity of alternative media strongly suggests that the world observed through social media is more interesting when authors insert themselves into it.

Although the problem of the relationship between media and individual or group identities may seem more of a sociological than a linguistic question, the unique pragmatic dimension of the allusions in media makes it an important element in the process of identity construction. In addition to the local and the global identity the authors talk of mixed or frontier identities, the "dramaturgical" representations performed by individuals and groups in daily *mise-en-scène*.[11] For example, Mikhail Epstein spoke of a collective, liberating, and emancipating "consciousness" that rejects the separatist concept of cultures, showing the intrinsic incompleteness of each.[12]

During the last two decades, a number of key symbolic processes occurred widely throughout Russian society, when ideologies and rhetorical practices were thrown down, unmasked, and scrutinized. New themes, new linguistic practices, and new identities became prevalent, and the cleavage between the official and alternative discourses was enacted. The competing discourses help us rationalize why and ultimately how people seek alignment with some and separation from others, how they discursively manifest their intentions of inclusion and exclusion of social actors.

In contemporary Russia, the official public sphere coexists with the parallel public sphere. The former includes the media of "marginalized groups," which are groups of people who, being excluded from a universal public sphere, form their own public spheres. If official media are primarily owned by the state or close to the state power elite group, and subordinate to censorship,[13] alternative or "counter-public" forms of media represent alternative debates to the dominant official discourse,[14] while also opposing the traditional organization forms of media production. One of the meeting points for these two types of discourses is a pool of classical allusions and the conventions and patterns of their usage, confirmed and established through their widespread reiteration.

Literary allusions actively participate in the process of shaping national and cultural identities representing the past through various ideological, political, and cultural perspectives. The specificity of contemporary Russian society requires special attention to the political and ideological implications with regard to the function of cultural production and, particularly, literature in that society. Eric Hobsbawm's emphases on the danger of historians' involvement as myth-makers in identity politics may also be well applied to journalism with literary references.[15]

For the purpose of my study I want to focus on the use of classical allusions and references and to observe how it functions in particular speech genres within different media discourses of the last decade. I accept the assumption that every society has its own system of speech genres that vary from culture to culture.[16] The theorist whose work comes most readily to mind in relation to the speech genres pertinent to Russian culture is Nancy Ries.[17] Ries, after studying the post-Soviet discursive universe, came to the conclusion that Russian authoritative discourse developed its own powerful discursive frames of talking about the individual, his or her private life, and interpersonal relations. As she remarks, the effects of Soviet speech genres on individuals and their emotions not only were organized by various social settings, but also were constituted through literature and arts. She points out that "Russian genres are themselves blurry, unfixed, protean, and interpenetrating";[18] nonetheless verbal and written performances "are distinguishable and generalizable as generic and thematic patterns, patterns that constrain and reproduce cultural structures, emblems, stances, and values every bit as much as do more traditional mythopoetic genres."[19] She makes a clear distinction between "certain key points, attitudes, ideas, and approaches to life, which American speech genres supported and contained, but which Russian genres did not."[20] She made an insight on how to fit the Russian talk she adopted into her speech genres. As she observed Russian interlocutors during the time of perestroika, she managed to compile a generic classification of Russian speech of that time.[21]

I argue that classical literature in Russia has always been not just a neutral commodity as it is in the West, but has been considered a precious asset, a repository of shared values. Since quotes from Russian classics are frequently and easily recognizable and highly appreciated by the audience of both official and alternative media, one can assume that this discursive practice has a peculiar role as a rhetorical device. Russian literature has provided the nation's forum for public discourse, an important site of contact between literary intelligentsia and refined audience. Public discourse in contemporary Russia is still marked by an open, vibrant, sometimes caustic exchange of the classical references. What this would seem to suggest, then, is that media practitioners through rhetorical techniques—be it mimicking the classics, appealing to their authority, or alienation from the classical tradition through pastiche or other stylistic inventions, or aligning of classical context with politics (to varying degrees)—keep engaged with intellectual culture.

For a century the literature not only created a new class of consumers—sophisticated and cultural readers—but also explicated the most essential part of upbringing and identity. It may be relevant to note that the Russian canonical writers (Pushkin, Gogol, Dostoevsky, Tolstoy, and Chekhov—just to name a few) were part of the secondary school curriculum. Names of classics were used as a guarantee of quality and truth of verbal statements, as well as for verification of the whole system of education. By the same token, each literary piece placed on the school curriculum obtained the status of classic. However, there was something particular in the reading of classics in the Soviet school. The literature reading list that included the variety of classical titles was regarded to be antiquated and even bourgeois, along with the Soviet authors who primarily promote the realization of communist aims and ideals, as it has been handed down to school kids, generation by generation, each time in conformity with the prevailing literary tastes of young readers, whose education could not conceivably be considered complete without this literature component. Classical literature was so authoritative that it was supposed to go beyond any criticism, making it advantageous for persuasion. The functions of the masterpieces determine their paramount usage in public discourse in the gap where prescribed interpretation tends to be treated as a point of criminality. The mechanism through which such inflexible normativity of interpretation was possible is, of course, reading literary texts from the premise of establishing authorial intent. The Soviet reader, as Evgeny Dobrenko has shown,[22] had an unmatchable, if perverse, creative power over the text; the extension of this power is the creation of a whole new character out of the text's author.

In an attempt at estrangement from the official cult building of the classics and explaining the effect of the attitude to the disparity between the literary figures and the cult surrounding them, I would add that learning legends about them was part of the reading experience for the younger and older generations of the Soviet readers. In the schools verses of classics were studied not for the sake of their talent and original, unique gift, but according to the kindergarten teacher's, the grade school teacher's highly selective and carefully interpreted versions of them. The lines of the classics were heard and read in radio announcements, headlines of newspaper articles, slogan placards at the factories, and posters in the passport department of the police station. The legends were based on surrounding their names with a certain halo and making of those names and images a daily encounter in Soviet life. Therefore, if for an average reader the relationship with classical canon was predicated on a distinctly Soviet mode of reading,[23] it is possible to assume by extension that there was an explicitly anti-Soviet audience capable of being critical, or disengaged through irony and sarcasm, advocating an individual interpretation of classics rather than a collective normative one.

To some degree the perestroika has laid its impression on every branch of Russian intellectual life. This new influence is perhaps most marked in literature. In the post-Soviet treatment of classical Russian literature one can observe more individual freedom in the choice and handling of classical themes and characters. In contrast to the Soviet period there has been a reaction against the canonization of classics that had been accepted as a part of the political change.

The system of samizdat and habits of reading banned books existed until 1988; only toward the end of perestroika did freely available classics appear in massive print runs. Books by authors of entirely different persuasions and from a wide range of periods were published simultaneously. And what happened when all the authors were cited in media and public discourse simultaneously, as though they were contemporaries? In introducing contradictory theories or approaches from different times and places, readers often fail to ask in what sense they are relevant to contemporary Russian problems. Although old and new works were cited in journalism, its authors still largely looked to the classics for their theoretical tools, while the average reader was not aware of the original sources and names mentioned in a public discourse. While the narrow literary circle has really systematic grasp of the national literature, Russians often felt they first need to gallop through the entire nineteenth and twentieth centuries before they can discuss and analyze available intellectual sources. Indeed how does one understand Dostoevsky's Christian perspective without knowing the doctrine of the "resurrection of the dead" by Nikolai Fedorov, or what is the point of referring to Alexei Losev without considering figures like Pavel Florenskii and Sergei Bulgakov in a philosophical rather than a strictly religious context?

As a consequence, new readers spoke and thought in a new idiom that included buzz words and mostly a mix of Soviet newspeak, Russian religious philosophy, and the occasional terms from Western humanities. Complicated concepts such as "self-constructing personality" (Nikolai Berdiaev), "dialogue," "carnival," "polyphony" (Mikhail Bakhtin) trickled down to the media; yet since most readers did not understand them, these terms ended up as glamorous all-embracing metaphors. This may sound surprising, since classical literature is regarded as a core subject in school curriculum. Insufficient literature background among average readers was a serious problem.

The problem would be far less dramatic if Russia had a critical mass of readers who have a command of classical sources, enabling them to judge the quality of literature. It is perhaps a symptom of the essential change of relationship with the classics themselves that in many contemporary Russian novels and poems the Russian classical canon has been revised, rewritten, and "distorted." If we look back to the late nineteenth-century Russian literary and journalistic discussions in the official public sphere, one of the trends to consider is the multiplicity of worldviews and philosophies (utilitarianism multiple versions of socialism, nihilism, slavophilism, Tolstoyan humanism, mysticism, etc.) that were in conversation and argument with each other, primarily through literary criticism. In the public discourse, there were clearly defined arrays intensely focused on certain philosophical perspectives, and a link to ideologically friendly media of the same persuasion; Slavophiles and Westernizers, for example, formed distinct and separate clutches situated across from each other in the network. With characteristic ambiguity, contemporary public discourse in Russia demonstrates significant overlaps between competing approaches, making distinctions between them highly conditional.

The contemporary paradigm of school education has stressed the humanistic nature of education and developing common values, but nevertheless the standardized instruction and rote memorization has left an average student with plenty of quotes from the classical literature. The analysis and creative interpretation of the main characters has been touched on only briefly. Dominating the public discourse, they are prominently presented in a considerable portion of schooling because they still seem pressingly relevant to the most immediate concerns of the present age. Russians proclaim their pride in quoting lines of classical literature, although not everyone would probably overtly justify this ability. Even though rote learning and memorization lead to the blind acceptance of certain ideas and tenants and do not leave room for critical analysis and creative interpretation, it is tempting to keep quoting from the key moral and intellectual voices as if they possessed powerful healing magic but could simultaneously extrapolate what happens in the real world.

Russia is not the most reading nation in the world as it used to be. Nowadays, skeptics are convinced that Russian youth are mostly unfamiliar even with the classics of Russian and Soviet literature and art. Critics accuse the entire generation of embracing opacity, glorifying surfaces, and rejecting the meaningful word. The older generation interpreted this as a troubling sign that this generation appears inauthentic. Recently, experts are witnessing an "alarming tendency" for people to read less, especially the classics. According to spokesman for the Moscow Writers Union Aleksandr Gerasimov, "Russians read more of their newspapers and news online, and they are developing apathy toward reading serious literature, thick books written not only by contemporaries but by classic writers as well."[24] In his opinion, "such indifference can lead to erosion of entire cultural layers, to depletion of knowledge about literature, to the loss of national self-identification."[25]

This situation reminds me of the state of Russian literature that Tatyana Tolstaya metaphorically describes in her novel *Slynx*, which reimagines dystopian fantasy. In Tolstaya's dystopian novel, a naive and carefree character, who is vaguely positioned in history and also resituated more specifically in time and place, fails to understand why Pushkin should be memorialized. Since he was born after the apocalypse that wiped out modern Russian culture and threw the country back to feudalism, he has no idea what "a pushkin" is, or why the elder members of the intellectual elite who remember culture and literature want him to carve out an idol to represent Pushkin. The explanation he got from his mentor is that for the Russian intellectual tradition, "Pushkin is our everything."[26]

Paradoxically, the late nineteenth-century discussion on the changing role of literature in the society is resurrected. More than one hundred years ago Dostoevsky parodied what he perceived to be the mistaken focus of these philosophies: the lack of appreciation of art, as he states in the oft-quoted phrase from a satirical piece he published in his journal: "A pair of boots are, in every sense, better than Pushkin."[27] Dostoevsky intends this entire argument to be ironic. Since this is one of the focal points of the Other's philosophy that he is trying to refute, Dostoevsky added to his argument by hinting at the notion of "art for art's sake" as opposed to the materialistic reasoning. This allowed Dostoevsky to extend the scope of his attack to left-leaning utopianists, who focused on materialistic solutions to humanity's poverty and despair. Some scholars claim that the new millennium is a grotesque distortion of this tradition. For example, Mikhail Epstein argues that "the entire life of society becomes an empty self-presentation."[28] This brings me irresistibly to the scholarship of Russian canon. Lyudmila Parts[29] studies a range of post-Soviet texts that use the "image of Pushkin" to critique late and post-Soviet cultural reality. Russian classics matter not as authors of actual works, but as "cult figures who are nothing but symbolic entities by and through which culture identifies itself and on which it relies to assure its identity and continuity."[30] This suggests that the process of metaphorization of the Russian classical tradition has a long history that I will discuss further with plenty of examples.

I bring this comparison up to suggest that although the classical references have been preserved in the public discourses, the ways classical heritage appears in the contemporary media reflects on the Soviet era prescriptive on interpretation and assimilation. The Russia of today is utilizing both its Soviet literary heritage, and its pre-revolutionary rich literary and philosophical traditions. Moreover, on the one hand, a certain form of Russian identity is thus constructed around veneration of the classical canon, as knowledge of literature and beliefs are intricately linked to a viable notion of education. On the other hand, as Ilya Kalinin notes, classical literature fails to generate any kind of communal significance and it cannot structure any community at all.[31]

One particularly striking example of a campaign to encourage Russians to read classics is the following.[32] To address the problem, the newspaper *Moscow News* launched a new ad campaign with billboards bearing quotes from famous people, not just Russians. Among the notable entries were Benjamin Franklin's "Большая империя, как и большой пирог, легче всего объедается с краев" (A great empire, like a great cake, is most easily diminished at the edges), but also Fyodor Tyutchev's "Русская история до Петра Великого—одна панихида, а после Петра Великого—одно уголовное дело" (Russian history before Peter the Great is nothing but one funeral service, and after Peter the Great is one criminal case alone), and Ivan Krylov's "Услужливый дурак опаснее врага" (A helpful fool is more dangerous than an enemy). These and a few other "disrespectful" quotes, such as "Честность неотделима от свободы, как коррупция от деспотизма" (Honesty is inseparable from freedom of corruption against despotism) by Anatole France and "Россия—страна фасадов" (Russia is a country of facades) by Marquis de Custine, "were chosen to recall the generic problems of Russian history," the newspaper's editor, Vladimir Gurevich, said.[33] "Few people, including myself, have seen these banners on the streets," Gurevich told RIA.[34] In Russia, where the authorities have been actively engaged in propagating their own concept of history, removal of challenged banners evokes the preemptive censorship or silencing of the voice of oppositional journalists. Apparently, billboards were removed because the message of the campaign implied that there was a sense of decline and corruption in the government. However, the scandal may have given more attention to the promoting banners because, although few people have seen these banners on the streets, their content is available to thousands of Internet users. It seems to be a perfect illustration to the axiom that when journalistic discourse is harshly censored and controlled, the only outlet for political and philosophical debate among the intellectual elite in public discourse is available through opaque Aesopian language.

Although the Russian Academy of Education granted individual schools considerable autonomy in developing curriculum, the literature syllabi specify every single work to be covered and give detailed lists of required readings. The reading list is focusing on the nineteenth- and twentieth-century masterpieces, thus schoolchildren read classics such as *The Storm* by Alexander Ostrovsky, *Fathers and Sons* by Ivan Turgenev, Nekrasov's poetry, tales by Saltykov-Shchedrin, and the critics by Vissarion Belinsky. Those authors were severely critical of autocracy and implied that if reforms were not forthcoming a revolt would be justified through man's natural right of self-defense. It is perhaps not surprising then that the respective members of the Public Chamber delivered a scathing criticism of the existing ways of teaching Russian literature in schools, maintaining that Russian literature should wield a positive influence on the pupil's personality and boost patriotism among the population. One of the avid critics of the curriculum, Pavel Pozhigailo,[35] voiced the opinion that school literature classes should be more effective in improving the morals of Russian society; in other words, they should suit the ideological needs of the state. To avoid confusing interpretations in literature classes, he suggests designing guidelines for teachers with no more than one sanctioned interpretation of the literary work that teachers would be allowed to offer students. He also calls for the revision of literary canon, offering teachers to confront characters' inner contradictions. His recommendations to avoid studying Gogol and Dostoevsky in secondary school fuel public discontent. But what triggers major public disputes is his statement that one of the "potentially harmful books" that can be left out is Mikhail Bulgakov's *Master and Margarita.*[36] The concerns of the ideological function of studying literature, for which family values and humanism, as well as national pride and a respectful attitude toward authorities are the key values, constantly do make an appearance in media. Nevertheless, professional school teachers and the academic community argue against the state-approved study program and once established interpretation of the literary works, the reader-oriented theories do not seem to have any impact on the authors of the curriculum.

I have argued that the new media witnessed the emergence of the dialogue with classical tradition. However, I tend to see the intertextual reference to the Russian literature in media not as an attempt to reinforce the old tradition, but more as a way to provide a metaphor for the current state of Russia. If it is obvious that media discourse is stuffed with classical, traditional, even archaic patterns of cultural mentality, it is also apparent that these patterns constitute the very basis of the mechanism of media persuasion and verification (or falsification), and thus create an inevitable, natural part of the consciousness, and especially the unconsciousness of a mass reader. During the periods of cultural instability, cult names served as pivotal figures who ensured the unity of culture. Nikolai Gogol's only full-length play is Russia's greatest stage comedy and its most devastating satire; *The Inspector General* is referred to most frequently when the journalist tends to mirror Russia's habit to collude in corrupt practices out of self-interest, or inertia, or both.

Many of Chekhov's characters have multiple meanings: the veneer of farce covers over both tragedy and compassion, both judgment and reflection, such as the eminently popular Lieutenant Colonel Vershinin in *Three Sisters*, who spends much of the play dreamily predicting how, "Через 200–300 лет жизнь на земле будет невообразимо прекрасной, изумительной" (in two or three hundred years, life on Earth will be unimaginably beautiful, marvelous)[37]—while utterly failing to act in the present. Another character, Trigorin, may think about such things as the World Spirit, the Earth in two hundred thousand years, but is unable to resist the temptation to reel off clever plots tied to the observation of petty details. In "Seagul" Chekhov puts the disparaging judgments on Trigorin's worth for comic effect: "Мило, талантливо... но... после Толстого или Золя не захочешь читать Тригорина" (*Treplev:* Charming, talented . . . but . . . after Tolstoy and Zola you don't want to read Trigorin).[38] In current journalism the simple isomorphism between the literal and the literary meaning of the names signal the Aesopian quality of the language. I believe that the return to Aesopian strategies in contemporary journalism must be linked to the intensification of dissent and must be read in the context of necessity to avoid infringing the censorship regulations. Aesopian reading indicates the explicity of two reference frames—one denoting the immediate object of the literary text, the other one targeting a political reality protected by censorship. Although Aesopian symbols emerge rarely in the journalistic texts—otherwise their accumulation would cancel the very condition of Aesopian reading—they are most frequently to occur in foreword or afterword sections, and at key points of an argument. Up to a certain point, the manifestation of Aesopian techniques evokes the limitation of the freedom of expression, the repression of individual thinking, and the falsification of history under the pressure of current political imperatives.

Authored quotes along with anonymous ones reside in Russian readers' minds, traveling through society by means of the spoken word. The rigid "words of the Other" are used as a "national-patriotic" persuasion, or as a tool of satire, appearing through their particular mode of bricolage.[39] These lines were such an essential part of the Russian childhood that today they easily roll off the tongues. While these famous quotes are reproduced in public discourse to add new perspectives on things, they also slowly blur the past, and, as the political actors attempt to prove, open up new horizons.

In order to better understand the media's reference to Russian classical literature, I focus on the public sphere to analyze the main themes of the discussion around politics and public affairs. Speeches of politicians have long been recognized as an important tool to influence public opinion and construct realities.[40] In what follows I offer to focus on the allusions that appear in today's public discourses on questions of historical and cultural memory. I refer to those who have the ability to speak with authority, in the public sphere today. Much of what motivates Russian politicians with regard to the ideal role of the state is seen in the references to nineteenth-century Russian thinkers and philosophers.

The topic of cultural memory and the role of Russian literature in it is likely to be of great importance to the Kremlin administration. An article on ethnic issues, with numerous references to the Russian literary traditions, was published in *Nezavisimaya Gazeta* on January 23.[41] The author, then prime minister Vladimir Putin, said that Russia has "always been described as a 'reading nation,'" and proposed taking a survey of the country's "most influential cultural figures" to compile "a 100-book canon" that every Russian school graduate will be required to read. Mandating a core reading list may appear as an incentive, or a desire to civilize Russian youth. However, in the context of the political appeal to preserve "the dominance of Russian culture," Putin's declaration looks like a manipulative indoctrination. Apparently, Putin does not look at literature as something transcendental, profoundly human, and visionarily global, but rather as a tool to instigate an ultranationalist ideology where the desired writers represent spiritual core values.

In the same article Putin referred to some of Russia's earliest philosophical and religious works, such as *The Sermon on Law and Grace* and the *Primary Chronicle.* The current Russian leadership, in other words, is using everything it can extract from history to boost the country's imperial traditions. Moreover, in recent years Russian politicians, including Putin, have begun to support a geopolitical strategy that puts Russia in the center.

In order to support my argument, I present the discussion on the possible impact of the language performance of a politician on the conventional modes of political practice. A number of studies show that Putin has been redefining the language of the Kremlin in a very personal way.[42] One may argue that analysis of Putin's political performance may suffer from a distorting lack of distance and thus conclusions of the role of agency in bringing about change in the political culture can be an exaggeration but not outright falsehood. I further demonstrate the usage of references to classics to effectively illuminate the political or moral judgment in Putin's public speeches. With respect to Michael Gorham's study on Putin's language,[43] my analysis supports the idea that discourse orientation in the political communication is what makes the politician's rhetoric so effective. Gorham cautions that Putin's "exceptional oratorical prowess stems from an ability to speak in a variety of voices depending on the context of his utterance, to shift in and out of language registers or speech styles to reflect the broader ideological and political sentiments of his immediate interlocutors and broader listening and viewing audience."[44] Quintessentially, the success of his political performance is not so much in the language, but in cognitive orientations to the addresses, assessment of the interlocutor's point of view, and a subject of political action being discussed. What occurred to me is that, nowadays, the state-owned media and even the national leader inject a portion of "classics" in the public discourse.

In February 2012, discussing the alleged assassination plot with the reporters on Russian state-owned television Channel One, Putin assured journalists that he is not afraid of terrorists, and cited Pushkin's *Eugene Onegin*, saying, "Иных уж нет, а те далече" (Alas, now some are no more, and some are distant). During a rally of his supporters at the Luzhniki stadium in Moscow on February 23, 2012, Putin cited Mikhail Lermontov's poem *Borodino* and ended the speech with Vyacheslav Molotov's famous Great Patriotic War slogan, "Победа будет за нами!" (Victory Shall Be Ours!). Then while celebrating his victory in the presidential race, he quoted the verses of Sergey Esenin, "Если скажет рать святая, брось ты Русь, живи в раю. Я скажу, не надо рая, дайте Родину мою" (If the Holy army yells, "Abandon Rus and live in paradise." I'll say, "I don't need paradise, give me my homeland"). However, this reference was made without a clear logical connection to his main point. Via patriotic formulation he moved on to praise those who actively voted for him, which he favorably contrasted to the passive absorption of opposition. Allusion, regarding the topic of the country that is totally possessed by enemies, has been frequently projected in the election campaign. It is not quite clear why Putin referred to Esenin's "holy army." It could be more comprehensible if considering this rhetoric as a strategy of perpetuation that introduces patriotic frame. According to Ruth Wodak et al., strategies of perpetuation "attempt to maintain and to reproduce threatened national identity, i.e. to preserve, support and protect it."[45]

As I mentioned above, a familiar expression can be curtailed, for example "И клятву верности сдержали" (And kept our oath of loyalty). Lermontov's lines from the patriotic poem *Borodino* had been written in the wake of the 1812 war against Napoleon. In the original verse it says: "'Ребята! не Москва ль за нами? / Умремте ж под Москвой, / Как наши братья умирали!' / —И умереть мы обещали, / И клятву верности сдержали / Мы в бородинский бой" (Boys, isn't it Moscow behind us? So let's die before Moscow as our grandfathers did! And to die we promised. And we have kept the oath of allegiance to the Battle of Borodino!). In an editorial in *Novaya Gazeta* titled "Engaged with Death," the newspaper's editor, Andrei

Kolesnikov, points out that Putin and United Russia's campaign is based on patriotic slogans borrowed from the 1812 war against France. The slogan at the pro-Putin Luzhniki rally, "Let's protect the country," was inspired by Lermontov's famous poem, "Let's Die Protecting Moscow." As Kolesnikov further underscores, "What do they want us to die for? Why are we being asked to die for Russia? What does it actually mean in the context of a political campaign?"[46] The editorial suggests that the "Defend Russia" rhetoric is aimed at Putin's core electorate: people over the age of fifty-five, pensioners, residents of small- and medium-sized cities. "This is the Russia which will follow Putin into a crusade against his perceived enemies," says the author. "The enemies which only exist in their imagination." To summarize the editorial position: The feeling of unlimited love of the native land is deeply rooted in the spiritual nature of the Slav, and it is sung and described by classical writers and classical poets in their works, such as *War and Peace*, *Poltava*, and numerous others. In the context of the contemporary public discourse the politician intensifies the classical context conflating love for the Motherland with hatred toward the enemy combatant. By doing so, he exploits the subversive potential of the powerful allusion to cater to what he thinks the audience needs to see in this poem, namely, the opposition is the Napoleon-style enemy, assailing everything a real Russian holds sacred. Replacing the context of the contemporary events with the historical past, he disrupts the expected tone of the classical allusion at its very core. Furthermore, not surprisingly the majority of modern history studies in Russia are engaged in elevating historiosophy as superior to other historical modes.[47]

In the first years of presidency, Putin was considered "ideologically amorphous—that is, neither left-wing nor right-wing."[48] However, now he, surprisingly, fits into a long-standing Russian tradition of liberal conservatism. Theorist Richard Sakwa commented on "a unique synthesis of liberalism and conservatism"[49] embodied in Putin's rule. An opinion circulates that ideas of Russian conservatism, especially those of the philosopher Ivan A. Ilyin (1883–1954)[50] have not lost their prestige for President Putin's administration due to the philosopher's predictions about the disintegration of the Soviet Union and his ideas of Russia's historical mission. Putin regularly quoted Ilyin, a proponent of multiculturalism, in his writings and speeches.[51] Whether Western philosophers consider the doctrine of Eurasianism by Lev Gumilev or more recently by Dmitry Shlapentokh,[52] it would seem that President Putin is more likely to be influenced by Orthodox nationalistic ideas recognizing the state-founding role on the Russian nationality. In the influential daily *Nezavisimaya Gazeta* Putin published a lengthy article, headlined "Russia: The National Question,"[53] where he underscores Ilyin's quote to emphasize Russia's historical respect for all creeds and colors: "Не искоренить, не подавить, не поработить чужую кровь, не задушить иноплеменную и инославную жизнь, а дать всем дыхание и великую

Родину—всех соблюсти, всех примирить, всем дать молиться по-своему, трудиться по-своему и лучших отовсюду вовлечь в государственное и культурное строительство" (Not to eliminate, not to suppress, not to enslave other people's blood, not to stifle the life of different tribes and religions—but to give everyone breath and the great Russia to honor all, to reconcile all, to allow everyone to pray in their own way, to work in their own way, and to engage the best in public and cultural development).[54]

Putin also quotes the famous Russian historian Vasily Klyuchevsky, who noted, referring to the Time of Troubles, "Когда надломились политические скрепы общественного порядка, страна была спасена нравственной волей народа" (When the political ties of public order fractured, the country was rescued by the moral will of the people).[55] Then Putin reminds his readers that National Unity Day[56] "на самом деле—это 'день победы над собой,' над внутренней враждой и распрями, когда сословия, народности осознали себя единой общностью—одним народом" (is in reality the day of victory over ourselves, over internal animosity and strife, when classes and nationalities acknowledged themselves as being one community—one nation).[57] The essence of the "national question" for Russia, as Putin stressed, is the civilizational identity that is based on the preservation of a Russian cultural dominance where differentiation between "us" and "them" is determined by a common culture and shared values: "Стержень, скрепляющая ткань этой уникальной цивилизации—русский народ, русская культура" (The core, the binding fabric of this unique civilization—is the Russian people, Russian culture).[58]

If that sounds like an echo of the nineteenth-century theory of Pan-Slavism, then it is not surprising to learn that Putin also alluded to the chief Russian theoretician of Pan-Slavism, Nikolai Danilevsky,[59] who stated that Russia as a separate civilization must absorb and then assimilate Europe. In his perspective, the Slavic cultural-historical type was regarded as superior. Putin has called for Russian people who "are nation-forming—on the basis of Russia's existence. The great mission of Russians is to unite and bind our civilization," while Danilevsky advocated a policy of strength in that Russia could fulfill its historical mission by transforming itself into a mighty empire.

Russian academics, journalists, and politicians have shown great interest in the theory and practice of conservatism in general and Russian conservatism in particular.[60] In 2004, the philosophy faculty of St. Petersburg State University founded the Center for the Study of Conservatism, which holds an annual conference and assists in the publication of books and articles on the theory and history of Russian conservatism and its significance for post-Soviet Russia. This rhetoric is indicative of the Russian mainstream. In my opinion, this is signaling "empire-preserving nationalism," which is best captured in what Hugh Seton-Watson called official nationalism.[61] Many scholars have built on the theoretical framework he constructed. Particularly pertinent is the most recent article by Nancy Condee, an editor of collected essays that explore discursive, visual, social, and other features of nationalism. She argues that "official nationalism provides the most historically familiar ideological system to ensure that the unmanageable business of nation formation is muted. But more importantly that such muting can itself be naturalized as the philosophical workings of sobornost (communitarianism) the Russian idea, or other nineteenth-century constructions of knowledge. Nationalism is thus assigned a place remote from social institutions, from what many Western scholars, in their won conceptual short hand, would call civil society."[62]

Not surprisingly, Putin and his administration (e.g., Vladislav Surkov[63]) seem most to admire another major figure in the liberal-conservative canon, Pyotr Stolypin.[64] Putin has quoted approvingly a statement to the tsar, attributed to "Imperial Russia's last great statesman" Stolypin: "Give me 20 years of calm, and I will reform Russia." Putin ordered his cabinet ministers to personally contribute money to a Stolypin monument to rise this April outside Moscow's White House.

In his fundamental study dedicated to Russian conservative traditions Pipes emphasized that Russian conservatism of the nineteenth century has been reinforced in the political behavior of the contemporary Russian establishment.[65] Pipes expresses the view, which recent events confirm for him: Russia, "for reasons rooted in either her social structure or her culture, or both, is committed to authoritarian government."[66] Identifying a belief system or philosophical justifications for Russia's attachment to an authoritarian form of government, Pipes points to the religious doctrines (particularly, the religious conservatism of Dostoevsky and the aesthetic, cultural conservatism of Konstantin Leontiev) that have practical implications in Russian civil conservatism. Although it is not my goal here to retell the history of authoritarian legacy in Russia, a detour is necessary in order to make clear that we expect to have repercussions in Russian society today.

For many, the notion of civic society since the perestroika period has been widely spread in Russia with the help of mass media and the democratically minded intellectual elite. Journalists of "the golden era" had generally imagined a reader who saw the appearance of market economy, and forms of democratic politics, as well as the public debates over ideology and politics.[67]

However, by the time Putin came to the power, the changes in the mentality of the readership reflected the perception of democracy. As sociological polls demonstrate, Russians tend to interpret human rights somewhat differently than the Westerners and believe socioeconomic rights are more important than political freedoms. For example, in 1994, the breakdown of the importance of certain human rights was as follows (in percent): education and social welfare 64, well-paid labor 49, guaranteed living standard 33, freedom of press 18, freedom of conscience 14, free exit from the country 11, free elections 9.[68] In 2007, according to the Levada Center research project, when asked to choose a definition for "democracy," some 54 percent of the sample cite "either a 'fair system of state governance based on the participation of all citizens on equal terms,' or a 'series of guarantees to observe citizens' rights and freedoms by the authorities/government.'"[69] Only 9 percent cite such fundamental democratic principles as the "free competition of political parties for voters" and "separation of powers (the executive, judiciary and legislature) and accountability of the authorities to its citizens." In their paper "The West in Russian Mentality," G. Diligensky and S. Chugrov note that Russia's democratic institutions are not rooted in long democratic practice.[70] Russians have their own ideas of democracy, reflecting the coexistence of long-standing ambivalence regarding democracy with the centuries-old traditions of authoritarian rule. Most frequently Russians appear to see little application of democratic values to their lives. Only 37 percent of Russians feel democracy exists in their country at all, and 12 percent of those interviewed said democracy is suitable for other nations, but not for Russia,[71] though, 56 percent supported the protests for free elections, and 64 percent agreed that attending demonstrations gave people the opportunity to express their opinion. At the same time 72 percent of those polled had endorsed Vladimir Putin, a strong leader, who was best equipped to solve Russia's problems—as opposed to a democratic government.[72] However, this view appears to be contradicted as an average Russian is reluctant to play any role, neither in the formation of independent associations, nor in self-government at the municipal level. While Russians say it is very important to live in a country with honest elections, most Russians are convinced that all problems the country faces should be solved by state authorities.

As Nadia Diuk states:

> It is conventional wisdom among historians that Russians perceive the "state" as a concept around which all ideology and all values revolve. Throughout history, Russians have either venerated the state or tried to decapitate it, but it has remained a fixture in Russian political consciousness until the present day. For this reason, the notion of building a civil society that operates independently of the levers of state power seems to be a much more alien concept in Russia than, for example, in Poland or Ukraine.[73]

At the risk of oversimplification, it seems that most of official discourse gives attention to the ideology of Russia's uniqueness and resurgence of faith in Russia's traditional form of government, strong centralized authority. At the same time, affirmation of Russian national culture goes along with the widespread belief in the values of Orthodox Christianity. The division of Russian philosophical and literary tradition into the religious and the secular branches can in many ways be traced back to the second half of the nineteenth century.

In the tradition established by Putin, the references to conservative philosophers and to Orthodox doctrine and imagery in his campaigning and public messages provide ample evidence suggesting that Putin has Orthodox sympathies. The important point is that Putin's religious rhetoric flows out of his personal religious convictions, whereas those who disagree with the president on religion typically find his religiosity disconcerting. It is noteworthy that he was the first post-perestroika leader of a secular state according to its 1993 constitution, who openly exhibited his religious sentiments, and talked about the relationship of church, state, and nation at an Orthodox Christmas service in 2000. He proclaimed that "[Orthodoxy is] an unbending spiritual core of the entire people and state." "The language suggests that all those within Russian territory are, de facto, Orthodox, promoting a view of the Russian Orthodox Church as a privileged sociocultural institution for both state and nation."[74] The Orthodox Church has not explicitly offered its backing to any particular political party, but according to a 2010 poll, it is the second most trusted public institution in Russia. Eventually one can recognize—at first more intuitively than fully consciously—that once suffused with ideology at every level, the Russian political elite has embraced politically tinged orthodox Christianity to fill this awkward vacuum left by the disappearance of communism.

Over the course of Putin's rule, it has become increasingly clear that the Orthodox Church is playing a similar role to the one it played during the Imperial period. I have not encountered any publications that condemn Putin's use of religious imagery; however, the question is: Is there anything aside from political expediency behind the newly religious attitude of Russia's rulers or is the goal of such rhetoric to reinforce the international perception of Russia as a Christian nation? Kremlin ideologists gloss over the role of the Orthodox Church "as the only major social institution to have survived their nation's turbulent history."[75] Meanwhile Russian liberal readers have less tolerance for overtly religious overtones in public discourse and expect a more nuanced assessment of Russia's historical connections, particularly careful phrasing of the idea of Moscow being the Third Rome and its profoundly anti-Western orientation to avoid misunderstandings. Putin, who speaks this way, only confirms suspicions that such simplicities of faith, and a habit of seeing a hideously complicated Russian world in black and white fashion, may bring the survival of religious nationalism.

In positing that a Soviet religious identification differs from a post-Soviet one, we may assume that religious changes are tied to changes in the political realm.[76] However, data and multivariate analysis show that the collective search for religiosity in both private and public spheres may be in a state of flux. The Soviet government made a sustained effort to eradicate religion. In the Soviet cultural context spirituality was cherished, but religious spirituality was disapproved. In the judgment of Aleksandr Panchenko, "From the start of the 1960s, large numbers of popular anti-religious brochures were issued by central and regional publishing houses. These texts allow us to observe the arguments and rhetoric"[77] that prevailed in official ideology. Panchenko states, "Soviet ethnographers and folklorists" regularly recorded unofficial religious practices in a spirit of relative neutrality, presenting these as signs of *dvoeverie* (dual faith), that is, the survival of robust traditions of paganism under a thin veneer of monotheistic veneration. At the same time, Soviet attitudes toward superstition were, in an important way, quite clear-cut; the more permissive attitudes to nonofficial religious practices set in after 1991 transformed their social and political status.[78] The Soviet prohibition on religion only made it more attractive. Many "spiritual explorers" who first learned yoga, then studied Sanskrit, then read the New Testament and Nikolay Berdyaev,[79] were drawn to Christianity. In the days of the pre-perestroika Soviet Union, amateur spiritualists who were bored with state atheism and revolutionary ideas of Marx and Lenin turned to Dostoevsky and Berdyaev, discovering new dimensions and developing a highly idiosyncratic overview of Russian intellectual history.

In contemporary Russia, where the majority of the population are not observant followers of any religion, the number of atheists or those self-identifying as non-religious is difficult to estimate. This may be caused by many factors, one of which is the fact that religiosity is more private and a less common topic for discussion in Russia. Although it is often claimed that less than 10 percent of ethnic Russians attend church services more than once a month and only 2–4 percent are considered to be integrated into church life, they self-identify as Russian Orthodox. As members of other ethnic groups, Russians often choose to self-identify as adherents to Orthodoxy for cultural reasons; meanwhile, they are dubious of the importance of religion in their lives.[80] Thus, as an alternate hypothesis, one might also reason that given the recent dramatic changes in government structure, religious doctrines may be uncertain and will, therefore, have no discernible effects on the interpretative power of the readership. According to this line of thought, among older readers we will not be able to find evidence of patterned differences between the Soviet and post-Soviet nature of media consumption.

Although comparisons of pre-perestroika and current discourse provide a good overview of the relative frequency of religious remarks, explicit religious references are scarce, while implicit mentions of the divine and religious concepts may have two possible connotations: religious and secular. Today, although a significant number regard themselves as Christians, the majority are not practicing Christians. People of all education levels appear to believe deeply in things mysterious and supernatural, and indulge in superstitions. Some of these superstitions are relatively innocent, shared by other Western cultures, such as knocking on wood three times in order to avoid tempting fate after making a favorable observation, a boast, or a declaration concerning one's own death. Superstitions include fear of cats and of the number thirteen. An owl screeching from a belfry could portend trouble. Illness is seen as God's punishment and the illness of a child as punishment for the mother. Practically every Russian talks about superpower forces and evil energies that affect people's health.

Interesting statistics are found in Belyaev's study dedicated to religiousness in today's Russia.[81] According to the poll conducted by the Levada Center in September 2011, 69 percent of respondents call themselves Orthodox, although 47 percent say they never attended church services. Only 3 percent of the respondents go to church on a weekly basis, 7 percent attend services once a month, 11 percent once a year, and 10 percent even less often.[82] These results can be viewed as an important confirmation of the hypothesis that in present-day Russia, heterodox or esoteric religiousness has become the dominant form of religiosity. For example, the number of convinced non-believers is low (less than 10 percent). Traditional religiousness is adhered to by about 15 percent of the population, while about 20 percent of the population is heterodox religious. Another 27 percent show both traditional and esoteric religiousness and about 30 percent of the population does not have any well-defined religious views.

While governing structures influence church powers, it seems that everyday customs and rituals held more and more sway in the lives of ordinary people, reflecting on religious beliefs along with folk customs. In recent years, a large number of pilgrims have thronged to sacred places and to relics of numerous saints. Many local sacred places have rapidly become the objects of spiritual tourism organized by the Orthodox dioceses and various travel agents. The coexistence and competition of different religious cultures or discourses related to a local sacred place are investigated by Jeanne Kormina in a case study of the Pskov region.[83] She argues that "pilgrims who came from urban centers, local priests and church activists, ordinary locals and migrants, chose different types of stories, or even genres, when they talked about the sacred."[84]

In October 2011, a holy relic arrived from a Greek Orthodox monastery on Mount Athos in Greece for a month-long tour of Russia. Hundreds of thousands of Orthodox believers—overwhelmingly women—visited the Cathedral of Christ the Saviour to kiss a glass-covered reliquary that they believe holds the Virgin Mary's belt, which possesses miraculous power. For most believers such a pilgrimage is a way to achieve the realization of spiritual or religious understanding, to show their devotion, and to venerate the relics. It also attracts those who have lost their way or suffered a great loss, or no longer have faith in medical care and await a miracle, or hope to be cured of ills like cancer, debt, or drunken husbands. As Sophia Kishkovsky reports,

"The blogs and Facebook pages of Russian Orthodox intellectuals have overflowed with debates about whether hysteria over the belt was a disturbing sign that many Russians' faith is based on superstition."[85]

On the eve of the 2012 presidential election, three members of the feminist punk band Pussy Riot performed in the same cathedral on the ambo, recorded, and then disseminated the video of their performance on the Internet.[86] A part of the purpose of the band's protests was to draw attention to the misuse and manipulation of religion for the purposes of political gain and power. The Russian Orthodox Church has, partially at least, been supporting Putin and his politics from the pulpit; if they take political action, they should not be surprised if political action comes back in return. All three women were sentenced by a Moscow district court to two years in prison after being convicted of hooliganism and inciting religious hatred. The Pussy Riot trial drew worldwide condemnation of constraints on political speech in Russia. Rallies in support of them were held in dozens of cities around the world; pictures of real people and monuments wearing Pussy Riot–style hats have spread on social networks. The Pussy Riot case has helped to energize the opposition. Secular liberals embraced them as the authentic voice of upwelling of dissent since disputed parliamentary elections last December; the conservative audience considered this performance an act of defiance. Meanwhile the high-profile trial mitigated media attention to centuries-old issues of the Orthodox Church's attitude toward the government and society, as well as to personal problems of those "who are making a serious effort to think about how to correlate their citizenry with their Christianity and whether it should be done in the context of a new democratic or traditional autocratic mentality."[87]

Alyssa DeBlasio[88] has noted that while the rapid transition of thinkers from the dogma of Marxism to the ideology of Orthodoxy brought a deep realization among non-religious philosophers of an expanding distinction between the language, methodology, and subject matter of Russian philosophy of the late-Soviet/early post-Soviet period, the "philosophical boom" reflected on a growing realization of the religious/secular binary opposition within the new philosophical paradigm. In Russia, the question of religious identity was never easy and simple. This is especially true for the fluid and complex, changing post-Soviet society. In the twenty-first century, apparently, ethnic and religious identity does not directly correlate with political affiliation. As it appears during the protests against the allegedly rigged parliamentary elections, many Orthodox believers sympathize with the protest movement, which is strongly anti-Putin; however, the same people were deeply offended by the form of the Pussy Riot protest. This stint also has a very sad political effect; as the journalist Andrei Zolotov put it, "It has become so easy now for the retrogrades to lump together the blasphemers with the political protesters, promoting, intentionally or unintentionally, the totally false and simplistic, but politically advantageous divide: those who are for God, Church, and Russia are for Putin and those who are against Putin, are insulting God, insulting us Christians, they are against God, Church and Russia."[89]

Liberal opponents of the Orthodox establishment think the state may simply use the church as ideological cover. On the one hand, the current political situation has forced restoration of civil culture for Russians who are sick and tired of chaos and voluntarism of authorities. On the other hand, Russia is a conservative country. To illustrate this point, I offer responses to a 2012 survey question: "Which of the following activities would you categorize as ethically unacceptable?"[90] Seventy-five percent of respondents considered abandoning a child the worst act of immorality. Suicide scored a 64 percent unacceptability rating, and homosexuality came in third, with 62 percent of respondents against it. One of the interpretations of the survey results is that religious maxims exert the most powerful impact on the Russians; Russian people are most often guided in their moral assessments by religious maxims. In the post-Soviet transition economy Russians are more likely to tolerate divorce and extramarital affairs, and less likely to show disapproval of euthanasia. Interesting is the case of personal habits, such as boozing or gambling, in which there is still room for moral assessment, though it is less emphatic. Permissive moral values reflect liberal religious and political ideologies. Apparently, the underlying ambiguity about tolerance and perception of the values reflects the manner in which the current public discourse in Russia has been shaped.

The results show that the emergence of Western-type democratic institutions is a crucial but not sufficient prerequisite for Russia's transition toward democracy. To an outside observer it may seem incomprehensible why and how the majority of the nation is still ruled by a communist illusion. The reasoning is the lack of the break from the past state ideology. Certainly there was a time when a new train of thought was implemented in Russian minds: during the late 1980s and the beginning of the 1990s, when the political and social changes were due to start or even seemed to have begun, the new political movements and parties were not internalized successfully, but were constructed within an "old ideology" based on principles of state monopoly. In the 2012 presidential elections, when Putin won more than 63 percent of the vote, the Russian choice was once more a cause for surprise to the rest of the world. Why does the Russian mentality seem to cherish the idea of a paternalistic state? Though Russian democratic ideals are usually somewhat unstable, they strongly correlate with concrete needs and aspirations. If a certain part adheres to the ideals of freedom (Decembrist movement), the majority of Russians stick to what they dream of but lack in everyday life (this may be one of the essential characteristic features of every social ideal). The majority of Russians clearly preferred socioeconomic guarantees provided by the paternalistic communist state to socioeconomic rights for political freedoms. As it is clear from public opinion polls, the majority of Russians consider such democratic values as human rights to be the locus of democracy, and at first glance this does not differ greatly from a Western point of view. Russian perception of the word "freedom" has the potential for internal contradiction. The linguistic digression on the word "freedom" in Michael Gorham's article seems to be of great value here, in which the decontextualization of the word allows us to find an actual social meaning. Gorham points out that the Russian concept of freedom is symbolically ambiguous.

> Its mixed, largely non-Russian origins left it open to criticism as a Western import that disregarded more time-honored Russian attitudes to the word and allowed it to be associated with metaphors of linguistic, social, economic and moral excess—as encapsulated by the two keywords most central to the attacks on the wild years of the 1990s, *proizvol* [whim] and *bespredel* [criminal slang for lawlessness].[91]

As we see, this linguistic division remains, for the most part, unexamined and unchallenged. Western and Russian terms align as oxymoronic in the perception of democracy. Unfortunately, one of the most important components of the Western civil culture—respect for law and universally accepted social norms—has found no substantial support in Russia, although according to a Pew Research Global Attitude Survey, 71 percent said that it was very important to live in a country where the courts treat everyone the same. These observations demonstrate that the persistent stereotypical notion of law as an obstacle to policy has still not yet been overcome in Russian society.[92] Such a mentality is neither pro-democratic nor anti-democratic; it is clearly vacillating between pro-socialist nostalgia and temptations of new life and aspirations. Primitive moralizing and moral stance in political discourse fit in this context. Igor Kon, a prominent Russian philosopher and psychologist, comments on the moral culture in Russia: "I suspect that the moral consciousness in Russia will remain tinged with anti-bourgeois sentiments for quite a while. It is likely to vacillate between two poles: the conservative-religious and socialist (though not communist!)."[93]

Each factor mentioned above has an impact on readership separately, and they work together to shape an image of Russian media readership that is not coherent. The great divide among experts is based on the media sources Russians turn to for information. On the one side, these are television viewers, the older and more conservative Russians, who are addicted to TV production not because it is a reliable information source, but because Soviet films are now being shown by popular demand, according to broadcasters. The demands are linked with nostalgia for the USSR and popular re-evaluation of the legacy of the Soviet Union. A misremembered past appeals to those born in the years of the Soviet Union, or even after its collapse. On the other side, there are new readership groups that began to emerge in the first decade of the twenty-first century, who almost exclusively turn to the Internet for everything from news to entertainment. This audience lost faith in television as an information source, and is disenchanted with its association with Soviet-style media that set the official ideological tone.[94] Given the young people's preoccupation with the "open" Internet, it would not be an overstatement to say that the "closed" media system, including state television and state-sanctioned press, is going out of fashion. Internet social media has greatly impacted Soviet interpretation of a readership group of people often considered backward and immobile, an interpretation I believe to be largely false and one that could be decisively argued with the introduction of Internet alternative media models and networking digital databases.

However, here I am interested in focusing on another aspect of the readership. If media appealed to authority figures from the classical tradition, it may be doubted how successful it would have been in targeting current cosmopolitan twenty-somethings. The Levada Center reports on the particular "symbolic" catastrophe in the post-Soviet space. As the prominent sociologist Boris Dubin puts it, "Libraries, schools, institutions, literary criticism lost not only their former symbolic value and authority but also their former role in structuring the reading of the masses, in providing and disseminating influential models."[95] Critics accuse the entire generation of embracing opacity, glorifying surfaces, and rejecting the meaningful word. The older generations interpret this as a troubling sign that this generation is inauthentic.

But in December 2011, contrary to the popular belief that young people are apathetic and disengaged from politics, many young citizens of Moscow and St. Petersburg gave politics a great deal of consideration. Young people assume an increasingly important role not only as readers of their fathers' and grandfathers' narratives, but also as active agents in glossing those versions of the past for their own social and political purposes. The Russian public sphere was certainly greatly influenced by the movement of the New Decembrists, a growing audience of young, educated people, university graduates, who read mostly alternative media. Michael Idov, a contributing writer at *New York Magazine*, describes the December activists as a new class, "those who barely remembered the Soviet Union," and "when they talk about the protests, their speech still whiffs of the collegiate absurdity; they are clearly attracted to plays on words and ironic absurdities."[96]

The New Decembrists are not rebels or revolutionaries. They represent neither punk nor hippie culture, but their dissent, code, and style of life signify counterculture, an alternative discourse. They "realized that building one's comfortable, beautiful world is impossible without participating in the running of the country," as editor-in-chief of *Esquire Russia* Andrei Loshak puts it.[97] The New Decembrists are a minority among intellectuals in general and university students in particular. Although the oppositional rallies and demonstrations of civic dissent in which they participate are peaceful, their opinions do not coincide with that of the government. Humor and a sense of irony are empowering for Russia's new opposition, and as Mr. Krasilshchik, the young editor of the arts and culture magazine *Afisha* and one of the original organizers of the December protests in Moscow, commenting on the discourse of the Decembrist Movement, says, the ubiquity of satire gives demonstrators a feeling that "it's a protest, but at the same time not really a protest. We're joking, but we're also serious."[98] As a result, the government views them as potentially intolerant toward the Kremlin.

Where Bourdieu identifies heretical discourse as having the task of challenging the doxa and producing a new common sense, we may do well to concentrate on the rhetorical devices and styles of Russian alternative media that manifest the heterodox discourse. Apparently, social media has given birth to a new public space with its own, alternative news flow. "Attractor bloggers"—Alexei Navalny, Anton Nosik, Andrei Malgin, Doctor Liza (Glinka), Marina Litvinovich, Oleg Kozyrev, and Yevgeny Roizman—spread the news across social media thanks to their own successful strategies. Launched in 2009, Slon.ru, a popular Russian website that provides commentary on politics, business, and economics, was consciously modeled after a handful of Western online niche publications, such as Business Insider and TechCrunch, and does not just report the news, but offers a unique take on stories that have already broken.

Discussed in chapter 11, *Citizen Poet*—initially an Internet project that became a sensation in Russia in 2011—consists of the discourse aimed at the Russian politics. The reason for the selection of this satirical project is the fact that it features well-known Russian actor Mikhail Yefremov reading poems from the Russian classics. The poems were adapted for the project by the writer Dmitry Bykov. What's more, this project, with its estimated 1.1 million visitors per month, attracts the exact same audience discouraged by television programming and the general dearth of information available through traditional media.

Masha Lipman, an expert on Russian media from the Carnegie Endowment, says, "To anybody who's curious to know more, to have an alternative idea of what goes on in Russia as opposed to the government's view and what's shown on television, there's no shortage of information. It's a demand problem."[99]

Russia's alternative media, consumed by quite a limited range of population, gained more credibility at that point. Political satire began to appear on Russian-language websites before the disputed election, and it has flourished since. I suggest that in an analysis of alternative discourse we should consider not only direct manifestation of dissent, but also the discourse—or representational system—that facilitated resistance by not speaking about it straightforward, but presenting it as something funny. One of the most popular sources of online humor is KermlinRussia,[100] a satirical Twitter account that began in June 2010 by mocking the posts of President Dmitry Medvedev. As one of the KermlinRussia authors puts it, "Putin stopped being scary. He started to become silly." From a purely comedic standpoint, the two young professionals behind KermlinRussia almost relish Mr. Putin's return to the Kremlin, as his macho theatrics—tagging a polar bear in the Russian Arctic, for example—make for easy satirical fodder. One of the posts mocked the almost North Korean reverence that the state-run television shows for Mr. Putin's public relations stunts: "В рязанском лесу, который лично тушил премьер, уже сняли три урожая брёвен" [In the Ryazan forest, where a fire was put out by the prime minister himself, three harvests of logs have already been gathered].[101] So many new antigovernment jokes, Internet memes, and videos have appeared in late November and early December that *Afisha* compiled and published a "dictionary of memes,"[102] which came out after the Duma election. I discuss the entries from the dictionary in chapter 10. In keeping with the amorphous, essentially leaderless nature of Russia's 2011 protest movement, the sharpest anti-Putin humor was not produced by traditional media institutions, but simply appears on the Internet or on handmade signs at demonstrations. Informal youth-group singing, tape-recorded guitar songs to abstruse slogans and anecdotes achieve wider circulation than the rigid news of official newspaper discourse. And because it did not bear the state imprint, the very modality of this oral style had more punch.

The new artistic production was created both by amateurish and by skilled satirists. Despite the fact that opposition was eclectic in nature and social representation, its members spoke with one powerful voice, not weakened by dissent or excessive subtlety, unencumbered by complexity. It was not time for half-tones and self-conscious irony, for this discourse, as any propagandistic one, depicted a world of stark contrasts: poets and writers were valorous and self-sacrificing while the Kremlin administration was mocked and foolishly described.

The language of the small genres of alternative discourse is rough, direct, and rich in obscenity: qualities that had been cleansed from official public discourse. The distinction of the alternative discourse from the official one lies in its nature—it is dynamic, vivid, and often coarse while it is assumed to threaten social order. Though alternative discourse is in recent times identified with liberalization, the assumption is not always true. Rather than opposing the reigning order, it could challenge and force it to adapt. When new discursive forms are brought in from the periphery, the official media, if they are to retain an audience, will have to adapt the new forms to their own purpose. The multiple evidences of this type of discourse can be found in media project *Citizen Poet* (see chapter 11).

NOTES

1. Pierre Bourdieu, *Outline of a Theory of Practice* (Cambridge: Cambridge University Press, 1977).

2. Pierre Bourdieu, *Language and Symbolic Power* (Cambridge: Cambridge University Press, 1991), 131–32.

3. Janett Hoskins, *Biographical Objects: How Things Tell the Stories of People's Lives* (New York: Routledge, 1998).

4. Bourdieu, *Outline of a Theory of Practice*, 164.

5. Bourdieu, *Language and Symbolic Power*, 128–29.

6. Lara Ryazanova-Clarke, "Re-creation of the Nation: Orthodox and Heterodox Discourses in Post-Soviet Russia," *Scando-Slavica* 54, no. 1 (2008): 223–39.

7. Russian: *Сам Издательство* (Sam Izdatel'stvo), literally self-publishing. It was used to reproduce and distribute censored works of literature and political criticism in the former Soviet Union. Those who received a manuscript would do so with the implied promise that they would type five carbon copies before passing it on.

8. Serguei Oushakine, "The Terrifying Mimicry of Samizdat," *Public Culture* 13, no. 2 (2001): 191.

9. Ibid., 191–214.

10. Certain salient orthodox properties of the Russian official discourse produced during Vladimir Putin's presidency have already been discussed in connection with the official language policy and its implementation in contemporary Russia in Lara Ryazanova-Clarke, "Crystallization of Structures: Linguistic Culture in Putin's Russia," in *Landslide of the Norm: Language Culture in Post-Soviet Russia*, ed. Ingunn Lunde and Tine Roesen (Bergen, NO: Slavica Bergensia, 2006); Ryazanova-Clarke, "The State Turning to Language: Power and Identity in Russian Language Policy Today," *Russian Language Journal* 56 (2006): 37–55.

11. Stuart Hall, *Representation: Cultural Representation and Signifying Practices* (London: Sage, 1997).

12. Mikhail Epstein, "Collective Improvisation and Transculture Consciousness," in *Transcultural Experiments: Russian and American Models of Creative Communication*, ed. Ellen B. Berry and Mikhail Epstein (New York: St. Martin's Press, 1999).

13. Olessia Koltsova, *News Production and Power in Post-Soviet Russia* (London and New York: Routledge Curzon, 2006).

14. O. Negt, *L'espace public oppositionnel* [Oppositional public space] (Paris: Payot, 2007).

15. Eric Hobsbawm, *On History* (London: Weidenfeld & Nicolson, 1998), 10.

16. See the discussion of speech genres distribution in Dell Hymes (1964), Gary Gossen (1972), and Joel Sherzer (1983, 8–14).

17. Nancy Ries, *Russian Talk: Culture and Conversation during Perestroika* (Ithaca, NY: Cornell University Press, 1997).

18. Ibid.

19. Ibid.

20. Ibid.

21. Ibid.

22. Evgeny Dobrenko, *The Making of the State Reader: Social and Aesthetic Contexts of the Reception of Soviet Literature* (Stanford, CA: Stanford University Press, 1997).

23. Ibid., 153.

24. "Sotsial'naya reklama, propagandiruyushchaya chtenie, poyabilac' v Moskve," Novosti@mail.ru, March 14, 2010, http://news.mail.ru/inregions/moscow/90/society/3811269/ .

25. Ibid.

26. Tatiana Tolstaya, *Kys'* (Moscow: EKSMO, 2004).

27. "Otryvok iz romana" [Excerpt from a novel], May 1864, http://smalt.karelia.ru~filolog/epokha/1864/Shedryn.htm.

28. Mikhail Epstein, *After the Future: The Paradoxes of Postmodernism and Contemporary Russian Culture*, trans. Anesa Miller-Pogacar, Critical Perspectives on Modern Culture (Amherst: University of Massachusetts Press, 1995), 196.

29. Lyudmila Parts, *The Chekhovian Intertext: Dialogue with a Classic* (Columbus: Ohio State University Press, 2008).
30. Ibid., 7.
31. On cultural tendencies to connect the Soviet past, nostalgia, and the project of modernization of Russia, see the discussion in Ilya Kalinin, "Nostalgic Modernization: The Soviet Past as 'Historical Horizon,'" *Slavonica* 17, no. 2 (November 2011): 156–66.
32. Read about the ban of the Moscow billboard campaign that allegedly encouraged Russians to read at http://lenta.ru/news/2011/03/20/badad/.
33. "S bilbordov v tsentre Moskvy snimayut tsitaty klassikov," Grani.ru, March 20, 2011, http://grani.ru/Politics/Russia/m.187125.html.
34. Ibid.
35. Pavel Pozhigailo is president of the Fund for the Study of Stolypin's Heritage; deputy minister of culture and mass communications; state secretary member of the Public Chamber; chair of the Commission on Cultural and Historical Heritage Protection of the Public Chamber; president of the Committee on Culture of the Civic Chamber; and president of VOOPiK, the society for the preservation of monuments.
36. Sergei Podosenov, "Ostrovskogo i Turgeneva staviat v shkolakh na osobyi kontrol'," *Izvestia*, March 6, 2013, http://izvestia.ru/news/545948#ixzz2U3S8JtrU.
37. Anton Chekhov, *Ivanov, Chaika, Diadia Vania, Tri sestry, Vishnyovyi sad* (Moscow: Khudozhestvennaia literatura, 1982).
38. Ibid.
39. Claude Levi-Strauss, *The Savage Mind* (Chicago: University of Chicago Press, 1966), 16–36.
40. See Putin's linguistic profiles and communication styles in Michael Gorham, "Putin's Language," *Ab Imperio* 4 (2005): 381–401.
41. Vladimir Putin, "Rossiia: Natsional'nyi vopros," *Nezavisimaya Gazeta*, January 23, 2012, www.ng.ru/politics/2012-01-23/1_national.html.
42. Gorham, "Putin's Language"; Helena Goscilo, ed., *Putin as Celebrity and Cultural Icon* (New York: Routledge, 2012).
43. Gorham, "Putin's Language."
44. Ibid., 382.
45. R. Wodak et al., *The Discursive Construction of National Identity* (Edinburgh: Edinburgh University Press, 1999), 33.
46. Andrei Kolesnikov, "Obruchennye so smert'yu," *Novaya Gazeta*, February 27, 2012, www.novayagazeta.ru/comments/51312.html.
47. See the discussion on the emergence of a new intellectual paradigm in Russia in Alyssa DeBlasio, *Between Philosophies: The Emergence of a New Intellectual Paradigm in Russia.* (PhD diss., University of Pitsburgh, 2010).
48. Natalia Shipitsyna, "Liudi v serom," *Moskovskii Komsomolets,* July 14, 2004.
49. Richard Sakwa, *The Crisis of Russian Democracy: The Dual State, Factionalism and the Medvedev Succession* (Cambridge: Cambridge University Press, 2011), 58.
50. See Ivan A. Ilyin, *Sobranie sochinenii v 10 tomakh*, ed. Iuri Lisitsa (Moscow: Russkaia kniga, 1993–1999).
51. In 2005 he played a role in the return of Ilyin's body to Russia and its reburial in Moscow with great pomp and circumstance. Later, he personally paid for a new headstone on Ilyin's grave.
52. See Marlène Laruelle's *Russian Eurasianism, an Ideology of Empire* (Baltimore: Johns Hopkins University Press, 2008) and Dmitry Shlapentokh's *Russia Between East and West: Scholarly Debates on Eurasianism* (Leiden and Boston: Brill, 2007).
53. Putin, "Rossiia: Natsional'nyi vopros."
54. Ibid.
55. Ibid.
56. The national holiday celebrated on November 4 calls for tolerance between various ethnic and religious groups in the Russian Federation. This holiday commemorates a 1612 uprising when Russia overcame a catastrophic split in the society, expelled the Polish-Lithuanian occupation force from Moscow, and brought an end to the Time of Troubles. Many in

Russia do not know the origin of the holiday, and confuse it with the November 7 holiday, which marks the anniversary of the Bolshevik Revolution.

57. Putin, "Rossiia: Natsional'nyi vopros."

58. Ibid.

59. Nikolai Danilevski (1822–1885) is an ideologue of the pan-Slavism and Slavophile movement. He characterized the Slavic type as being at the youth stage, and developed a socio-political plan for its development, involving unification of the Slavic world, its capital at Constantinople, ruled by an Orthodox emperor. According to Danilevsky, humanity can be divided into several autonomous groups, each of which has its individual history. Danilevsky introduced the concept of "cultural historical type," which equals the concept of "civilization."

60. See Igor Osipov, "Aksiologiia rossiiskogo konservatizma," in *Filosofiia i sotsial'no-politicheskie tsennosti konservatizma v obshchestvennom soznanii Rossii*, ed. Iurii Nikiforovich Solonin (St. Petersburg: Izd-vo Sankt-Peterburgskogo gos. Universiteta, 2004), 106–18, here 115–17. See also Galina Talina, "Russkaia samoderzhavnaia monarkhiia pervykh Romanovykh glazami sovremennikov i potomkov," in *Samoderzhavnoe tsarstvo pervykh Romanovykh*, ed. S. V. Perevezentsev (Moscow: Izd-vo Sotsial'no-politicheskaia mysl', 2004), 7–74, esp. 31–36; and Mikhail Zyzykin, *Tsarskaia vlast' v Rossii* (Moscow: Izd-vo zhurnala "Moskva," 2004), 74.

61. H. Seton-Watson, *Nations and States: An Inquiry into the Origins of Nations and the Politics of Nationalism* (Boulder, CO: Westview Press, 1977), 83–87, 148.

62. Nancy Condee, "Tales Told by Nationalists," in *Soviet and Post-Soviet Identities* (Cambridge: Cambridge University Press, 2012), 37–53.

63. Vladislav Surkov is the former influential Kremlin adviser. Known as the "gray eminence," he is widely believed by analysts to have been behind the creation of the controversial pro-Kremlin youth group, Nashi, and largely responsible for the many, and often ugly, forms that "Putinism" took and the ways that it treated its political adversaries. Surkov was particularly involved in the creation of the concept of "sovereign democracy," which is not quite as popular a term as it once was but which is still the default ideological position of the Kremlin.

64. Pyotr Stolypin (1862–1911) was a sophisticated conservative liberal who took over as prime minister and stabilized Russia after the revolution of 1905. As the prime minister of Russia from 1906 to 1911 he introduced a series of modernizing economic reforms in the midst of revolution and did not flinch from using extreme violence to suppress it. One night at the opera in Kiev in 1911, a radical entered the prime minister's box and shot him fatally in the chest.

65. Richard Pipes, *Russian Conservatism and Its Critics: A Study in Political Culture* (New Haven, CT: Yale University Press, 2005).

66. Ibid., xii.

67. See discussion in L. Belin, "The Russian Media in the 1990s," *Journal of Communist Studies and Transition Politics* 18, no. 1 (2002): 22. G. Simons and D. Strovsky, "Censorship in Contemporary Russian Journalism in the Age of the War against Terrorism: A Historical Perspective," *European Journal of Communication* 21, no. 2 (2006): 189.

68. *Monitoring Obshchestvennoe mnenie*, VTsIOM, Intertsentr, Akademiia Narodnogo Khoziaistva, Moscow, 1993–2000.

69. "Voices from Russia: Society, Democracy, Europe," EU-Russia Centre/Levada Center Research, February 2007, p. 6.

70. G. Diliguenski and S. Chugrov, "'The West' in Russian Mentality," Office for Information and Press, Brussels; Institute of World Economy and International Relations, Moscow, 2000, www.nato.int/acad/fellow/98-00/diliguenski.pdf.

71. Levada Center Project, 2007, 2, 8.

72. James Bell is the director of international survey research for the Pew Research Center's Global Attitudes Project and the Pew Forum on Religion & Public Life. "Russians Back Protests, Political Freedoms: And Putin, Too," Pew Research Center's Global Attitudes Project, May 23, 2012, www.pewglobal.org/2012/05/23/russians-back-protests-political-freedoms-and-putin-too/.

73. Nadia Diuk, "Is There a Key?," *Journal of Democracy* 20, no. 2 (April 2009): 59.

74. Beth M. Admiraal, "The Failure of National Religious Policy in the Post-Soviet Region: The Experiences of the Jehovah's Witnesses in Russia and Greek Catholics in Romania," *Religion in Eastern Europe* 32, no. 1 (February 2012): 21. Retrieved from www.georgefox.edu/academics/undergrad/departments/soc-swk/ree/Admiraal_Failure_Feb%202012.pdf.

75. Geraldine Fegan, *Believing in Russia Russia—Religious Policy after Communism* (New York: Routledge, 2013).

76. Ibid.

77. Alexander Panchenko, "'Popular Orthodoxy' and Identity," in *Soviet and Post-Soviet Russia: Ideology, Consumption and Competition* (Cambridge: Cambridge University Press, 2012), 326.

78. Ibid., 321.

79. Nikolai Berdyaev, *The Origin of Russian Communism* (Ann Arbor: University of Michigan Press, 1960); Nikolai Berdyaev, *The Russian Idea* (New York: Lindisfame Press, 1992).

80. For more on the role of the church in the development of the Russian state, see Irina Papkova, *The Orthodox Church and Russian Politics* (Washington, DC: Woodrow Wilson Center, 2011).

81. Demyan Belyaev, "'Heterodox Religiousness' in Today's Russia: Results of an Empirical Study," *Social Compass* 58 (2011): 353, http://scp.sagepub.com/content/58/3/353.

82. Ibid., 369.

83. J. Kormina, "Pilgrims, Priest and Local Religion in Contemporary Russia: Contested Religious Discourses," *Folklore* 28 (2004): 31–33, www.folklore.ee/Folklore/vol28/pilgrims.pdf.

84. Ibid.

85. Sophia Kishkovsky, "In Russian Chill, Waiting Hours for Touch of the Holy," *New York Times*, November 23, 2011.

86. See the discussion of this performance in V. Akulova, "Konformism v protestnoi obertke?," 27 February 2012, http://www.openspace.ru/art/events/details/34649/; D. Vilenskii, "Aktsionism—to ot sily 2% aktualnogo iskusstva," http://www.sensusnovus.ru/culture/2012/04/27/13364.html; A. Epshtein, "Arest uchastnits gruppy 'Pussy Riot' v Khrame Khrista Spasitelia rfr ratalizator khudozhestvenno-grazhdanskogo aktivizma," http://www.nlobooks.ru/node/2585; A. Epshtein, "Mobilizovannaia Bogoroditsa: Pank-mobelen gruppy 'Pussy Riot': Feministskii protest v kontekste klassovoi bor'by 'Neprikosnovennyi zapas,' http://www.nlobooks.ru/node/2285; Elena Gapova, "Delo 'Pussy Riot': Feministskii protest v kontekste klassovoi bor'by 'Neprikosnovennii zapas,'" http://www.nlobooks.ru/node/279.

87. A. Zolotov, "You Know It When You See It," *Spirit of the Times* (blog), February 23, 2012, http://en.rian.ru/andrei_zolotov_blog/.

88. Alyssa DeBlasio, "Writing the History of Russian Philosophy," *Studies in East European Thought* 63 (2011): 203–26.

89. Zolotov, "You Know It When You See It."

90. "Otkaz ot cvoikh detei, samoubiistvo I gomoskesualizm moral'no nepriemlemo dlya bol'shei chasti rossiyan," Levada Center, September 14, 2012, www.levada.ru/14-09-2012/otkaz-ot-svoikh-detei-samoubiistvo-i-gomoseksualizm-moralno-nepriemlemo-dlya-bolshei-chas.

91. Michael Gorham, "Language Culture and Identity in Post-Soviet Russia: Economies of Mat," in *Post-Soviet Russia: Culture and Identity* (Cambridge: Cambridge University Press, 2012), 237–54.

92. For details, see Diliguenski and Chugrov, "'The West' in Russian Mentality."

93. Igor Kon, "Moral Culture: Public Morality and Private Responsibility," http://cdclv.unlv.edu//archives/nc1/kon_moral.html.

94. See the discussion in Ekaterina Kratasiuk, *Reprezentatsia proshlogo v reklame, ili istoriia kak brend. Sovremennye strategii kul'turologicheskikh issledovanii* (Moscow: Izd. RGGU, 2009).

95. B. Dubin and N. Zorkaia, *Chtenie v Rossii 2008: Tendentsii i Problemy* (Moscow: Analiticheskii Tsentr Iuriia Levady; Mezhregional'nyi Tsentr Bibliotechnogo Sotrudnichestva, 2008), 39–40.

96. Michael Idov, "New Decembrists," *New York Magazine*, January 2012, http://nymag.com/news/features/russian-revolutionaries-2012-1/.

97. In Jonathan Earle, "Journalists Toe Fine Line with Opposition Politics," *St. Petersburg Times*, March 28, 2012, www.sptimes.ru/story/35373.

98. "Prospekt skharova vse, chto bylo na mitinge I vokrug nego," Afisha.ru, December 24, 2011, www.afisha.ru/article/24online/.

99. See the discussion on the freedom of press in Andrew Roth, "Warriors of the Keyboard: The Problem with Russia's Free Press Today Is on the Side of Demand," *Russia Profile*, December 14, 2011, http://russiaprofile.org/culture_living/50997/print_edition/.

100. See the discussion in Julia Ioffe, "Meet the President," *Foreign Policy*, January–February 2011, 91.

101. @KermlinRussia, "V ryazanskom lesu, kotoryi lichno tushil prem'er, uzhe sniali tri urozhaia breven," Twitter, August 12, 2010, https://twitter.com/KermlinRussia/status/21015323222.

102. Aleksandr Gorbachev and Pyotr Favorov, "Novaya politika: Slovar' memov," Afish.ru, February 29, 2012, www.afisha.ru/article/new-politics-glossary/.

Chapter Five

New Models and Old Constraints

In this chapter, I focus on the characteristic elements of contemporary rhetoric, primarily in its print media outlets, with a view to establishing the significance of the historical continuity between the Soviet journalistic tradition and media discourse today.

In contemporary journalism, both the heritage of the Soviet era and the years with increasing freedom of the press in the 1990s are apparent. I refer to media scholarship that defines new and old journalistic practices[1] and empirical research in the area of journalism.[2] Since it will be relevant later, it is worth mentioning at this point that media scholars assume that, although the two generations of journalists—old and new—are conducting journalism in different ways, they both lack objectivity, which again leads to a lack of pluralism. My study is also heavily informed by insightful commentary on Russian civil society and on objectivity and pluralism in the post-Soviet era offered by Sarah Oates.[3] However, according to media researcher Svetlana Pasti (2005), who conducted her survey among St. Petersburg journalists, the two styles of journalism differ in how the journalists view the audience: those from the old generation are still combining facts and commentary, using Soviet-style journalism, while the new generation is going toward the Western model, with the separation of facts and commentary. Pasti found that both generations may publish unverified information because they trust their sources (especially the authorities), both generations collaborate with the authorities on local and national levels, and both generations perceive their role as a servant for the political elite, as well as a propagandist for the power holders in elections, while being critical of those in power or representing the views of the opposition is not part of their role, as they understand it. Pasti gives a very thorough analysis of the results, which reveal the continuing dominance of the publicist role, where the journalist is the writer's own exclusive preserve, not a technical product. The journalistic authorship is an integral part of the professional culture of Russian journalism rooted in the classics of Russian literature and publitsistika, inherited from the Soviet school of journalistic genres and turning all genres into publitsistika genres without rigid distinction within them. Meanwhile, contemporary publicist reporting does not necessarily represent a plurality of opinions.[4] The findings of this study support the views of other researchers that objective news reporting is not attainable in the media (Oates 2007). Meanwhile Voltmer (2000) suggests that the lack of both objectivity and critical, investigative reporting are due to the Soviet-era heritage, where criticism was symbolic only, and objectivity was not considered a journalistic virtue. Rather than striving to be the fourth estate providing a check on the other powers, the Russian media are perceived as supporting the state more than filling the role of the state's watchdog (Oates 2006). Oates is referring to the Russian media as a "tame lapdog of the state."[5]

This practice is obviously conditioned by the particular political situation in which the Russian journalists find themselves. Journalistic professionalism in Russia is viewed differently from the way it is viewed in the Western countries. In addition to questions of personalities, a generation of younger journalists who came of age during Putin's presidency accept an unspoken set of Kremlin rules of what cannot be covered by state media outlets; this is unlike their predecessors, the veteran reporters, who grasped media freedom as the Soviet Union collapsed. Yulia Ioffe,[6] a Russian-American journalist and blogger, reported on the Russian state-funded news network Russia Today (RT), seeing it as being the Kremlin's mouthpiece. According to her knowledgeable source, "There is no censorship per se," says another RT reporter. "But there are a lot of young people at the channel, a lot of self-starters who are eager to please the management. You can easily guess what the Kremlin wants the world to know, so you change your coverage."[7] "Self-censorship today in Russia is at an all-time high," says high-profile TV host Vladimir Pozner, who began in the business when Soviet censors used to decide what subjects he and other journalists were allowed to report.[8] "Journalists are not journalists at all but bureaucrats, obeying a logic of service and submission," says Parfyonov, the former NTV presenter who now produces sardonic historical documentaries shown on state television and told TV executives at a black-tie event.[9] As Russia's leading nationwide news channels all came either directly or indirectly under state ownership during Putin's presidency, it came as no surprise that journalists say they risk being similarly sacked if they break the rules. As part of a broader regime security effort, the Kremlin administration turned to the media to deliver stricter "message control" to highly sensitive issues such as coverage of the war, Mikhail Khodorkovsky's trial, or the AIDS epidemic in Russia.

Considered the "fourth estate" in the state issues, the media in the socialist Soviet Union have been burdened with a crucial responsibility in molding popular values. Being always along the prescriptive normative lines, the media protected themselves by denying the opposition access to public opinion, and not allowing any room for polemics thus further endorsing the notion that there is "one right way" that was sponsored by the regime and consumed by the millions. Among those who explore the dynamic relationship between culture and politics, and those who closely examine the aesthetic dimensions of "representation of power" (Dobrenko), are Boris Groys, Sheila Fitzpatrick, James van Geldern, and Svetlana Boym. Evgeny Dobrenko notes that the survival of the special role played by literature can be explained by the fact that the official discourse appropriated its "treasures," and the classical themes were interpreted as either ideologically palatable or ideologically unacceptable.[10] If the "monologic" (in Bakhtinian sense of the word) discourse of the early era of the Soviet Union took a discursive base and reworked the tradition of its predecessors—early twentieth-century traditions of avant-garde art[11]—contemporary media discourse draws from wider sources, reproducing the particularly, and sometimes most unimaginable, episodes of Russian heritage, and fascinates readers by the breadth of cultural context inherent in certain catchphrases, quotations, references, or allusions. Evocations of the socialist-era media reveal surprisingly striking parallels between the "authoritative discourse" of media, which heavily relied on literary tradition of socialist realism, and the contemporary official public discourse of state-run media, which incorporated a wide range of associations and allusions from Russia's immediate and distant past. Some classical phrases appear in commentaries on the episodes of the current Russian situations, inviting the reader to recover something of the original meaning of the literary texts as they pertained to subject, author, and audience within the foreign context of the media articles. While Sheila Fitzpatrick stresses common interests and experiences among political and literary figures,[12] James van Geldern points to Russia's rich tradition of mixing political discourse and popular entertainment.[13] He has concluded that echoes from distant times and cultures are heard at unexpected moments: revolutionary posters borrowed from commercial advertisements; socialist rituals mimicked Orthodox Christian rites.

Svetlana Boym[14] made a similar observation in the context of discursive perspective of autobiography. She remarks the peculiar cult of poets and the sources of the changing cultural myths surrounding the poets in non-literary discourse as a positive element in the development of Russian culture. She endorses the conventional formalists' view that "the artistic structures offer an ideal model for describing the multifaceted processes of society."[15] I share this view, and the point that I want to particularly stress here is that literary texts "are a kind of crystallization of floating, formless cultural codes that exist in a society."[16] While I agree with these observations, I would like to suggest that a journalist serves as a manipulator of a literary message, calling attention to the arbitrariness of norms and conventions of the classical texts. The points above will be additionally substantiated by examples drawn from my research.

Jeffrey Brooks[17] gives interesting insights into the development and deployment of artistic devices in state discourse and links between political message and the interplay of culture and tradition. As he emphasizes, "The existence of a single overarching discourse, concentrated in the leading newspapers and legitimated by the full punitive power of the state, was a chief feature of Soviet society. Within this discourse Pravda was paramount."[18] I am inclined to agree with Brooks that "presenting classical writers as cultural heroes differed from prerevolutionary intellectuals' views."[19] Brooks states: "The new authority of the classical writers, particularly the leading nineteenth century Russian writers, emerge from such accounts as vital, independent personalities with strong moral feelings about the issues of their day."

The old-fashioned serious journalism revealed the totalitarian tenets of the state both in media content and in form. While the language of state-controlled media had once been demarcated by neutrality and rationality, it frequently read as openly aggressive and xenophobic. Everyone kept reading the slogans like this one in the media, and skimmed the newspapers to get the official line rather than for the news. There was a time, however, when neither believing in the original Soviet promise nor criticizing the current Soviet reality was possible. However, the astute Soviet reader used to scrutinize the leaden texts of Soviet-era media for a clue of what was really going on from what was not reported. The media formed an indivisible fusion with the party and its doctrines and had no power of its own to question such monstrous formulas as "демократический централизм" (democratic centralism), "окончательная победа социализма и полная гарантия от интервенции и реставрации капиталистического порядка" (the final victory of Socialism and a full guarantee against intervention and the restoration of capitalism), "превратим Москву в образцовый коммунистический город" (turn Moscow into an exemplary communist city), and the like. In fact, it is difficult to think of socialist media headlines, no matter how asserting they were, existing in a competitive market and designing their messages to make them attractive to potential readers. Along with repetitive, uninventive, stereotyped, monotonous, and trite headlines, there was a proliferation of predictable patterns of language, which had echoed the ideas and campaigns of the party leaders. Illuminating evidence of abstract nominalization[20] and slogan-like titles can be drawn from the central newspaper *Pravda*: "Решения 9-го Пленума в жизнь" (Implementing the 9th Plenum decisions into life); "Руки прочь от Берлина" (Keep your hands off Berlin); "Куба: дорога к революции" (Cuba: the road to revolution).[21]

In the Soviet-era media ideological aphorisms were easily singled out by readers. This political sub-language was described and characterized with particular emphasis on the dichotomy known as "diglossia" in which two parallel idioms—"Russian" and "Soviet Russian"—coexisted and served distinct communicative functions.[22] Everyone kept hearing the popular official Soviet song with refrains that became aphorisms, though I am not sure many understand the elusiveness of the lines like "есть у революции начало, нет у революции конца" (there is a beginning to the revolution; there is not an end to it). Virtually every Soviet citizen participated in both spheres on a daily basis. Most importantly, the Soviet-Russian discourse was characterized with unequivocal cynical reasoning that created a perfect source for tautological statement. A telling example is a slogan, such as "Мы говорим Ленин, подразумеваем партия. Мы говорим партия, подразумеваем Ленин" (When we say "Lenin," we imply the party. When we say the party, we imply Lenin). In critical discourse analysis of certain grammatical forms like passive structures, nominalizations, strategies of replacement, and distancing strategies draw special attention due to their ideological potency and their role in "framing" various forms of potentially ideological discourse. Although one cannot simply read off ideological meaning from grammatical forms, it has been proven through empirical research that such linguistic forms as metaphors, argumentative fallacies, rhetorical devices, and presuppositions facilitate a critical interpretation of the social context of media texts in a controlled way, or Soviet media "empty" (read false) reporting. Several rhetorical effects become central in this respect, some of which are nominalization, passivization,[23] satire, or criticism in party slogans such as "Всё во имя человека, всё во благо человека" (All in the name of a man, all for the good of a man) and have crept into the media discourse and were a tool to promote a reasoning for moral orders of socialism, so the aphoristic phrases played a conducive and vital role in constructing and promoting a certain set of views and attitudes and were a unit of a specific sub-language. In opposition to this ubiquitous discourse of "empty signifiers" there was a no less widespread discourse of folklore tradition (political anecdotes, chastushki, etc.). My point here is that official discourse delivered cynical reasoning and oppositional discourse did not have a better way but to address the ideological component of official discourse with deadpan jocular irony. This was the only comeback oppositional discourse could manage.

It is common in analyses of Soviet media discourse to explore tensions in the relationships between the individual and the political regime. A certain opposition to a dominant and ruling ideological discourse was expressed in a counter- or opposing discourse introducing revitalization and carving out the doublethinking. Messages of nonofficial sphere shaped a peculiar type of humor and satire. The strategies of such a discourse co-opted Soviet readers into understanding the nature of constraints and linguistic tools of circumventing them. Commonly recognized but rarely registered in written sources, widespread but hidden from outsiders, truths about socialism's failure were acknowledged in this type of discourse. This counter-discourse found material in anecdotes of the era of stagnation and in Soviet leaders' use of language.[24] It even had its own officially published satirical outlet—*Krokodil.* By introducing satirical treatment of social pathologies, discourse dictated where, how, and what to smile at. Thus, in many respects, it was a form of controlled critique and a tool of entertainment and enlightenment of the public. Censorship would never allow the formal admission of failure of socialism as a system, but the political regime did not attack satirized and humorous depiction of defects and rigidities of the regime. Russian satire did not have a function that it had in other societies—to criticize; but the printed word that revealed social ills to the public was similar to satirical outlets in other societies. The satirical novel *The Twelve Chairs,* written by co-authors Ilya Ilf and Evgeny Petrov, is one of Russia's best-loved books. In it, Ostap Bender searches for diamonds stashed inside one of twelve missing matching chairs. Paradoxically, the national space that the novel creates, known as the New Economic Policy (1921–1928), is a complex simulacrum of Russia during perestroika, associated with the general feeling of post-Soviet anarchy and relative cultural and economic openness. The book's greatest feat is its keenest paradox—the ultimate effect is precisely the opposite of openness. Nowadays, Bender has become more than just a fictional character; he is an imitation of the "culture hero" and "alive and well all over the world." Ilf and Petrov's novel became one of the largest and most influential sources of counter-discourse and can be seen as a polar opposite to the official sublanguage. Ilf and Petrov became the mouthpiece for those were longing for a path to a new world, which lies beyond the revolution, which is still well-known and remembered. The main character and one of the most celebrated tricksters of the Russian literature, Ostap Bender, once claimed, "У меня с советской властью возникли серьезные разногласия. Она хочет строить социализм, а я нет" (I had very serious differences of opinion with the Soviet power. It wants to build socialism, and I do not). Ilf and Petrov had written *The Twelve Chairs* in the 1930s, but the book did not become a masterpiece right away. Their famous hero embodied "the mechanism of cynical survival and deception that existed behind the ideologically approved simulacra of the state-run economy and 'classless' society," as Mark Lipovetsky explains.[25] Richard Stites points to a conjunction of official heroes and fictional ones in Russian Stalinist literature.[26] All facets of the "image of socialist Russia" were a mirrored reflection and simultaneously were distorted. Furthermore, Ilf and Petrov created the character who speaks "southern" (Odessan) jargon. Aside from phrases, intonation, and accent, grammar is part of Bender's language mask as well. On a pragmatic level, the language masks of the characters combine cliché formulas and prearranged signals, making the characters recognizable. The dialectically tinged language is consistent primarily by grammatical errors, rather than structurally with Ostap's non-standard language. On another level, benderisms reproduce and reaffirm certain key social and cultural themes. Memorable catchphrases taken from *The Twelve Chairs* are well known and have been incorporated into everyday language and media discourse. Since Russians typically make extensive use of aphorisms and catchphrases from sources conventionally perceived as witty, this book is immensely popular. More often than not countless quotes taken from *The Twelve Chairs* communicate a range of subtle messages about identity and worldview, personal aspirations, and social expectations.

Readers are free to shift constantly from one interpretation of a quotation to the next, and yet, as one progresses deeper into the story of the novel, each interpretation begins to seem more sophisticated than the other. For example, Bender is one who knows "четыреста сравнительно честных способов отъёма денег у населения" (four hundred comparatively honest ways of taking money away from the population). This famous quote comes from *The Golden Calf*—another famous satirical novel by Ilf and Petrov. Bender's sarcastic expression "Может быть тебе дать еще ключ от квартиры, где деньги лежат?" (Perhaps you'd also like the key to the apartment where the money is?) is used as a formula of rejection when someone has expectations of you or makes unreasonable demands. Bender's personage has become more than just a fictional character as he philosophizes about his lot in life and shares his understanding with others: "Жизнь, господа присяжные заседатели, это сложная штука, но, господа присяжные заседатели, эта сложная штука открывается просто, как ящик. Надо только уметь его открыть. Кто не может открыть, тот пропадает" (Life, gentlemen of the jury, is a difficult thing, but this difficult thing, gentlemen of the jury, can be opened up as simply as a drawer. One only has to know how to open it up. Those who fail to do it, perish). Most prominently, con man Ostap Bender represents the literal tradition of tricksters and comes to symbolize the driving force behind the "Wild West" capitalism of the 1990s in the country.[27] The constant reappearance of the benderisms in various contexts of the current media reveals that journalists are capable of taking an outsider's view on the subject.

I brought up Soviet-era aphorisms and stiob style as examples of the Soviet reporting cut-and-dried style. (The stiob style is discussed in more detail in chapter 10.) The rhetorical strategies that tailored propaganda in those "empty" media fell into highly predicted patterns. But there is another aspect to it, too. In the official discourse, ideologically charged language surrogates were widely exploited as the authorities stipulated requirements for any media. Journalists, therefore, tried to tread the safe ground of acknowledged doctrines and abstained from any urge to be original or inventive either in headlines or in the body of text. They were also engaged in educating the public how to react to certain themes and concerns. For decades, the language of newspapers lacked novelty as well as subtlety of expression, and was designed to introduce and reinforce moral/political standards. Gorbachev's perestroika did not change the Russian language itself, but brought out the conditions of usage. On the one hand, striking and bright modes of expression became welcome. The new journalistic discourse has replaced them with language full of irony, pastiche, and simulation. Gorbachev's glasnost created the opportunity for the discussion of many subjects previously considered strictly taboo like criticism of the horrors of Stalinism, like inhumanity, paranoia, and betrayal, just to name a few. Glasnost made these topics open for promulgation. On the other hand, fascination for sensationalism, conspiracy theories, and the popularity of detective novels in Soviet popular culture at that time reflected the decisive breaking down of ideological hegemony.[28]

The framework of references in the Russian press changed very quickly after 1991 with such resources as Soviet political language and popular culture (including television advertisements) becoming available to journalists, who were at the same time freed from the requirement to be serious and to avoid irony. The speech outburst swamped the whole nation. Borders disappeared between various forms of language and the situations in which they were used. Consequently, social distinctions in speech became fewer, but individual distinctions observed were greater. Live speech replaced the always-correct "newspeak" (Orwellian term to define specific political language) that was steeped with repeated patterns, and speech manner—that is, style—in many ways became a reflection of a journalist's personality.[29] For example, during glasnost, the Mayakovsky legend served once again as a reflection of changes in state ideology. Ironically, Soviet rulers and opposition alike appealed to the same poetic symbols: Mayakovsky's verse and alleged beliefs were cited in support of the putschists' call for defense of the old regime, while those who resisted the putsch also recited from Mayakovsky in their speeches. Moreover, *Pravda* and *Izvestia* would pull out the old, standard quotations about "коммунистическое далёко" (the communist far future) and "весна человечества" (the spring of humanity). Alternatively, *Kommersant* used the widely known phrase about *byt*, or the daily grind, from Mayakovsky's suicide letter ("The boat of love has crashed against the daily grind"). The word "*byt*" takes on the additional connotation of philistinism in an advertisement to sell foreign consumer goods: "Ваша любовная лодка не разобьётся о быт, если на её борту бытовая техника Siene" (Your love boat will not crash against the daily grind [*byt*] if it is equipped with technology for everyday use [*bytovaia tekhnika*] made by [Siene]).[30]

The 1990s have seen an ever-growing research interest in art's role in transforming "dry ideology into the fuel of images and myths intended for general consumption."[31] By the time the official ideological symbols had been openly criticized and ridiculed by the discourse of glasnost, the new sub-discourse had developed—Russian rock. During the Soviet Union, rock was the only medium not under complete state control and rock musicians have long played a prominent role in Russian politics. Russia's few politically outspoken rockers consistently expressed their anti-establishment views, and have always struggled against an oppressive state and one of the genre's functions before perestroika was seen as that of assisting a civic awakening. In many ways Russian rock is special, with lyrics playing a far larger role than in Western rock music. In their lyrics rockers acknowledge the ability "to see behind the façade" and articulate tacit knowledge and complicated paradoxes of the Soviet ideology. Lines drawn from the lyrics of Boris Grebenshchikov (*Akvarium*), Yuri Shevchuk (*DDT*), and Vyacheslav Butusov (*Nautilus Pompilius*) became known as stock expressions. Here is just one example of an excellent symbol of empty form and recognition of one's own complicit behavior in the stagnation period that was brilliantly grasped by Butusov: "скованные одной цепью, связанные одной целью" (joined together into a straight chain forged together for a common purpose).

It is my perception that throughout the 1990s the Russian media, while retaining their fondness for the traditional type of aphorism, had moved closer to the Western model in so far as they had started to make more use of catchphrases from radio and television programs, including advertising slogans (e.g., Twix chocolate bar commercial "сладкая парочка" [a sweet couple]; "Я не халявщик—я партнёр" [I am not a freeloader; I am a partner]).[32] Everyone, without even noticing repeated phrases, from commercials and media parodied this style. Consider, for example, "Новое поколение выбирает Пепси" (Pepsi—the choice of the new generation), as an example of advertising a range of foreign-made products. Advertising was viewed as part of the Western communicative style and Russian speakers began to structure and organize their messages in a compact way.[33]

Interestingly, the authoritarian tendencies in Russian society during Putin's presidency brought back the nostalgia for Stalin's (imagined) successful statehood strategies and Stalin's rhetoric. Although the Yeltsin government was successful at repressing overt Stalinist rhetoric, the discourse of the *Izvestia, Moskovsky Komsomolets, Zavtra* of the past years features Stalin-sounding rhetoric. A close reading of references to the rhetoric of "the competent manager" makes it clear that journalists are simply using a persuasive analogy, in much the same way that the dictator might have done under similar circumstances. The overall stylistic tone of Stalin's language is purely "bureaucratic," in Evgeny Dobrenko's words.[34] I would say that this bureaucratic spirit to a great extent defined the nature of the totalitarian vision of the world and as such is transmitted and kept alive in a multitude of ways—not only through references to Stalin's words, but also through cultural practices, historical narratives, memoirs, and images associated with him and his time. Personally, every former citizen of the Soviet Union is very well familiar with catchphrases drawn from Stalin's speeches, mostly through the journalistic discourse that cited Stalin's catchphrases, creating an ad hoc new language formula to describe present-day reality. The identity of the older generation was formed around the historical past and evolved around Stalin and his role in Russian history. Just as in the aftermath of the October Revolution, people often looked back on pre-revolutionary values and the language that expressed them, nowadays the incessant use of socialist jargon and references to Stalin's time is either evocative of nostalgia for a more secure past, or being critical, ironic, or sarcastic about it. Surprisingly, Stalin's discourse has a presence unfortunately not only in the discourse of the "power," but also in the discursive practices of media practitioners, either in the mockery of indoctrination or in the direct non-ironic borrowings.[35]

Comparing the list of expressions in the mainstream papers *Izvestia, Moskovsky Komsomolets,* and *Zavtra* from 2010 through 2012, it becomes apparent that Stalin's phrases were reproduced with various degree of precision: "Смерть одного человека—трагедия, смерть миллионов—статистика" (One death is a tragedy, one million is a statistic); "Лучшее решение всех проблем—это смерть, нет человека—нет проблем" (Death is the solution to all problem. No man—no problem); "Вы не можете делать революцию в ш ё лковых перчатках" (You cannot make a revolution with silk gloves); "Благодарность—это такая собачья болезнь" (Gratitude is a sickness suffered by dogs); "Писатели—инженеры человеческих душ" (The writers are engineers of the human soul).

Upon looking at the references to Stalin's texts in contemporary media and public discourse, the reader will notice that they have been preserved almost intact and lend themselves perfectly for framing the narrative of the recent political speeches and editorials. At first, the unusual distribution of the speech patterns of Stalin's linguistic remnants in contemporary Russian public discourse can be attributed to a long-time effort on the part of the authoritative media discourse to control public language. As observed by Grenoble, "Soviet leaders knew that language counts, that it is a crucial part of both a nation's and an individual's identity, and it could be manipulated to serve as a powerful tool for the State."[36] If we look at the contemporary authoritarian discourse that is replicated on the deeper layers of the doxa's frame, it shows high frequency of powerful Stalinist dicta, which acquired special status. Evidently, these linguistic mechanisms used to control the citizens' minds in an uncanny Orwellian sense (Orwell 1949) are tangentially engaged with mechanisms of the discourse of the Third Reich, for instance. In fact, in his *The Language of the Third Reich*, Victor Klemperer[37] anticipates this very argument. He remarks that "Nazism permeated the flesh and blood of the people through single words, idioms and sentence structures which were imposed on them in a million repetitions and taken on board mechanically and unconsciously."[38]

Compare this with an example of a Stalin-style catchphrase redeployed and reified in the following headline: "Кадры решают все" (Cadres are the key to everything). This infamous Stalin quote, or just a kind of folk-embodiment of a widespread attitude, makes a headline to an interview with an activist from the web portal *Pravoslavie i mir* (Orthodox Christianity and the world).[39] The article focuses on the discussion that the church's activists need to equip themselves with better skills in public relations. Compare this with a 2008 *Izvestia* headline: "Головокружение от успехов" (Dizzy with success).[40] Paradoxical as it may seem, the headline introduces the report on the value-added tax reduction and compensation for reduced revenue from the stabilization fund. This headline with its residual connotations from Stalin's article published in *Pravda* on March 2, 1930, in which he called for a temporary halt to the process of collectivization, is one of the examples of catchphrases that remained dormant since Khrushchev's Thaw period until the 2000s. I have come to think that the conclusion could have an unanticipated discovery that demonstrates profoundly negative consequences of such a deployment in the current social climate.[41]

As we see, the rhetoric that served Soviet propaganda is now back to serve new authorities. The modern-day reception of the Soviet-era catchphrases is quite an interesting topic itself, but this topic is outside of this study's scope. My point here was to discern and discuss voices from particular places and time included in contemporary media that characterize the cultural rhetoric of the society.

When taken together with the fundamental problem of linguistic representation, such "socialist" allusions are illustrative of the rhetorical persuasion. The development of meaning depends on the apprehension of the readers; however, unfamiliarity with Stalin's idiom does not lessen an effect of propaganda power. Current work in the field of trauma studies[42] raises a related question: How does narrative mediate between incoherent experiences and the difficulty of assimilating past to present? Such considerations reflect an interdisciplinary awareness that examining connections between the national past and the present involves questions of organizing narrative. The variety of ways in which Stalin's image and language are rendered in a number of contexts is a certain indication of the existence of the "new" Russia newspeak, which reflects both an impoverishment and an elaboration of Russian as a communicative tool; it overlaps but is not quite the same as Soviet-style Russian newspeak. Ilya Kalinin, discussing the presence of the Soviet past in present-day Russia, underscores that powers in reinterpretation and restoration of historical past support the objective of nostalgia for the Soviet past, while in the masses a return of the lost past is perceived as a comically heterogeneous cultural legacy.[43]

As we see the rhetoric that served Soviet propaganda is now made to serve as a reminder of that type of ideological discourse, based on communist values and the language that expressed them. Contemporary media style has a lot in common with Soviet media language. In current media discourse old catch phrases and aphorisms are commonly used as recurring reactions to paradoxes of socialism; they are also cited in the context of the acknowledgment of the failed purpose of socialism. I explore selected strategies of current media discourse, demonstrating how the new rhetoric of the democratic order can thrive on strategies associated with the old communist newspeak. Many of the examples cited above are illustrative of the idea that there is much reflection going on about the verbal legacy of socialism. Fragments of that past molded in the language formulas have a tendency to reemerge in completely new, different contexts where they are no longer perceived as part of the whole, but rather an instance, a fragment, a message, a warning from the past. What used to be obligatory formulae of expression, therefore, has now become the individual choice for a journalist. The constant reappearance of the slogans, mottoes, quotations from that time in the new reformed newspaper headlines reveals that journalists are capable of taking an outsider's view on the subject. Further on in my analysis of allusions that reflect on the verbal legacy of socialism, I present evidence that the ironic overtone would be inevitable in most contexts. I also present rather compelling confirmation of the incessant use of socialist jargon being evocative of nostalgia for a more secure past, while simultaneously being characterized by critical, ironic, or sarcastic tone. Thus through allusions, we are able to observe the highly contradictory process of simultaneous rejection and attraction of the immediate past. It is obviously conditioned by the particular political situation in Russia, but here we largely move out of the discourse analysis and practical stylistics perspective and enter the field of political science.

NOTES

1. See the discussion in K. Voltmer, "Constructing Political Reality in Russia," *European Journal of Communication* 15, no. 4 (2000): 469–500; I. Zassoursky, *Media and Power in Post-Soviet Russia* (Armonk, NY: M. E. Sharpe, 2004).
2. Svetlana Pasti, "Two Generations of Contemporary Russian Journalists," *European Journal of Communication* 20, no. 1 (2005): 89–115.
3. Sarah Oates, "The Neo-Soviet Model of the Media," *Europe-Asia Studies* 59, no. 8 (2007): 18.
4. Pasti, "Two Generations of Contemporary Russian Journalists," 101–2.
5. S. Oates, "Media and Political Communication," in *Developments in Russian Politics 6*, ed. S. White, Z. Gitelman, and R. Sakwa (Basingstoke, UK, and New York: Palgrave Macmillan, 2005), 114–29, 115.

6. Julia Ioffe is Russian-born journalist and blogger who spent much of her childhood in Moscow. When she was seven years old her family emigrated to the United States. She earned her degree in history from Princeton University, specializing in Soviet history, and later began her career as a fact checker for the *New Yorker*, before moving to Columbia Journalism School's Knight Foundation Case Studies Initiative. In 2009, she went back to Russia on a Fulbright scholarship, and spent three years in Moscow as Moscow correspondent for *Foreign Policy* and the *New Yorker*. She currently serves as staff writer for the *Washington Post*, *Forbes*, and the *New Republic*.

7. Julia Ioffe, "What Is Russia Today?," *Columbia Journalism Review*, September/October 2010, www.cjr.org/feature/what_is_russia_today.php?page=all.

8. Mikhail Antonov and Vladimir Pozner, "Segodnia pyshnym tsvetom rastsvela samotsenzura," Novyi Smysl, www.sensusnovus.ru/interview/2012/01/06/12390.html.

9. Full text of the speech is available at http://neterpi.ru/articles-id-11.html.

10. Evgeny Dobrenko, *Metafora vlasti: Literatura stalinskoi epokhi v istoricheskom osveshchenii* (Munich: Otto Sagner, 1993), 74.

11. See Boris Groys, *The Total Art of Stalinism: Avant-Garde, Aesthetic Dictatorship, and Beyond*, trans. Charles Rougle (Princeton, NJ: Princeton University Press, 1992).

12. Sheila Fitzpatrick, *The Cultural Front: Power and Culture in Revolutionary Russia* (Ithaca, NY: Cornell University Press, 1992), 248, 256.

13. James van Geldern, "Cultural and Social Geography in the Mass Culture of the 1930s," in *New Directions in Soviet History*, ed. Stephen White (New York: Cambridge University Press, 1992), 64.

14. See Sveltana Boym, *Death in Quotation Marks: The Cultural Myth of the Modern Poet* (Cambridge, MA: Harvard University Press, 1991).

15. Ibid., 26.

16. Ibid.

17. Cited in Jeffrey Brooks, "Socialist Realism in *Pravda*: Read All About It!," *Slavic Review* 53, no. 4 (Winter 1994). See also discussion in Jeffrey Brooks, "*Pravda* and the Language of Power in Soviet Russia, 1917–28," in *Media and Revolution*, ed. Jeremy Popkin (Lexington: University of Kentucky Press, 1995); Brooks, "*Pravda* Goes to War," in *The Heart of War: Soviet Culture and Entertainment, 1941–45*, ed. Richard Stites (Bloomington: Indiana University Press, 1995).

18. Brooks, "Socialist Realism in *Pravda*," 981.

19. Ibid., 979.

20. *Nominalizations* occur when sentences or parts of sentences, descriptions of actions, and the participants involved in them are turned into nouns. They help to impersonalize actions, to eliminate agency, and to transform processes into objects. In the following example the nominalization is used to hide the agents of unpopular measures undertaken by government and to represent the whole case as something necessary and inevitable.

21. See Miller Owen, preface to *Identity of the Literary Text*, ed. Mario J. Valdes and Owen Miller (Toronto: University of Toronto Press, 1985), viii.

22. See the works by Tomas Venclova, Patric Sériot, John Dunn, Maksim Krongauz, "The Transformation of Russian from a Language of the Soviet Type to a Language of the Western Type," in *Language and Society in Post-Communist Europe*, selected papers from the Fifth World Congress of Central and East European Studies, Warsaw, 1995 (Macmillan: Basingstoke, 1999), 3–22. John A. Dunn, "The Role of English in Modern Russian," in *Sprachwandel in der Slavia*, ed. Lew N. Zybatow (Frankfurt-am-Main: Peter Lang, 2000), 87–101.

23. *Passivization* is the rendering of verbs in the passive form; it also obscures the agency and focuses the attention of the reader on certain themes at the expense of others. In addition, the passive constructions permit the removal of reference to the causing agent.

24. See the discussion of ethnic humor and oral folklore in Emil Draitser, *Forbidden Laughter* (Los Angeles: Almanac Press, 1980); Seth Graham, *A Cultural Analysis of the Russo-Soviet Anekdot* (PhD diss., University of Pittsburgh, 2003).

25. Mark Lipovetsky, *Charms of the Cynical Reason* (Brighton, MA: Academic Studies Press, 2011).

26. Richard Sites, *Russian Popular Culture: Entertainment and Society since 1900* (New York: Cambridge University Press, 1992), 66–72.

27. See the discussion of Ostap Bender as an example of the New Soviet Man in Sheila Fitzpatrick, "The World of Ostap Bender: Soviet Confidence Men in the Stalin Period," *Slavic Review* 61, no.3 (Autumn 2002): 535–57.

28. On the impact of pulp fiction on late Soviet culture, see ibid., chapter 7, "Perestroika and the People's Taste."

29. The scholarship of the language of Soviet totalitarianism is substantial. For Sériot, for example, "langue de bois" or newspeak is the language of the other, an aberrant language as opposed to the "language of the people." P. Sériot, "Dereviannyi iazyk, iazyk drugogo i svoi iazyk: Poiski nastoiiashchei rechi v sotsialisticheskoi Evrope 1980-kh godov," *Politicheskaia lingvistika* 5, no. 25 (2008): 160–67, www.philology.ru/linguistics1/serio-08.htm. Wierzbicka describes this totalitarian language as the language of manipulation, which is opposed to the alternative language, which she describes within the frame of normality (*narodnyi iazyk, antitotalitarnyi iazyk*). A. Wierzbicka, "Antitotalitarian Language in Poland: Some Mechanisms of Linguistic Self-Defense," *Language in Society* 19 (1990): 1–59. Furthermore, Yurchak (pp. 36–37) uses the term the "Soviet authoritative discourse" referring to the Soviet didactic discourse, a long-standing, uniform, and legitimate phenomenon, which had shaped the knowledge shared and adhered to throughout the decades of Soviet society. With "all types of information, new and old were presented as knowledge previously asserted and commonly known" (p. 61). A. Yurchak, *Everything Was Forever until It Was No More* (Cambridge, MA: Harvard University Press, 2006).

30. Cited in Svetlana Boym, *Common Places: Mythologies of Everyday Life* (Cambridge: Cambridge University Press, 1994), 282.

31. Igor Golomstock, *Totalitarian Art in the Soviet Union, the Third Reich, Fascist Italy and the People's Republic of China* (New York: HarperCollins, 1990), xii–xiv.

32. It is a phrase from a commercial that promoted vouchers of MMM, a Russian pyramid scheme with one of Russia's first television ad campaigns. One investor, Lyonya Golubkov, a blue-collar character boasting of the money they made on MMM, said proudly: "I'm not a freeloader; I'm a partner."

33. It was a subject of detailed discussion, see S. Malykhina, "New-Coined Aphorisms and Old-Fashioned Euphemisms in the Russian Current Media Discourse," a paper delivered at the AAASS Annual Convention, Boston, MA, November 2009.

34. Evgeny Dobrenko, "Total'naia lingvistika: Vlast' grammatiki i grammatika vlasti," *Russian Literature* 63, no. 2–4 (2008): 585.

35. See the discussion by Gassan Gusseinov on cultural and historical terms and complex forms of linguistic and rhetorical practices used in Stalin's discourse and its vitality at www.indepsocres.spb.ru/gusein_e.htm.

36. Lenore Grenoble, *Language Policy in the Former Soviet Union* (Dordrecht: Kluwer Academic, 2003), 1.

37. Victor Klemperer, *The Language of the Third Reich: A Philologist's Notebook*, trans. Martin Brady (London: Continuum, 2002), 15–16.

38. Ibid.

39. E. Zhosul, "Kadry reshauit vse," September 6, 2012, www.pravmir.ru/elena-zhosul-kadry-reshayut-vse-1/.

40. A. Livshits, "Golovokruzhenie ot uspekha," *Izvestia*, April 9, 2008, http://izvestia.ru/news/335298 .

41. Good summaries on Stalin's style can be found in Richard Bandler and John Grinder, *The Structure of Magic I: A Book about Language and Therapy* (Palo Alto, CA: Science and Behavior Books, 1974); Dina Khapaeva, *Goticheskoe obshchestvo: Morfologiia koshmara* (Moscow: Novoe literaturnoe obozrenie, 2007).

42. Santner offers a critique of a certain mode of German historiography that has sought to minimize the trauma, downplay the question of responsibility. Eric Santner, "History beyond the Pleasure Principle: Some Thoughts on the Representation of Trauma," in *Probing the Limits of Representation Nazism and the Final Solution*, ed. Saul Friedlander (Cambridge, MA: Harvard University Press, 1992).

43. Ilya Kalinin, "Nostalgic Modernization: The Soviet Past as 'Historical Horizon,'" *Slavonica* 17, no. 2 (November 2011): 156–66.

Chapter Six

Allusions in Headlines

In this chapter I describe functions and features of allusive headlines, present examples, and discuss some key parameters of their contexts. The aim of this chapter is to demonstrate that the ways that journalists apply allusions in headlines clearly reflect on the framing process; however, the frequent disconnection between the headline and a narrative may lead to informational discretion.

The analyzed segments were entered into a database. The headlines and the context in which they were found were then singled out in the database and now constitute the general data corpus. A restricted corpus made up of a few dozen headlines with interplay in them was later singled out of the general corpus. Among the challenges that allusive headlines present in terms of translation are frequent unclear correlations between the allusive headline and the content of the text and lack of conventional equivalents commonly accepted and culturally specific equivalents in a source and a target language. Moreover, in many case, the literal translation fails to represent the pun or interplay of the literal and implied meaning. I have commented widely on general questions of cultural and historical context as well as the articles' content, which often takes the form of linguistic and historic digression in order to shed light on the original source and a journalist's shortcomings. It is my belief that the allusiveness of contemporary media is more often invoked than analyzed, and a reading that focuses on the problems of interpretation and recontextualization forces one to ask genuinely interpretive questions.

My interest in headlines containing allusions to classics derives from the assumption that media impact comes not only from the information brought to the audience but also (and more likely) from the way the media organize and package this information. Within the article, nowhere else is the framing effect registered as quickly and comprehensively as in the headlines and kickers. Considering that the Internet is the most important source of general information, I searched the electronic versions of these outlets, and I would like to elaborate on the peculiar effect of an online version over a printed one. It is the widespread opinion that the attractiveness and effectiveness of online media headlines depends on the selection of words and phrases that captivate and motivate the audience. Although there are no special studies to be found on the framing effects of media headlines, some experiments—conducted by the specialists in communication studies, inspired by the results of framing research in cognitive psychology (in particular, Kahneman and Tversky 1984)[1]—showed that viewers may, after a certain period, "remember" obtaining certain information from the article body, while they have in reality obtained it from the headlines, kickers, leads, or pull quotes. Headlines are observed to relate to a wide variety of topics, both domestic and international, related to political figures, groups, events, and ideologies. Some of the topics are found consistently throughout the data while others are linked to specific events. I have collected examples that show specific authorial frames of reference and interpretive norms.

I primarily consider references related to Russian classics that help to structure news stories on different stages from problem formulation to resolution. I start with a group of allusive headlines with classical references in them that can be described as aphoristic. The headline is part of a journalistic piece; therefore the complete the analysis of the entire frame, it is insufficient to focus on the headline itself. The unfolding storyline, indeed, resembles a big nasty welter composed of a sequence of the ironic twists and some complex reversal of roles, stances, and directions. I want to look at the discourse of mainstream media to examine how it utilizes classical allusions—at least linguistically if not explicitly rhetorically.

My first example concerns the idea and the metaphor which is an essential element of post-imperial Russian geopolitical discourse. In 2011 *Novaya Gazeta* published an interview with a prominent Russian culturologist Igor Yakovenko discussing the impact of the metaphor "empire" resurrection in the public discourse in the former Soviet Union and post-Soviet Russia. The interview presented in the rubric "Politics" is pointedly titled "Конечная остановка: 'Москва—Третий Рим'" (The last stop is "Moscow the Third Rome).[2] This theme has been selected because hints at the ancient Russian messianic idea and its Orthodox roots were implicit rhetorically in the public discourse throughout the Imperial and Soviet periods.[3] In the post-Soviet mainstream discourse this concept received new and unexpected relevance. This theme defined and popularized in the first half of the sixteenth century; since that time the change in how to view this concept reflected the paradigm shifts with one conceptual worldview replaced by another—from paradigm demonstrating an almost exclusive Orthodox focus to the nationalist interpretation of the "Byzantine inheritance." A journalist provocatively cited Ronald Reagan describing the USSR as the "evil empire" (the view that reflected the Western perspective of the USSR as internally repressive and externally expansionist). The reporter also challenges the interviewee with questions whether or not Russia wants to restore its imperial grandeur and whether or not such archaic stereotypes are useful today. The position of the interviewee can be summarized as follows: historically, Russia has judged itself and has been perceived by others as an empire. Yakovenko admits that after the fall of the USSR many of the Soviet psychologists and historians called the Soviet state, an empire and traces the genealogy of this doctrine placing it in historical and cultural context. What does the headline of this article add to the framing effect? The title is reminiscent of commonly known text. In Soviet public discourse the idea was less popular than it has become in the recent decades. This doctrine is one of the first historical formulaic ideas of nomination of Muscovy as the Third Rome (following the original and Constantinople).

Although the idea did not officially appear in either in Church or government statements, it was destined to unite all Christian realms under its sway, and the doctrine also elevated the Russian tsar to a position of both spiritual and secular preeminence. The following passage was found in the letters sent by a monk from Pskov, Philotheus (Filofei), to the Pskov representative of the Moscow grand prince Vassilij III (1479–1533), to Vassilij himself and to Ivan IV the Terrible (1530–1584): "All Christian realms will come to an end and will unite into the one single realm of our sovereign, that is, into the Russian realm, according to the prophetic books. Both Romes fell, the third endures, and a fourth there will never be." As Marshall Poe puts it, "Scholarly opinion concerning the doctrine is divided: though many specialists argue that 'Third Rome' was never very important in Old Russia, one can still read, particularly in textbooks, that Filofei's doctrine was the official ideology of Muscovy."[4] In the last decade the topic gets high key coverage while the context tends to be "rhematic" and focus on the unknown rather than on the "thematic" repetition of the national myth. Unlike in the stories of the Soviet period, Filofei's doctrine is seen as a factor unifying the nation through constructing and claiming the unity of the Slavic territory and joint legacy. In Russia, newspaper articles and editorials cite the doctrine of the "Third Rome" as a symbol of Russian renewal, and employ it as a Russian Orthodox geopolitical metaphor to explain the neo-Eurasianist prospects for Russian foreign policy. This catchphrase is frequently employed in the discourse to justify that Russia should regain its great power status. In the West, scholars, philosophers, and publicists view Filofei's writing as the "roots" of what they believed to be a fundamental characteristic of the "Russian idea"—the religious-political idea of Moscow as the Third Rome.

The wealth of information encoded in the headline could hardly have been rendered through less evocative means of expression. The headline also contains patriotic overtones, and affords the journalist the possibility of a double allusion—on the one hand, to a universally known myth, and on the other, to the dilemma that was faced by Russia's politicians. We are dealing here with an allusion that is, actually or intentionally, aphoristic.

The next aspect of headline framing which contributes to contextualization is highlighting the background historical parallel. Often journalists seek the causes of different societal problems in "mentality," "consciousness," "complexes" of people, extensively referring to national literary-historical discourse. This type of allusions is also interesting in terms of the constitution of identities. The "national features" mentioned in editorial titled "Pria slovesnaia" (Verbal skirmish)[5] (*Nezavisimaya Gazeta* 2007) are seen as causes of societal problems. The article describes Sen. Hillary Clinton and Sen. Barack Obama the 2007 Democratic presidential debates in Philadelphia. However, the main point made is an official avoidance of debate in Russian political sphere with references to "inferiority complex," "slavish obedience," "lack of fighting qualities," and the like. The society is presented as apathetic, weak, and unable to engage in the discussion of social problems and their solution, and events are related as if viewed by an outsider. The author insists that the functions and nature of political debate are radically different in the West than in Russia. Basically, the journalist focuses on social and informal norms that Russian politicians often adhere to, which limit the extent and diversity of a discussion. The journalist clues the readers that given the fact that the strong political leadership with one-party dictatorship still dominates formal discourse and mass media communications in Russia today, linguistic behavior totally subordinates and leads—through token agreement and hedge opinion—to the avoidance of disagreement, thus affecting the democratic plurality of a political talk. Ivan the Terrible's time comes alive in the context in more than one sense. Labeling the political debates with a vernacular expression of the sixteenth century diplomatic discourse brings the unsettling mixture of connotations to the subject matter at hand. The clash between the optimistically presented old-fashioned debate and the critical view of the contemporary practice creates the desired stylistic tension. In this particular context the use of the expression "verbal skirmish" borrowed from Ivan the Terrible and Prince Andrey Kurbsky's correspondence creates the style of discourse that devalues the subject and fails to use the issue of political debates to construct a nationally unified, shared meaning.[6]

The following headline provides an example of a stand-alone unit that possesses ultimate explanatory power, and is revealing of the text that follows: "Тьмы низких истин нам дороже нас возвышающий обман?" (A deception that elevates us is dearer than a host of low truths) (*Uchitel'skaia*

Gazeta 2009).[7] A journalist cites Pushkin, whose authority is undisputable, to refresh the conventional truth and who is a symbol of the Russian cultural heritage. Since Pushkin says that uplifting deception is dearer to him, so the reader is offered to proceed from the supposition that truth is a traumatic experience. This important point was underlined in the first paragraph of the article that regards the age-old discussions concerning the teaching of history in schools. This is not only the question of how history should be taught in schools, but also what history should be taught is as significant, for the eradication of some historical topics is to risk losing this common identity for future generations. With strategic use of question mark the media practitioner sets the legitimacy of his subject matter into question while simultaneously opening the polemical understanding of his or her position. As a mini text, headlines have to keep their semantic integrity intact. On the one hand, it is a self-sufficient independent text that can stand and be analyzed on its own, thus functioning as a mini-text capable of denoting essential information. On the other hand, the headline foretells a larger text and announces its topic or sums up—in a most precise and clear-cut form—its content. The author's implied subversion does not pass unnoticed. This formulaic expression is ambiguous since it is unclear whether the allusion constructed as recognized and valued metaphor that has relevance to current situation with the textbooks and national historical past, or this expression is a rhetorical manipulative tool, which, in addition to other overtones, invests the texts with pervasive irony.

In some instances attempts to construct narratives of national relevance while the discourse unified and supported by common knowledge, result in an opinion-driven frame led by political attitudes or ideological stances of a journalist. The following example demonstrates how the narrative was reassembled around the topic introduced in the allusive headline. The use of distorted quotation may be enough to set up an allusion that has passed into common parlance, whereas the changes used to alert the reader to a change in register. Some quotations undergo structural changes, but the fact that they are additionally supplied by the cues to the "members resources"[8] makes them totally recognizable.

The story of favoritism in the Kremlin's inner circle, and how the children of the well-known Russian politicians benefited from their parents' positions is reported by a 2003 *Komsomolskaya Pravda* in the article titled "Я тебя породил, я тебя и пристрою!" (I gave you life, it is on me to get you a job/I will get you a job).[9] The original quote, by an epic character Taras Bulba from the eponymous novel by Russian-Ukrainian writer Nikolai Gogol (Mykola Hohol'), reads, "I gave you life, it is on me to take it." These words are pronounced in the novel's most tragic moment, when an old Cossack Taras Bulba killed his younger son, who surrendered to his passion with a Polish girl and renounced his family, nation, and faith. The implied suggestion of the quote is "I am your father; therefore I am to preserve honor in the family." Although the book abounds in description of violence, tortures, murder, and brutality, the key idea of the novel is a romantic concept of brotherhood among Cossacks. The single small change in the quote—the informal nuanced *пристрою*—imbues the heading with irony or sarcasm creating a great effect by literalizing the meaning of the phrase and at the same time keeping its transferred sense vibrant.

The issue at hand is not whether the old Cossack's exclamation is good or bad, but how the way in which his comment on the family is revealing about the exceptional feature of the "Russian" character. Overall the article does not contain open criticism; data are fused in one lengthy homogeneous text with no highlighting of background data, no underlining of main ideas, no detailed information about political agents and multidimensional picture of events necessary to critically evaluate the performance; however, with the allusive headline it is possible to twist the whole topic around and bring up unfathomable depths that otherwise remain unclaimed.

The next example, an allusion to Ilf and Petrov's novel *The Twelve Chairs*, "Заграница нам поможет" (Somebody from abroad will help us) (lenta.ru 2008),[10] was chosen for examination due to the theme of the article, which is dealing with the U.S. position toward the independence of South Ossetia. The Russia-Georgia War of 2008[11] coincided with the visit of the U.S. secretary of state Condoleezza Rice to Tbilisi, where she assured that the George W. Bush administration will help Georgia to rebuild. As the national conflict discourse has been the topic through which fundamentally patriotic frame has been projected in post-Soviet media, its rhetoric lends itself perfectly to strategies of nation building and strong statehood. The headline of the Russian account of the war is referring to the humanitarian aid in the conflict. A journalist has to employ the verbal irony to capture the simultaneous presence of two dimensions of meaning: what is said and how. Kierkegaard captures this sense of simultaneity in his assertion that "the ironic figure of speech is like a riddle and its solution possessed simultaneously."[12] The headline catches an intertextual reference to the source text, and to the expression that Ostap Bender utters.[13]

Like the previous headline the next is also a reference to a benderism "И этот лед тронулся"[14] (The ice has been broken) (*Ezhenedel'nyi zhurnal* 2002). This dry translation cannot provide all the connotations that the source text seems to suggest. The article offers a story about the initial period of modernization in the world's most totalitarian state—North Korea. The reference to the benderism in the headline and of this article evokes the spirit of Ostap Bender as the driving force behind the "Wild West" capitalism and post-Soviet anarchy in Russia. A typical for mainstream discourse stories of the foreign affairs reports in the narrative that made it impossible for readers to identify the agents responsible for the issues. The benderism functions as a formula for explaining the North Korean way of reform. The journalist's reference to Ostap Bender keeps open the implicit comparison between the expectations of the North Korean leadership and a fast-thinking swindler. The main point of the article is that North Korea, one of the most tightly controlled countries in the world, needs outside help for its reforms to work.

According to the factual information of the article, the regime in Pyongyang has carried out limited economic reforms and has made sporadic efforts to improve relations with the United States in the hopes of gaining increased aid. This fact is echoed in the quote from the article: "Северокорейский лидер и раньше, случалось, говорил о возможности реформ, равно как и о примирении с окружающим миром, надеясь добиться помощи и кредитов от богатых соседей" (This statement by the North Korean leader was made sometime in the past. Subsequently, however, after North Korea confessed to having a nuclear bomb program, it faced further international economic isolation. This crisis would likely make it harder for this impoverished country to gain the international support that it needs to revive its moribund economy, so Korean leaders hope that "someone will help us."[15])

Adopting Ostap Bender's style, the journalist sets the tone for objections. By beginning the article with the colorful quote, the journalist draws the readers' attention to his own assessment of North Korean modest reforms. The journalist is suggesting that the North Korean project be flawed from the start. To illustrate his point the reporter borrows the benderism, and by doing so, positions the events generally described within the frame of lack of control. Remove the quotation, and most of the article's effect is negated. These stories typically present the locus of control of the issues as lying beyond the access of an average reader, in the hands of uncontrollable forces or faceless "North Korea," "Korean leaders"—some generalized or unclear agents which could not be recognized and, consequently, scrutinized and controlled by the public. Vague names made it impossible to identify the agents in charge, and, hence, put the locus of control over the issues out of sight of the public. In addition, the nominalization "international economic isolation" permits to conceal the causing agent and shows only the result of the decision. The main body of the article contains further signals of a discursive jumble of unresolved puzzles.

The following headline employs the same highly evocative benderism—(see the discussion above and in chapter 5). The headline "Заграница нас научит" (The West will teach us), which is a remake of a line discussed previously (The West will help us), heralds a new move in governmental policy in sending students to study abroad. As I hinted at earlier, the substitution of the verb is contextually justified by the new political considerations. The article copes with the program that stimulates Russia's science and education sectors. As it says, Russia announced a new grant program for the students to attend one of the top three hundred universities. The universities will select the students, who must return to Russia to work for at least three years after graduation, or else must pay back all of the grant stipend.

The examples below raise a question about doubtful allusion and its effectiveness. Since to identify allusion is to assume a journalists intention, it makes sense to analyze some headlines in detail. As a rule, allusive headlines are a kind of linguistic hybrid. In it, two linguistic consciousnesses must be present, with each belonging to a different system of language: one is that of the journalist, and one the other of the author being cited. As Bakhtin claims, "There are not only (and not even so much) two individual consciousnesses, two voices, two accents, as there are two socio-linguistic consciousnesses, two epochs."[16] It is typical for allusive headlines to give an advance notice of the upcoming article's frame, but present the story in an emotional and expressive manner, painting a broader picture of events, depicting some key social problems without revealing the information on the ways of problem alleviation. To prove my points let us consider some striking examples.

The author of the article "Рождение за три моря" (Giving birth beyond the three seas) (*Moskovskie Novosti* 2012)[17] takes for granted that readers are familiar with *A Journey beyond the Three Seas*—a gripping travelogue of adventures reported by the fifteenth-century Tver merchant Afanasy Nikitin.[18] In the context of the article the headline refers to the difficulty of finding a good maternity hospital, since the woman in labor is transferred to a specialized maternity ward far away from her home, but makes no explicit moral judgment about this issue. The substitution is based on the phonemic similarity between the two Russian words: *хождение* (journey) and *рождение* (giving birth). The title of Nikitin's travelogue suggests that it is not a pun, but is another means of creating additional stylistic charge or expressiveness.

Editorial interference is presented in the following headline "С вином виновытые" (Guilty with wine) (*Minskii kur'er* 2012). Its stylistic effect is based on homonymy, that is on the simultaneous actualization of two meanings of a homonym "*вино*" (wine) and "*вина*" (guilt). Here, the proverb "Без вины виноватые" (Guilty without fault) is used with an apt contextual substitute with wine. The article's headline that reveals the effects of alcohol on Russia's population is making it clear that the pun is intended to draw the reader's attention to the title, and that "wine" rather than "guilt" is the subject of the text.

A familiar phrase or quotation can be extended to fit the new context, as is the case with "Как нам обустроить Россию" (How shall we reconstitute Russia) (*Kommersant* 2005) written by the columnist Sergei Khodnev.[19] This headline is an apparent evocation of the title of Solzhenitsyn's essay written in 1990—"How Shall We Reconstitute Russia?"—in which he advocates the dissolution of the Soviet Union. The name "Rossi" has been used frequently in reference to Italian architectural style of a number of buildings and streets in St. Petersburg. As I hinted at earlier, the implied pun imbues ironic overtones and suggests that if Russia cannot attain overall success in perestroika, it could at least set some small things right, such as taking care of the architectural legacy.

Yet another attribute of allusive headlines is presented in the following section. Discursive distortion by means of "seeping of the speech into another discourse"[20] may invoke contextual environments least associated with a topic of the article. The next headline illustrates this point. Pushkin's quote *Я памятник себе воздвиг* (I have erected a monument to myself) (*Re-aktsia* 2007)[21] as a headline to the article of the Russian celebrities' hobbies is, in my view, intentionally misleading one. The first line of the poem is most commonly understood as Pushkin's poetic testament. On the surface, this quote seems to bear out the emotive tone of the poem that was completed in the last year of Pushkin's life, a time of financial worries and struggles to launch his new literary journal, *The Contemporary*, as well as anxieties aroused by the persistent rumors of his wife's infidelity. Scrutinized more closely, however, this article demonstrates that the ready-to-use familiar words in fact bear a double-edged irony because neither contemporary celebrities nor their hobbies are significantly impressive. The prototypical quote is referenced because of its obvious frequency in different contexts; the desired effect of the allusion is attained because it does not fail to catch the reader's eye.

Substituting one component of a set expression or idiom with a contextually suitable word is another frequently used device employed to attain additional expressiveness in the headline like this "За морем жильё не худо" (Housing is not bad overseas) (*Trud* 2004).[22] The original Pushkin's line from his fairy tale *Tsar Saltan* says "За морем житьё не худо" (Peace reigns overseas) and implies the tsar's convoy's observations of the lifestyle abroad. For present-day Russian society the substitution of the word "*житьё*" (way of living) by "*жильё*" (housing) creates a certain subtext. The vernacular word "житьё" imbues the headline with an informal, colloquial tone, adding to the sense of irony. The difficulty in absorbing the ironic stance may came not because this phenomenon was insufficiently known, or because the journalist's attitude was incomprehensible itself, but because the usage of the word in Pushkin's time varied from the contemporary usage.

The headline "Горе от крыла" (Woe caused by aircraft) (*Rossiiskaia Gazeta* 2009)[23] appears to be striking in its inappropriateness of playful tone related to the somber topic of the article. The title of Griboedov's play, *Woe from Wit* is used ironically to describe the incident of Russian military helicopter crashes into mountains in Dagestan. Phonetic similarity between the Russian words for "wit" and "wing" has prompted the use of the play's title in this case. The desired effect is attained because it does not fail to catch the reader's eye, as the allusion and its original use appear in a strikingly different context.

Another headline "Январь! Достать чернил и плакать" (It's January! Pick up your pen and weep) (*Moskovskii Komsomolets* 2012)[24] echoes the first line of a well-known Boris Pasternak's poem "February. " An apt metaphor "Pick up your pen and weep" is associated with connection between nature and man as a certain system in flux. The dreary February weather invokes the mood of dullness and randomness spilling over nature and man. It is precisely the mood that an editor mocks in the article dealing with the reflections on presidential candidate Putin's predicament during his election campaign in January 2012. Phonetic similarity of the names of the months has prompted the use of the poem ' s line. The mockery headline is consistent with the content of the article permeating sense of irony

The next headline is one that relies on the shape of the source text, intentionally ignoring the broad context—"Пир гламура во время кризиса" (Feast of glamour in time of crisis) (*Argumenty i Fakty* 2008) evokes Pushkin's title "Feast in Time of Plague."[25] This headline may not be perceived as allusive by the readers unaware of Pushkin's tragedy. This example shows that what is allusive for one reader may be merely a commonplace metaphorical idiom for another. In such cases, the journalist needs not to rely on the reader identifying the source, and authorial intention, but the alluding unit in any case functions as an attention-catching figure.

The headline "На кушетку к дедушке" (To the couch of Grandfather Frost) (*Mosckovskiy Komsomolets* 2008)[26] is highly evocative of Chekhov's popular children's story—"На деревню дедушке" (To Grandpa in the village). But this refers to a therapist's couch and ironically frames the story of a new service offered during Christmas season—one can invite a psychotherapist dressed up as Santa Claus for adults to complain and get professional help on Christmas Eve. The original wording has one of its components "to village" substituted with "to couch"—and both are complement with feminine-ending words. The therapist is framed as a family member, elderly and possibly not quite professional, as is implied by the use of the informal and endearing, but at the same time mocking, term "дедушка."

The article about the Russia-Ukraine gas deal, where Ukraine remained the main transit corridor for Russia's gas export, is appropriately titled "А газ и ныне там" (Gas is still there today) (*Rossiiskaia Gazeta* 2009).[27] It brings to mind the moral of Krylov's fable "The Swan, the Crab, and the Pike," which reads "The cart's still there." This line could not more accurately characterize the official relationship between Russia and Ukraine, when despite bitter argument, the possibility still remains where it was. Its use in reference to the gas conflict is particularly poignant and appropriate, as it is in tune with the fable's plot in which a swan, a pike, and a crab jointly attempt to move a cart laden with goods, but in their attempt, the swan strives skyward, the pike pulls toward the river, and the crab scrambles backward.

Another series of headlines are remakes of Pushkin's famous line from *Eugene Onegin*, in which Lensky, as he waits for Onegin to arrive, looks back on his happy youth on the morning of the duel and utters: "Что день грядущий мне готовит" (What does the day coming has in store for me?). In many variations the headlines may read, "What does the mail coming has in store for us?" "What does the rouble coming have in store for us?" "What does the year coming have in store for us?" "What does Russian version of SAT have in store for us?"[28] It is suggestive of well-grounded doubts about whether the growing importance of an event or a new decision can be justified. Phonetic similarity between the word in the source text and the substitutions has prompted the use of the poem's line in these cases.

Other changes may be introduced too, which imbue the line with jocular overtones. The headline "Свои люди—сочтутся?" (Isn't it all among friends?) (*Trud* 2006)[29] refers to a proverb and to the title of a play written by the classical nineteenth-century Russian playwright, Aleksandr Ostrovsky. He used proverbs for most of his titles, since proverbs in Russian culture are considered a reliable and expressive source of the collective mentality, or as formulas for rough-and-ready wisdom. This particular one translates in English as "It's a family affair; we'll settle it ourselves." Ostrovsky's famous title tentatively ends in a question mark in this headline. It is suggestive of well-grounded doubts whether the proverbial wit can be justified.

The article described contemporary fortune telling traditions pointedly titled "Раз в крещенский вечерок . . ."[30] (Once upon a Christmas night) (*Argumenty i Fakty* 2008) and echoes Vasily Zhukovsky's poem *Svetlana.* Zhukovsky's origin of the phrase can prompt its meaning, as it relates to a stunning mystical Eastern Orthodox Christmas ambience: "Once upon a Christmas night the girls were telling fortunes: taking their slippers off their feet and throwing them out of the gate." The period is highly abrupt in the flow of the poem and is an invitation for the reader to go beyond the headline to learn more about contemporary tradition of fortune telling.

The predicate-only verbal headline "Выхожу один я на дорогу . . . А зачем?" (I walk alone out on to the road . . . But why?) (*Trud* 2004)[31] imbues the headline with an informal, colloquial tone, adding to the sense of fragmentation and incompleteness of a heading. Lermontov's sense of spiritual presence and search for calm and peace has gone, replaced with the absences of an interlocutor, and of any sense of purpose or future. In this headline an original line is extended by adding the question "What for?" which is used in a strategic and manipulative way. The vague and shifting meaning of the syntactic structure is an inclusive rhetoric technique. The clash between the melancholic line of the verse and the critical view of the reporter creates the desired stylistic tension.

The explicitly critical view is apparent in such headlines as "В России 'Раскольниковы' опять убивают старух-процентщиц" (In Russia "Raskolnikovs" again murder old women-pawnbrokers) (*Komsomolskaya Pravda* 2009).[32] The headline made me immediately think of Dostoevsky's novel *Crime and Punishment*. Here, cleverly placed quotation marks put the alleged literary character in the context of a contemporary criminal story. In Russian classical literature Raskolnikov is an evocative symbolic name associated with a theory by which one is justified in killing. The strategic use of plural referring to a literary character has a perceptible negativity in its semantics, hinting at situation at hand as a trivial rather than exceptional. Changing the grammatical number of nouns "Raskolnikov" and "old lady" from singular to plural signals disintegration of a situation as a specific one, and qualifying it as a typical one.

A familiar expression can be also curtailed, but this is less common, for example "Любовь к родному пепелищу" (Love for one's own hearth and home) (*Rossiiskaia Gazeta* 2006).[33] Only half of Pushkin's famous quote is cited. The original runs: " Two feelings are amazingly close to us; In them the heart finds nourishment: / Love for its own hearth and home, / Love for the ancestral graves." One can find this headline more surreal than informative, but once in a while an allusive headline can bring things into focus better than the body of an article. This headline is evocative of o ne of the most iconic Pushkinian motifs, that is the idea of the family as a chain of generations. It also captures the spirit of domestic bliss and harmonious family life eloquently as it goes hand-in-hand with the context of the article, where Solzhenitsyn's son, who was born and raised abroad, visits graves of his ancestors in the region of Stavropol.

Familiar phrase or quotation can be extended to fit the new context and used as fly-on-the-wall view, for example, "Цинандали: горе от любви и горе от ума" (Tsinandali: Woe from love and woe from wit) (*Argumenty i Fakty* 2006)[34] and based on classical play's title is a flattering headline of a reportage of Griboedov's house and story of his loyal widow who was buried near him.

Quite often the figurative expression helps to prepare the readers to see the dramatic debates that took place long before the time when an article was written, as in the article entitled "Под сенью дружеских штыков"[35] (A friendly fence of bayonets) (*Ezhenedelnyi Zhurnal* 2002). This expression refers to a weapon the USSR left behind in Afghanistan. Over three decades have passed since senior members of the army elite of the former USSR declared that major combat operations had ended in Afghanistan. Yet even now military leaders are trying to justify why things did not turn out quite as they predicted: Afghan guerrillas and terrorists are using Russian guns as they continue to spread violence. This headline is highly evocative of a famous line from Lermontov's *Mstyri*, where he gives his romantic depiction of Georgia of the first quarter of the nineteenth century. Lermontov's mythology of Caucasus is based on heroic and romantic literary stereotypes:

> The land, and Georgia bloomed, and gone
> Her old fears were and old suspense:
> Of friendly bayonets a fence
> Did, bristling, rise in her defense.

The journalist employs the allusive metaphor to describe a peaceful life in the shadow of a great power; which, from the perspective of the Other, could be ironically justified due to the new political considerations. The allusion produces a literary-historical subtext suggesting broader perspectives of present dilemmas and possible answers to the implicit questions of "what or who is at fault" and "what ought to be done." Allusion thus functions as an evaluative framework, invoking a comparison and contrast of contemporary character and situations with equivalent ones of the past. In other words, it is a tool of Aesopian language that the reader must take pains to decipher. Some allusions are highly elliptical but nevertheless identify their source precisely, partly because of their close association with the historical context.

The impersonal construction in the following headline given to the article about economic reforms in social security service positions the reader among the participants of the story. "Пенсионером можешь ты не быть" (You don't have to be a pensioner) (*Rossiiskaia Gazeta* 2004).[36] Article discusses another step in implementing a pension reform. Government badly in need of "long money" offers reform through securing and increasing pensions by placing pension savings on the financial market, allowing money to roll over so that returns will be accumulated and later paid as supplements to pensions. With this, however, the question of increasing the retirement age rose. In what has become a famous poetic slogan "It is possible for one not to be a poet, / But one is obliged to be a citizen" (implying the lack of democratic institutions), the Russian writer/poet has never just been an artist, but a spokesman for the truth and a public conscience as well. The headline echoes a line from Nikolay Nekrasov's poem. In this particular context its use is highly ironic because of the substitution of "citizen" with "pensioner," as this is reference to the fact that, with the prospect of rising the pensionable age and with the statistics the life expectancy in Russia, men simply could not live to see their pensions. The media attitude to this government initiative is thus clearly revealed as the headline is permeated with strong ironic implications.

The headline "Сетевая революция: из веб-искры возгорится пламя?"[37] (Web revolution: A spark will set ablaze a flame) aptly summarizes the growing spread of the oppositional movement in Belarus. The article touches on the question whether the Internet facilitates political mobilization in Belarus, like it did in Moldova, Iran, Tunisia, and Egypt and suggests that it can. The patriotic overtones of the phrase "A spark will set ablaze a flame" still linger, but the whole phrase is jocular. Earlier on, the very same line from the song appeared in a highly political context. In 1827 Pushkin wrote a poem addressed to the Decembrists deep in Siberian mines and sent it to a far off penal colony. A line from Prince Odoevsky's reply to Pushkin's poem, where the line "And ignite anew the flame of freedom" was transformed into "A spark will set ablaze a flame." Pushkin's poem and Odoevsky's reply became the standard lore of Russian revolutionists. There is a concealed double play in its wording, for it alludes to a quote that Lenin borrowed in 1900 from the prince's reply and made it an epigraph for his Bolshevik newspaper, *Iskra* (Spark).[38] The reconciliation of two opposing forces within one semantic unit proves the fruitfulness of creative mediation.

The heading "Хождение по мукам инноваций" (Walking through the torments of innovations)[39] is a slightly transformed version of Aleksey Tolstoy's frequently cited novel titled *Walking through Torments*. Trying to locate the origin of Aleksey Tolstoy's title one can point out to the Eastern Christian legend, the souls of the dead sinners had to walk the road of sorrow in hell for forty days, with the devils subjecting them to all sorts of tortures. There was also a famous apocryphal story (Virgin Mary's Walk through the Torments), which described Our Lady's journey across Hell. Now, this title is employed in reference to a different addressee. The implication of this heading is that the implementation of new technologies will be as difficult as life in Aleksey Tolstoy's novel. For quite a long time, Russia has been trailing in sending students out to study. Current programs reflect the promise Putin made to increase Russia's funding of science and education and during the next year Russia will likely see one thousand students go abroad.

It has to be noted that biblical quotes and references frequently make their way into headlines enjoying different popularity. I will include the analysis of few biblical allusions which are mostly considered literary classical allusions rather than religious ones. Consider the following examples: "Чаша сия" (The cup of suffering) (*Zavtra* 2012).[40] The words were said in the Garden of Gethsemane: "If it is possible, let this cup pass away from me; yet not my will, but yours be done" (Luke 22:42). Theologians may differ on just what details Jesus knew of his impending suffering, but it seems that the author of the article, notable writer Alexander Prohanov, chooses the familiar language formula for its stylistic effect and to stimulate the readers' interest in the reported subject. "Эффект Лазаря"[41] (Lazarus phenomenon) takes its name from Lazarus who, in the New Testament account, was raised from the dead by Jesus. "Не хвалите да не хвалимы будете" (Don't praise and you won't be praised).[42] This headline is evocative of "Don't condemn, and you won't be condemned." The headline has two of its components imperative in "Don't condemn" and the passive participle "won't be condemned" substituted for another words, both of the same grammatical shapes. The admonishing tone of the title is obviously intended here.

Substitution of one of the components of a set expression or idiom by a contextually suitable word is a frequently used device employed to attain additional expressiveness. "One must not live on potatoes alone" (Не картошкой единой)[43] is the slightly paraphrased quotation from the Bible (Matthew 4:4), where it reads, "Man does not live on bread alone, but on every word that comes from the mouth of God"; this means physical nourishment is not sufficient for a healthy life, man also has spiritual needs. The substitution of bread with potatoes gives rise to complex semantic changes within the phrase. In its new form it becomes a free word combination, with each word assuming its direct meaning.

The discursive samples demonstrate that biblical quotations ceased to be allusive, as they lost their links with the source texts and been received into the language as an idiomatic expressions or proverbial sayings, as for example the common expression "salt of the Earth." Apparently, the capacity of well-formulated headlines apart from being informative, and appealing to catch the reader's eye, is to allude to the Bible to encapsulate core information. However, the practice of lexicalization of the biblical concepts along with the substitution of a word or two in the biblical quotes quite frequently ends in a failure of recognition the source. At the same time, even if the biblical quote is well known and easily recognized, its original meaning may be warped by its recontextualization. Given very rich allusive foundation, comic distortions of the biblical motives can be found in sardonic references to the political reality or in the cynical guffaws. But the sarcastic modality in the contexts of this sort is provided entirely by the reader's inference. The process and the results of such transgression may or may not make it easier to distinguish between a real biblical quote and a lexicalized reference which became an idiomatic expression.

Close analysis of newspaper headlines leads me to believe that to a certain extent current media language has been taking shape under the influence of post-modern literature and post-modern methods of reflecting the reality.[44] At the same time, these allusions allow for detachment, enabling a journalist to deal with a sensitive and potentially insoluble problem. Though in Russian post-modernism references to and recycling of the allusions and quotations allow public thinkers and other language constructors to build up an explosive overproduction of meaning in an utterance. Media subjects realized that the past cannot be erased, forgotten, or simply left behind.

As we see, many of the above-cited examples are stylistically marked. The headlines are made prominent by various linguistic means, one of the most frequent of them being the contextual change of one of the components of a set expression, idiom, or quotation. Given that the job of the honest journalist is one of the most dangerous professions in the post-Soviet space, we can assume that the use of ironical allusions within allegorical, if not satirical, language is obviously conditioned by the particular political situation in which Russian journalists find themselves.

It is apparent from the examples that the sources of expressivity in headlines have many dimensions including semantic opposition or contrast, contextual use of the expression with some changes in its componential structure and/or meaning, literalization of the figurative meaning, and change of the familiar reference of a phrase or an expression. All this twisting and bending of the catch phrases and stock phrases becomes apparent because the readers are aware of the prototypes of these words and expressions. Thus through newspaper headlines the reader is able to observe a highly contradictory process of simultaneous rejection and attraction of the immediate past.

NOTES

1. D. Kahneman and A. Tversky, "Choices, Values, and Frames," *American Psychologist* 39 (1984): 341–50.
2. www.novayagazeta.ru/politics/6343.html.
3. Nikolai Berdiaev stated that "Russian messianism" was the fundamental element in "Russian religious psychology," and the primary force behind Bolshevism. See the discussion in Nikolai A. Berdiaev, *The Russian Revolution* (Ann Arbor: University of Michigan Press, 1971 [1931]), and *The Origin of Russian Communism* (Ann Arbor: University of Michigan Press, 1960 [1937]), 144. Even though Berdiaev's writing on "Third Rome" was banned in Soviet times, it is now being published, read, and widely accepted.
4. Poe Marshall Moscow, "The Third Rome: The Origins and Transformations of a 'Pivotal Moment,'" *Jahrbücher für Geschichte Osteuropas* 49, no. 3 (2001): 412–29.
5. www.ng.ru/editorial/2007-11-01/2_red.html.
6. Ivan the Terrible was "a man of wonderful understanding in the science of book learning and very eloquent," as one chronicler writes. Even more surprisingly, he could enter into the debate not only by force of power, but also with power of his words. Ivan the Terrible kept correspondence with a fierce oppositionist, Andrei Kurbsky, who is sometimes seen as the first Russian dissident. Prince Kurbsky, who at one time stood at the head of Ivan's troops, fled to Lithuania in 1564 under the patronage of Polish King Sigismund Augustin, and from there wrote a letter to Ivan the Terrible condemning his government policies. Not only did Ivan the Terrible reply to Kurbsky, but also he thoroughly answered every accusation of his opponent. In lengthy letters Ivan the Terrible presented his own views as a statement, then as he turned to objections and, mirroring Kurbsky's arguments, ridiculed him, and contrasted traitor Kurbsky to faithful servant Basil Shibanov. However fearlessly Kurbsky conducted polemics with Ivan the Terrible, had he returned to Russia, he would have been slaughtered for being a maverick and an "ill-will enemy."
7. Evgeny Yamburg, "T'my nizkikh istin nam dorozhe," *Uchitel'skaya Gazeta*, August 18, 2009, www.ug.ru/archive/29059.
8. Members' resources are language resources, background knowledge, assumptions, and so on of the interpreter of the text. In Norman Fairclough, *Language and Power* (London: Longman, 1998), 11, 141.
9. L. Kaftan, "Ya tebia porodil, ya tebia i pristroiu," *Komsomolskaya Pravda*, June 5, 2003, http://komsomolka.com/daily/23046/4188/.
10. "Zagranitsa nam pomozhet," http://lenta.ru/articles/2008/08/14/us/.
11. This armed conflict between Georgia on the one side and Russia and the separatist governments of South Ossetia and Abkhazia on the other is also known as the Five-Day War, 2008 South Ossetia Conflict, or August War.

12. S. Kierkegaard, *The Concept of Irony*, trans. M. Lee (Princeton, NJ: Princeton University Press, 1965), 265.

13. The ironic headline is intended to remind readers of the episode from the novel involving the so-called Union of the Sword and the Plough. In the novel, Ostap gathers some wealthy townspeople for a meeting of the union—the secret society that Ostap Bender creates in Stargorod, ostensibly, to support homeless children. Then, he promptly pockets the cash and laughs at how easily the contributors were fooled.

14. Semen Verbitskii and Aleksei Pimenov, "I etot lyod tronulsia" *Ezhenedelnyi zhurnal*, no. 39 (2002): 22–23.

15. Leon Bogdanov, "Zagranitsa nam pomozhet," *Itogi*, no. 39 (2002): 23.

16. M. Bahktin, *The Bakhtin Reader: Selected Writing of Bakhtin, Medvedev and Voloshinov*, ed. P. Morris (London: Arnold, 2001), 117.

17. Galina Papernaya, "Rozhdenie za tri moria," July 11, 2012, www.vseokrovle.ru/pressa30.shtml.

18. He explored opportunities for trade and wrote the diary during the years he traveled, describing in detail all that he saw, which was to him wild, exotic, and nothing like anything else he knew. He died in 1472 on his way home to Smolensk, yet his travelogue of India, *Khozhdenie za tri moria*, endures.

19. Sergei Khodnev, "Kak nam obustroit' Rossi," *Kommersant*, April 15, 2005.

20. P. Sériot, "Dereviannyi iazyk, iazyk drugogo i svoi iazyk: Poiski nastoiiashchei rechi v sotsialisticheskoi Evrope 1980-kh godov," *Politicheskaia lingvistika* 2, no. 25 (2008): 160–67, www.philology.ru/linguistics1/serio-08.htm.

21. *Re-aktsia*, January 22–February 1, 2007.

22. Oleg Roldugin, "Za morem zhilie ne khudo," *Sobesednik*, no. 238 (3 March 2010).

23. "Gore ot kryla," *Rossiaskaia Gazeta,* January 19, 2009.

24. Matvey Ganapolsky, *Moskovskii Komsomolets*, January 12, 2012. www.mk.ru/politics/article/2012/01/11/659680-yanvar-dostat-chernil-i-plakat.html.

25. "Pir glamura vo vremia chummy," *Argumenty i Fakty*, December 17, 2008.

26. "Na kushetku k dedushke," *Moskovskii Komsomolets*, December 31, 2008.

27. "A gaz i nyne tam," *Rossiiskaia Gazeta*, January 16, 2009.

28. "Chto EGE griadushchii nam gotovit?," http://news.mail.ru/economics/8660395/.

29. V. Klimtsev, "Svoi liudi sochtutsia," *Trudovaia Rossia* 3 (2006).

30. "Raz v kreshchenskii vecherok," *Argumenty i Fakty,* January 16, 2008.

31. I. Nikolaeva, "Vykhozhu odin ya na dorogu: A zachem?," *Trud,* no. 234 (2004).

32. U. Skoibeda, "V Rossii Raskolnikovy opiat' ubivaiut starukh-protsenshchits," *Komsomolskaia Pravda*, January 13, 2009, www.kp.ru/daily/24225/426787/.

33. "Liubov' k rodnomu pepelishchu," *Rossiiskaia Gazeta,* August 14, 2006.

34. "Tsinandali: Gore ot liubvi i gore ot uma," *Argumenty i Fakty*, January 5, 2006, www.aif.ua/number/number/number_id/7.

35. "Pod sen'iu druzheskikh shtykov," *Itogi,* November 26, 2002.

36. I. Nevinnaia, "Pensionerom mozhesh ty ne byt'," *Rossiiskaia Gazeta,* no. 3629 (2004).

37. "Setevaia revoliutsia: Iz veb-iskry vozgoritsia plamia," http://naviny.by/rubrics/politic/2011/08/05/ic_articles_112_174643/.

38. David M. Bethea, ed., *The Pushkin Handbook* (Madison: University of Wisconsin Press, 2005), 294.

39. V. Kuryshev, "Khozhdenie po mukam innovatsii," *Nezavisimoe voennoe obozrenie*, September 21, 2012.

40. A. Prokhanov, "Chasha sia," *Zavtra,* February 15, 2012.

41. "Effect Lazaria," http://medvestnik.ru/archive/2012/1/4348.html.

42. "Ne khvalite, da ne khvalimu budete," *Segodniashniaia gazeta*, no. 6 (2006).

43. "Ne kartoshkoi edinoi," *Argumenty i Fakty,* November 26, 2008.

44. On the topic of Russian post-modernism, see Mark Lipovetsky, *Russian Postmodernist Fiction: Dialogue with Chaos* (Armonk, NY: M. E. Sharpe, 1999).

Chapter Seven

Onomastic Allusions

This chapter follows and analyzes the process of cultural adaptation and assimilation of Russian classical figures whose ideas were accepted and popularized in current media. Here, then, I focus on one of the features shared by mainstream and alternative media discourses, in which onomastic allusions occupied a special place. I am particularly interested in why specific names became part of the national culture and how the news media absorb references to well-known classical authors. Not only classical texts are widely employed both in official and alternative media discourses, but also noteworthy are the numerous uses of allusive names in the media. The most successful allusions seem to be those that can be recognized, identified, and grasped in their current context. Just like the names of the characters in the classics hold context clues in their linguistic, historical, and etymological roots, these context clues inform readers of the journalists' intentions and reflect the characters' purposes and their individual functions in the plot. The overwhelming potency of names reveals the process of naming as a practice to determine character and explore allusions that the names contain. Linguistically, names may not have much of a different meaning to a modern audience (e.g., main characters of Pushkin's *Eugene Onegin* are Tatyana and Onegin), but their "cultural afterlife" has changed. Textually, they live apart, but once their names (their identities) escape to our imagination their names are linked.

Classical onomastic practice is not an arbitrary act, and neither is the contemporary audience's reception and transformation of the meaning behind those names. Clearly, words' meanings—proper names included—are determined through a series of experiences both before and after an encounter with the word itself. Consider an example of naming in Dostoevsky's novels. Semantically, the name Raskolnikov from *Crime and Punishment* evokes the idea of schism in Russian, but contextually the name conjures up an idea of a Napoleon-like great man to whom the ordinary rules of common morality do not apply. Another example is the principal character of the novel *Idiot*—Prince Myshkin.[1] Dostoevsky deliberately creates dissociation in the identity of this character. Prince Myshkin is far from being monolithic; in fact this character evokes the opposite qualities. In the novel, Myshkin has been rejected in many instances, slapped in the face, and as another character says: "You'll be ashamed, Ganya, of having insulted such a sheep!" This last characterization equates Myshkin with the lamb of God. Prince Myshkin's main virtue has been described by the Russian word "*smirenie*". The word means the curbing of all passions, humility, and spiritual peace, therefore it is believed that Dostoyevsky ostensibly modeled Prince Myshkin after Christ. In secular vein, Prince Myshkin is also viewed as naive, irrelevant, withdrawn, and alienated, therefore designates the opposite. While for one reader the ostensible message is positive, the ostensible message for another reader is invariably negative. Since there are associations of the name that remained suppressed, this allusion becomes more flexible and quite ambivalent.

Thus, the expressiveness of individual proper names is not inherent in the names themselves as units of language, nor does it issue directly from the meaning of these names: it is either a generic expression, or an echo of another's individual expression, which makes the name representative of another's whole utterance from a particular evaluative position. The interpretation then invites multiple parties that re-invent and reassess the denotative meaning of the name. Thus in my discussion I focus not only on the meaning of the name, but also on the meta-message, which is signaled by some overt textual cues, both original and journalistic.

Paul Lennon[2] notes that a dictionary, giving definitions of some lexicalized allusions, may mention the source. Typically, lexicalized onomastic allusions tend to become the personification of a certain attribute, that is, Rockefeller of wealth, Al Capone of gangsterdom.[3] Like quotations, names from literature can acquire lexical meaning and become "lexicalized allusive metaphors."[4] Repeated allusive use of the name may result in recognizing the motif as general knowledge, which is detached from the source text. Such an allusion may function as a metonymical device or as allusive metaphors for the qualities associated with the names. In other words, we deal with shorthand notations for the scripts. Lermontov is associated with the quote "No, I am not Byron, I am another. . . ." Lotman offers us the context in which we should understand Lermontov's exclamation, insisting that in a striking parallel, Byron enters Russian culture as a cultural double.[5] As it turns out, Lermontov, who was immersed in both cultures—Russian and English—is a Russian as he was an organic part of the Russian culture and spoke its language, and, at the same time, in the context of Russian literature he would fulfill his function only if he was experienced as Byron.

The Pushkin myth was used for almost two centuries, as Ryazanova-Clarke argues, "as a symbol of Russian national identity, has also experienced a successful transposition into [post-Soviet] . . . culture. The name as well as the image of Pushkin, . . . represents metonymically the Russian language itself."[6]

The use of Tolstoy's name as a philosopher to index origin of the great ideas against the backdrop of mediocre philosophies has a long tradition in public and media discourse. While for many years following the Revolution, the fundamental and most prescient opposition to Tolstoy's works may have seemed simply to be that between religious belief and atheism, now, the ground has shifted: the controversy in Tolstoy's views are found in the familial sphere, and Tolstoy's relevance is less clearly visible today. The following example demonstrates how with the name of Tolstoy, an allusive chain is set, even in the absence of a referenced source:

> Лев Толстой морочил нам голову. Его знаменитый тезис о том, что «все счасливые семьи похожи друг на друга, каждая несчастливая семья несчастна по-своему», ученые опровергли. Оказывается, семьи больше похожи своими несчастьями, а вот счастье у кажой семьи будет свое.
>
> [Leo Tolstoy confounded our minds. Scholars disagree with his famous theory that, "All happy families are alike, yet each unhappy family is unhappy in its own way." Apparently, families look more alike in their misfortunes, yet each family has its own happiness.][7]

The inclusion of Tolstoy's name that have long ago turned into a veritable cult and its subsequent reworking can create what Bakhtin called "hidden polemic"[8] and underscore the openness of "another's discourse" of subversion and manipulation. Here, cleverly placed quotation marks put the alleged objective saying into question, while author's use of the scholarly context for the literary quote taps into the media tradition of degrading one's ideological opponents through the use of inadequate context.

Similar to the earlier experts, the next example is an article titled "Smerdyakovshchina"[9] (The Smerdyakov's effect) (*Ezhenedel'nyi Zhurnal* 2012). The article offers the story about the new policies in the Russian Parliament that reflect Duma deputies' Russophobia, for which a journalist compares them with Smerdyakov, who is notoriously known for his phrase "как было бы хорошо, если бы в 1812 году умная нация французская покорила бы глупую нацию русскую и присоединила к себе" (It would have been great if the intelligent French nation had conquered the stupid Russian nation back in 1812, and had annexed it). The heading borrows the name from Dostoevsky's character of *The Brothers Karamazov.* Smerdyakov is a name that speaks for the character of its bearer, for "*smerd*" in Old Russian means "slave" and its link with the verb "*smerdet'*" (to stink). A special term, "*smerdyakovshchina*," has been coined for the cases of general aversion to foreign subjugation. Views similar to those of this character are thus branded as slavish by the appellation itself. The effect is strengthened by the use of the highly derogatory suffix *–shchina*. The onomastic allusion is used as a rhetorical device of creating foregrounding,[10] with metaphorical coinage in the heading. The dynamics between the author's and discourse of another may be observed in polemical frame, where "another's discourse . . . is not reproduced with a new intention, but it acts upon, influences, and in one way or another determines the author's discourse."[11] Whatever the spark may be that ignited this story, the article's general outlook toward the Duma deputies is rather negative, although its headline clashes stylistically with the rather dry style of the main body of the article.

Certain names from recent history have become a stored allusive pattern, and at the same time metonyms for an episode in history. The name has acquired the status of metaphor/metonymy, hence their meaning as "semiotic rather than representational, communicated elliptically on the basis of shared knowledge and assumptions."[12]

The process of lexicalization, by identifying a name with a single quality, makes it potentially less ambiguous as an allusion and allows it to be used more widely. Khlestakov is identified with irresponsibility, light-mindedness, absence of measure; Oblomov with ineptitude, uselessness, and all-pervasive inertia; and Chichikov with vulgar, vile, and despicable avidity and greed for money. Consider the example where a journalist supplanted human or individual vices, follies, abuses, or shortcomings by proper names of literary characters that reflected culturally embedded scripts. The purpose and manifestation of such a rhetoric technique seems to indicate more than a manner of speaking, but philosophical and moral allegory:

> Скучной оказалась страна Россия, когда революция схлынула,—по-чеховски скучной и заселенной чичиковыми да маниловами, башмачкиными и собакевичами.
>
> [Russia turned out to be a boring country when the revolution subsided. It was in a state of Chekhovian boredom, populated by Chichikovs, Manilows, Bashmachkins, and yes, Sobakeviches.][13]

In some sense refined aristocratic characters, depicted by Turgenev, Chekhov, and Tolstoy, correspond to the notion that the Russian soul seems more familiar to the Western audience than other characters; these are more easily accessible to Western audience and can be successfully imported and assimilated to Western readers. Other characters, such as those from novels by Gogol and Saltykov-Shchedrin, seem to be bound to Russian realm. Perhaps these references are more parochial and less universal. The social reality they depict seems to be bound to a particular place and time. Practicing

Aesopian language, Saltykov-Shchedrin avoids common language clichés in order to produce sophisticated analogies between real and fictional societies. He skillfully takes advantage of hyperbole so real facts acquire fantastic contours and featured his characters with expressive nicknames with traceable origin. An illustration of this figurativeness can be found in *The History of a Town* by Saltykov-Shchedrin, which was read as a satirical description of the Russian government: in the images of the governors, their allusions and details, the reader perceives real persons and facts referring to the real historical events of the end of the eighteenth and the first decades of the nineteenth century.

This novel was written in a genre of the chronicle in Aesopian language, intentionally ambiguous enough to leave the censor as well as the modern reader uncertain about the meaning of many allusions. Although the author does not specify how the subversive meaning of this text is generated, "the initiated reader" is able to identify a background, a deep literary level and attach this level to a political context and not to a moral frame of reference. In fact, the reader is invited to investigate the Aesopian figurativeness based on the linguistic levels—phonetic, lexical, stylistic—so that the statement could be read dually.[14] As most of Saltykov-Shendrin's proper names operate by transferring implications, they have a power to fashion allegiances and control attitudes, and the nature and function of the names are worth considering in the translation. A typology of fictional personal names and toponyms in Saltykov-Shchedrin's *The History of a Town* has been proposed by translator Alexander Kalashnikov[15] He bases his translation on specific rhetoric connotation and verbal design of the stems-motivators that resemble in their forms "ordinary" words. For example, the city name Глупов (Foolov) is translated by rendering a stem in English and keeping a derivational Russian suffix -ov. Village Голодаевка (Faminovka) has a motivator "голод" (starvation). The following examples of last names are rendered taking into account their spelling in Russian. Угрюм-Бурчеев (Gloom-Grumblev) is an example of a blended word with two motivators, such as "gloomy" and "grumble." This fictitious last name of the governor is consonant with the name of his prototype, Arakcheyev.[16] Yet the last name of Governor Беневоленский (Benevolensky), has a Latin motivator, "bene volens," with its English counterpart, "benevolence," meaning kindness, generosity. This last name alludes to the prominent Russian lawmaker Mikhail Speransky, who was obsessed with lawmaking; however, this allusion would be shared by the readers who could see the similarity in Benevolensky's description with the facts from the biography of M. M. Speransky. Sometimes the stem-motivator fulfills only the expressive function, such as is the case with the last name of the governor Бородавкин (Wartkin), who had "an indomitable energy, always knew what and where took place and even being asleep kept one of his eyes open, which inspired fear in his family."[17] Curiously enough, his first name, Василиск (Vasilisk), that is, Basilisk, is associated with Basilisk, the classical mythological creature that can kill with its look. Those names and toponyms, besides being ridiculous, are embodiments of cruelty, dullness, and an evil hatred of the people. Comic and grotesque names immediately capture the intended meaning of the original as they contain the stems of expressive words. Sometimes the onomastic allusions are offensively sarcastic, or simply ironic references to a person's occupation or habits. These and many other allusions to Saltykov-Shchedrin's characters function as metonymy available in reserve of the classical literature, providing ready-to-go labels to symbolically represent the politicians and their decisions. Reevaluation of Saltykov-Shchedrin's skillful use of hyperbole and circumlocutions, such as *сердцевед* (sounder of hearts) for a police officer assessing political reliability and oblique references such as *внезапности* (suddennesses) for acts of administrative repression does not sound archaic in contemporary media discourse. On the contrary, his ingenuous employment of Aesopian language[18] is relevant for an "oppositionist" journalist nowadays.

In my next example, the phrase "неизменный Остап Бендер" is embedded in the generally seriously furnished context. The promise of experiencing an exciting surprise is "invariable Ostap Bender as an MC," which, in addition to other overtones, invests the texts with pervasive irony:

> Вообще есть спрос на стилистику 20–30х годов: оформление, бабушкины (иногда прабабушкины) туалеты. И неизменный Остап Бендер в качестве ведущего!
>
> [In general there is a demand for the style of the 1920s and 1930s: design, grandmothers' (and sometimes great grandmothers') and garment. And invariably, Ostap Bender acting as an MC.][19]

The overall tone of irony colors the reference to the novel and suggests the broader picture of the society associated with the name of a great conman and his role that aligns him with the wild Russian capitalism of the 1990s.

Another proper name, Shvonder, echoes the post-revolutionary chaos, the repercussions to new revolutionary order, and the dying aristocratic epoch, reflecting the effect of the Soviet system on the proletarian. In Mikhail Bulgakov's novella *The Heart of a Dog*, pesky Comrade Shvonder is the chairman of the housing committee who wants to take over several of the professor's rooms. The professor's insistence that having a dining room is critical to his lifestyle is not something to which Shvonder is sympathetic. Bulgakov's Shvonder, therefore, has acquired the status of allusive metaphor: It is a metonym for a period of the anti-intellectual atmosphere that the Soviet regime was creating. In the headline, "Bogdanov and Shvonders"[20] the name Shvonder, by metaphorical extension, became partially freed from the particular situation and immediate historical context, and available for re-application.

These characters from post-revolutionary Russia and Stalin's claustrophobic milieu are similar to their predecessors form Gogol, but infinitely cruder. For Russian readers these were truculent unsavory types, so convincingly authentic, and although they were clearly compounded of myth, this made them all the more colorful that their evocations of rogue, swindlers, household tyrants entered into the consciousness of the Russian audience and still have relevancy there today. However I would hazard a guess that these colorful characters are not perfectly recognizable in the West, and fail to strike a responsive chord in the Western public.

Evocative headline "Chonkins are always the stronghold of a regime"[21] refers to Ivan Chonkin, a character of the book by the popular Russian satirist Vladimir Voinovich. Private Chonkin is a patriotic, conscientious, simple, bumbling peasant. Being rogue and witty, he is a combination of Russian folk hero Ivan the Fool and Czech the Good Soldier Švejk. He is caught in a senseless web of intrigue, the world devoid of irony, and seems to embody the spirit of the whole Stalin era.

The next example relies on the pre-text knowledge frame connected with particular personas widely known on the Russian political scene. The Western press used to compare Vladimir Putin to the Russian tsar Ivan the Terrible as pre-text frame related to the infamous personality in Russian history, who personified authoritarianism. However, it is interesting to see the following example: "Сегодня, по прошествии пяти лет пути с Путиным, мы все идущие вместе с ним готовы вопрошать: 'Куда ты завел нас, Сусанин–герой'" (After five years of walking together with Putin we are ready to ask a question: "Where did you get us, Susanin-hero?").[22] This line is from the libretto to a patriotic-heroic tragic opera, *A Life for the Tsar*. The original Russian libretto, based on historical events, was written by Nestor Kukolnik, Yegor Rozen, Vladimir Sollogub, and Vasily Zhukovsky. The saying "Where do you lead us, Susanin-hero?" is based on the historical anecdote referring to a quasi-legendary hero of popular resistance to Polish infiltration in the seventeenth century. In the period of unrest and Polish invasion known as the Time of Troubles, Russia inherited, of all things, a name for bad tour guides. The Polish troops set out to kill the newly chosen tsar who was hiding in a remote village. Legend has it that a local peasant, Ivan Susanin, promised to guide them to the hideout. Instead, he led the Poles deep into the marshy woods and perished together with the soldiers. It would be difficult to find a Russian who has never heard of Ivan Susanin, a popular character in Russian music and literature. However, although this saying became a part of every Russian's patriotic consciousness, its contemporary usage seems rather different from the historical use: nowadays this saying is used to describe actions of someone who claims to know the way, but who eventually gets lost. This allusive name and the catch phrase also provide a way to analyze the stereotypes (conscious or unconscious beliefs) indirectly reflected in the language.

My next example is drawn from an article by a pro-Kremlin journalist Mikhail Leont'ev, who writes,

> Что такое Шуйский? Шуйский—это в какой-то степени Ельцин. Поздний Ельцин. В этих сравнениях всегда есть некоторая доля натяжки, но они здесь настолько яркие, что даже при всей рискованности в них есть смысл.
>
> [What is the role of Shuisky? To some degree, Shuisky is equal to Yeltsyn. Late Yeltsin. There is some strain in these comparisons, but they are so bright that despite the risqué implication, they are sensible.][23]

The onomastic allusion in the article above goes hand-in-hand with another onomastic allusion that grabs the attention of anyone familiar with Russian history, the word "*semibankirshchina.*"[24] The semibankirshchina, a play on words, alludes to the seven boyars (*Semiboyarshchina*) who acted as the government of Russia after Tsar Vasily Shuisky was overthrown in 1610.[25] The disconnection of the bankers from the power is further stressed in the main body of the article by the mentioning the external view of their misplaced behavior. This example demonstrates the manner of reporting language with an unsettling mixture of jargon and historical reference. It appears unjustified when the shockingly informal and negatively nuanced criminal metaphor *разборки* (turf wars), which is usually expected to be followed by a negatively connoted complement (e.g., *разборки авторитетов*) clashes stylistically with the cultural idiom evoking the historical figures. The article describes the bankers as random, unpredictable, and arrogantly uninvolved. The construction of the oligarchs who usurp their leading position is contrasted with the chaos they created in the economic life.

If we turn our attention to the onomastic allusions, where they may be interpreted in terms of pluralism, it would be no exaggeration to say that as readers we should come to terms with the value of pluralism. Journalists on occasion leave the reader to decide whether his/her arguments and the evidence s/he provides are persuasive or not. By focusing on the problem of pluralism, the divergent opinions, as we have seen, permeate all types of frames, including ironic. It is in the ironic context that journalists address different audiences.

NOTES

1. Etymologically, with its Russian root "mouse," it contains the human characteristics attributed to a mouse: meekness, powerlessness, and a quiet manner.

2. Paul Lennon, *Allusions in the Press: An Applied Linguistic Study* (New York: Mouton de Gruyter, 2004), 68.
3. Ibid.
4. Ibid., 67.
5. Yu. M. Lotman, *Universe of the Mind: A Semiotic Theory of Culture*, trans. A. Shukman (Bloomington: Indiana University Press, 1990), 137.
6. Lara Ryazanova-Clarke, "The Crystallization of Structures: Linguistic Culture in Putin's Russia," in *Landslide of the Norm: Language Culture in Post-Soviet Russia*, ed. Ingunn Lunde (Bergen, NO: Slavica Bergensia, 2006), 31–64.
7. L. Vasil'eva, "Semeinye pary shchastlivee odinochek," *Komsomolskaya Pravda*, no. 71 (2006).
8. Bakhtin's concept of hidden polemic best captures the dialogical, ideological, and sociological insights into language. In discussing Dostoevsky's poetics, Bakhtin underscores that in double-voiced discourse the discourse of another coexists distinctly with the author's discourse.
9. Golts A. Smerdyakovshchina, June 9, 2012, www.ej.ru/?a=note&id=11850.
10. Foregrounding is the rhetorical device of making something stand out from the surrounding words. It is generally used to highlight important parts of a text, to aid memorability, and/or to invite interpretation.
11. Mikhail Bakhtin, *Problems of Dostoevsky's Poetics*, ed. and trans. Caryl Emerson (Minneapolis: University of Minesota Press, 1984), 195.
12. Cited in Lennon, *Allusions in the Press*, 69.
13. Tatyana Tsherbina, "Razocharovannaia strana," *Novoe Vremia* 3 (2005).
14. Lev Loseff defines Aesopian language as "a special literary system, one whose structure allows interaction between the author and reader at the same time that it coneals inadmissible content form the censor." In Loseff, *On the Beneficence of Censorship: Aesopian Language in Modern Russian Literature*, trans. Ane Bobko (Munich: Otto Sagner, 1984), x.
15. Alexander Kalashnikov, "Proper Names in Translation of Fiction (on Material of Translation into English of *The History of a Town* by M. E. Saltykov-Shchedrin)," *Translation Journal* 10, no. 1 (January 2006), www.bokorlang.com/journal/35propernames.htm.
16. Count Alexey Andreyevich Arakcheyev (1769–1834) served under Paul I and Alexander I as army leader and artillery inspector respectively. Starting in 1816, he organized military-agricultural colonies, creating terrifying conditions in those settlements, and became known as an embodiment of wild tyranny, and oppression. *Arakcheevschina* (the Arakcheev regime) is used as a derogatory term for a military state.
17. Kalashnikov, "Proper Names in Translation of Fiction."
18. It is one of the most efficient forms of resistance of the intellectuals against censorship. As a term "Aesopian language" was first used by satirist Mikhail Saltykov-Shchedrin in his *Letters to Auntie* (1881–1882), in order to designate a "figurative language of slavery," an "ability to speak between the lines . . . at a time when literature was in a state of bondage." As for practice associated with this concept, it can be traced back to the Antiquity. See Loseff, *On the Beneficence of Censorship.*
19. M. Tumashkova, "Mobil'niki otobrat'—I po etapu," *Novaya Gazeta* 41 (June 4, 2007), www.novayagazeta.ru/arts/35385.html.
20. Sergey Nekhamkin, "Bogdanov i Shvondery," *Izvestia*, January 25, 2006.
21. Yan Shenkman, "Chonkiny vsegda oplot rezhima," *Ogonyok* 39, no. 5248 (January 10, 2012).
22. O. Chekrygin, "Otdaite den'gi detiam, chtoby oni rodilis'," *Novaya Gazeta*, January 30, 2003, http://2003.novayagazeta.ru/nomer/2003/39n/n39n-s01.shtml.
23. M. Leont'ev, "Byt' derzhavoi voobshce ili ne byt'," *Trud,* November 3, 2006, www.trud.ru/article/03-11-2006/109524_byt_derzhavoj_ili_voobsche_ne_byt/comments/1?query=%CE%C4%CD%C0%CA%CE%20%C8%CC%C5%CD%CD%CE%20%D2%C0%CA%20%D1%D2%C0%C2%C8%D2%20%C2%CE%CF%D0%CE%D1%20%D2%C5%CB%C5%C2%C5%C4%D3%D9%C8%C9%20%CC%C8%D5%C0%C8%CB%20%CB%C5%CE%CD%D2%DC%C5%C2&subj=0&author=0&sort=rel.
24. When Yeltsin came to power he invited seven tycoons to his government. Among them were Peter Aven, Boris Berezovsky, Mikhail Fridman, Vladimir Gusinsky, Mikhail Khodor-

kovsky, Vladimir Potanin, and Alexander Smolensky. Insensitive to the issue of "conflict of interest," their government appointments enhanced their business dealings. It would not be exaggeration to say that the "Big Seven," or *semibankirshchina*, as the Russians began to call them, came close to controlling 70 percent of the Moscow press and radio and 80 percent of the nation's TV.

25. A. Ignatenko, "Oligarkhi khotiat vlasti," *Moskovsie Novosti,* November 17, 2003.

Chapter Eight

Allusions in the Articles

In the previous chapter I suggested that the framework of references in post-Soviet press allowed the reporter to liven up a text through the introduction of a note of irony. But that's how allusions work in headlines. Similarly to the allusions in the headlines, excerpts of articles analyzed with a focus on allusions taken from the articles make clear that events framed by allusions in the body of the articles are often viewed as if by an outsider, or an ironic detached observer. Discursive samples taken from the body of the articles demonstrate that overall allusions construct predominantly moral frames proclaiming the universal "common sense" with minimal stylistic amplitude and with allusions presented a myth-producing potential.

Though there is great use of the frameworks and difference in employing classical quotations and allusions in the body of the articles. The article in *Sobesednik*[1] in the rubric "Life" of celebrities by Oleg Roldugin, about the former first lady of Russia Svetlana Medvedeva starts with a quote from Alexander Pushkin. Mrs. Medvedev adheres to the advice of the great poet in her public life: "Remain to praise and slander cool, And do not argue with a fool."[2] The first paragraph also describes Medvedeva as the most pious among first ladies of contemporary Russia. The way to describe Medvedeva's demeanor is an unquoted reference from Pushkin's poem. The fool in Pushkin's poem is one who takes the lofty style of his solemn verses at face value. In Pushkin's sense the word "stupidity" is banality, vulgar behavior of a crowd, whose stupid praise offended Pushkin more than reproaches. The poet's lines contain witticism, a sort of resolution. The irony and double meaning of Pushkin's words can be explained if we remember dramatic relationships with the reading public during his last years. Take a note that Pushkin's notion of stupidity remains the same in our time as well: stupidity is understood as idealism, un-sophistication, the lack of practice of reflection, the lack of traumatic experience. By applying the poetic formula to the contemporary context, a journalist reinforces the similarity between Pushkin's meaningful conclusion to what he experienced in his own life and what Medvedeva is supposed to be aware of. In addition to this parallel, the author suggests that Medvedeva's reasoning bears a resemblance to the poet's spiritual disposition. It appears that "praise and slander" are so unnecessary in Pushkin's life that he prescribes clever tactics: silence, the refusal to answer, and preponderate indifference. Does it tell us anything about the former first lady? I suspect that the whole point of this quote is that is capable of infinite recycling. This is perhaps why it appears often in public discourse. But it may also be a way of negotiating the gap between what has to be reported and what the reader knows in a society that is sufficiently open for it to be no longer possible to pretend that the gap does not exist.

The use of the literary allusions is one of the ways to draw the readers' attention to the published material. In what follows I discuss the articles from popular tabloid newspaper *Sobesednik*,[3] reporting on the recent tendency of Russian emigration. One reporter chose to quote "The Sail,"[4] one of Lermontov's best-known poems. Its opening lines are among his most frequently quoted. This miniature reflective poem offers distinct perspectives on the Romantic concept of freedom and has a developing structure: the first and second lines create an image of a sail and the view of the sea, while lines three and four invoke Lermontov's worldview with a distant sail as metonymous with the unnamed sailor's departure from his home, and the sea voyage as a metaphor to symbolize a life and the sea as nature's innate harmony. The sail and sea metaphors pack a complex worldview into a single image, but they are nonetheless still superficial to contemporary readers, though they could rely on much deeper and less obvious reasoning. It evokes a feeling of abandonment and seems informed by the sense of disillusionment that followed the Decembrists' revolt in 1825 and the discontent with the prevailing atmosphere of political reaction. The poem's lyrical hero can be interpreted as a persecuted wanderer striving for security and peace of mind.

The journalist, apparently, found a parallel development in the mood of the observing poetic hero and Elena Baturina, a powerful wife of former Moscow mayor Yuri Luzhkov, and Russia's richest woman, who fled the country in 2011. Baturina came under suspicion of fraud as investigators claimed to have found nearly $500 million in misappropriated funds in her personal bank account. The first paragraph of the article titled "It's Time to Shove Off" features a variation of the poem's opening lines: "One can clearly see what she wants to find so far away," and "It is basically clear what she abandoned (or whom she bilked) in her own country." Pun is another means of creating additional stylistic charge of expressiveness. It is a play on words, and its stylistic effect is based on homonymy, that is, the simultaneous actualization of two meanings of a homonym: *кинуть*—to leave, abandon, and bilk one's debts. What the journalist implies is that she bilked her creditors. The punch line of the story is that "the sail in blue obscurity of sea" is not alone. In other words, the number of those who would like to leave the country for good has increased, and there is much irony in this, for an essentially private matter has been turned into a scandal. The media attitude to this event is thus clearly revealed for strong ironic implications permeate the quote.

Let us consider an example where there is a literal allusion to Gogol's *Dead Souls*: "Только продолжают постораниваться и давать нам дорогу другие народы и государства" (Other nations and states keep drawing aside and making way for us).[5] In his novel *Dead Souls*, Nikolai Gogol imagined Russia as a *troika*, a carriage pulled by three-abreast horses, speeding through the countryside. Gogol admitted no knowledge of where Russia was going: "Russia, where are you flying to? Answer! She gives no answer." Gogol continues: "As Russia flies by other nations and states draw aside and make way for her"[6] but Russia's path was unique and the country was destined for greatness. The very vehicle that he compares Russia to, the *troika*, and other states, and their industrial might, stood firmly in Russia's path. The narrator in *Dead Souls* grants that Russia is the strongest state. On the other hand, the quotation contains a satire on what can be called "hierarchy of peoples and states." Gogol makes it possible to simultaneously accept and reject the rationality of the statement. A reader perceives a humorous effect through this distorting or rather contrived word "постораниваться." When the journalist mirrors Gogol's image of Russia, the multiple nuances become fairly obvious. While Gogol wrote in a positive way, the journalist is more reserved in his positive evaluations: there is a farcical element in such. In addition to creating a farcical idealized image of Russia, the allusion I present here highlights the problematic legacy of the country's domestic policy, with its government's unscrupulous actions that provoke other countries' condescension and apparent disapproval mixed with fear, leading them to avoid Russia, and to get out of its way. The ironic sense of the quotation is based on the contrast of its extensions in the source and target texts with all their logical and literary presuppositions.

Some quotations do not undergo any structural changes, but the fact that they are used in a totally different environment imbues them with irony or sarcasm, as the case may be with one particular quote, such as the heading "Komu—'Tatory,' komu—'Liatory,' a komu i natsproekt"[7] (What are tartars for one man are larters for another, but for many is a national project), which echoes the famous line coined by the mostly forgotten Boris Pilnyak in his novel *Naked Year*, where the peasant comes to town and reads: What are tartars for one man are larters for another."[8] The article focuses on realization of a priority national project aimed to improve public health care in a provincial town called Orel. The reporter is unaware whether or not doctors of Orel read Pilnyak, but, as he stated, they are for sure well-educated and definitely know from firsthand experience how one gets everything right, while another one not quite. In other words, medical professionals from Orel believe that as professionals, they were not treated fairly. By 2005 the Russian economy as a whole had grown about 7 percent annually over a few years; thus one could decide that the situation in the country was stable and this had created the preconditions for major solutions to the social problems. The decision to implement the salary increase for medical workers was taken to encourage them to stay at their posts, as the statistics show that municipal clinics were operating with only 56 percent of the staff they needed, and that at rural clinics the figure was only 35 percent. A journalist wrote about the pay raise for doctors and nurses working in municipal and village clinics, who respectively received salary hikes of 10,000 rubles and 5,000 rubles. It should be noted that Russian doctors never had the same status and money as their Western counterparts. This is especially true in provincial centers like Orel.

The reader well familiar with the contemporary literature can observe that this article headline contains yet another literary allusion appropriately titled "A State Affair; Is It Clear?" This brings to mind a very popular poem from the 1980s, "The Tale of Soldier Fedot, the Daring Fellow," written by one of modern Russia's best-loved actors, Leonid Filatov. Filatov created a satirical fairy tale to portray the sociopolitical situation in Russia. Revealing the mystifying quality of the ideology was not, however, his straightforward task; he created a fairy tale with carnival elements, which are not only common but also consciously political, and allowed critical engagement with the ruling ideology. Thus, Filatov employed the "folk laughter" (in Bakhtin's terms) in a deconstructive assault on the seriousness of the system. In this framework the headline is perceived as more expressive, as opposed to being just ideologically marked. Therefore the reference to Pilnyak may be put in a new context, in which it may take on a very explicit political significance. This allusion along with a playful headline can be enough to evoke a whole realm of social problems making the allusion essentially political and giving the clue to the journalist's attitude.

Irony in journalistic writing is usually not apparent upon the first reading; the surface evaluation of a situation that a journalist delivers may be quite different from the deeper meaning of his/her piece. The examples I have been discussing in the previous chapters bear witness that irony is often the distinctive sense of using another's words. My analysis reveals that irony is constructed by the context and allows a journalist to convey a certain response. Irony tends to be associated with people who are in opposition to or at least skeptical toward the authorities. In my collection of examples irony is invariably hostile, disapproving, or sarcastic. However, I assume that only by looking at the specific ironic utterance in its context is it possible to reconstruct a journalist's implications. It should be taken into account that sarcasm involves an act of pretense, that is, insincerity. However, unlike lying, sarcasm has no intention to deceive. In terms of theory of speech acts, sarcasm is game. However it is possible to be ironic or sarcastic without any overt sign of the speaker's insincerity. Let us consider the example of a put on:

> Тронная речь бессменного председателя [Союза кинематографистов] по интонации напоминала признания Чичикова о том, что много в жизни претерпел, а все потому что и сироте, и вдовице ни в чем не отказывал. Кроме того, Павел Иванович обладал чувствительным сердцем и, завидя нищего, обязательно давал ему грошик. Так Михалков рассказывал о какой-то нищей вдовице-актрисе и о не менее нищем знаменитом актере, которым он, конечно, помог. Похоже, что эти нищие и уволокли миллион.
>
> [A royal speech of an unchanging chairmen (of the union of cinematographers) in intonation reminded the appointed Chichikov of the fact that that he endured much in life and everything including orphans and widows he did not deny. Moreover, Pavel Ivanovich had a sensitive heart and seeing a beggar would immediately give him a penny. Thus did Mikhalkov retell about some beggar, widow and no less the impoverished famous actor, whom he, of course, helped. It seems, however, that these beggars and widows dragged away millions.] (K. Kedrov, *Novoe Vremya*, no. 45, 2004)

Readers familiar with the activity and rumors around Mikhalkov, his political views, and his social activities, as well as readers who subscribe to the outlet in which they are expressed (*Novoe Vremya*) will have no difficulty in "hearing" the author's contempt in each of the phrases I have emphasized. But many readers who are used to getting their ideology from network TV might take these remarks at face value.

The following passage is another example of a put on. Let us look at a saying that a journalist plays with and makes use of extreme formulation. The journalist raises the question of citizens' rights. It is patently the case that no man can be absolutely sinless, and that no one can be absolutely innocent.

> "Кто богу не грешен, царю не виноват?"—вопрошала старинная пословица. "Был бы человек, а статья найдётся"—отвечали наши старшие современники.
>
> ["Who is without sin before God, and guiltless before the tsar?"—asked an ancient proverb. "You can always convict a person of something"—answered our older contemporaries.][9]

In Russian culture there is a higher tendency to represent popular beliefs through proverbs. Russians tend to use proverbs and sayings more than Americans do, and as George Gibian writes, "the Russian still trusts proverbs, and does it think he is being a parrot when he chooses to pick out of his memory a ready-made folk formula and applies it to a given situation."[10] Irony in this passage is marked by its extremity to emphasize the impossibility of what is being asserted.[11] The journalist's attitude toward the Russian legal system is being interpreted by an old saying that may be restated as follows: one may disregard the law in exceptional situations, since under certain circumstances anyone might become the target of official repression.[12] The so-called wittiness of the passage alludes to the historical fact that in Russia laws could be treated as conveniences rather than absolute norms of conduct. It implies that laws are a creation of man and, accordingly, are imperfect by definition. On the one hand, the extremity of the sayings can be seen as ironic, and on the other, the content of sayings themselves usually tends toward the extreme. In this case the ironist invokes an alternative world where the certainties are not so certain. Irony is thus characterized by an expression of doubt where there should be certainty and vice versa.

In the article "Roundup for Justice"[13] Valeria Novodvorskaia discusses the aspirations of human rights activists and an unjust legal system in Russia. The following passage containing the allusions reads:

> И здесь мы с благодарностью и ужасом вспомянем Александра Грибоедова, это еще не реформы Алесандра II. Это оттепель Александра I (после павловской суровой зимы). "А судьи кто? За древностию лет / К свободной жизни их вражда непримирима. / Суждения черпают из забытых газет . . ." (времён Андропова и покоренья Праги и Будапешта).
>
> [I wonder what kind of judges such a society can provide for justice. That is where we can remember Alexander Griboedov with gratitude and horror. These are not yet the reforms of Alexander II yet; it is only the thaw of Alexander I (after the harsh Pauline winter). "And who are the judges? Because of their old age, their animosity to freedom is irreconcilable. They draw their judgments from forgotten newspapers ran up against this human factor" (from the time of Andropov and the conquest of Prague and Budapest).]

This passage resonates with my understanding of Russia's nascent democracy and how it cannot by itself guarantee a triumph of freedom or respect for citizens' rights. As Novodvorskaia points out, Russia's newly subjugated media generally describe President Putin's reforms as a productive policy that somehow will foster democracy, and this despite growing evidence that it will do exactly the opposite. The journalist finds a way to criticize the Russian government's policy by referring to key moments in Russian history. Alexander I of Russia (became emperor in 1801, died in 1825) was a popular ruler, well liked for his liberal ideas and concerns for the peasantry. His foreign policy was moderate. Alexander I at various times sided with and against Napoleon, but the French invasion of Russia in 1812 galvanized Russian opposition to the revolutionary ideas associated with the Napoleonic regime. The government of Tsar Alexander II (came to the throne in 1855, assassinated in 1881) enacted a series of liberal reforms, the most important of which was the liberation of the serfs throughout most of the Russian empire. Alexander II rethought Russia's foreign policy: the country concentrated on strengthening its borders. However, high-handed imposition of land reforms in Russian Poland aroused hostility among the landed gentry and groups of young intellectuals in that region. Eventually, Novodvorskaia mentions the name of Yuri Andropov, a top Soviet official who played a part in suppressing the Hungarian and Czechoslovak attempts at liberation in 1956 and 1968, respectively. Andropov's image in the Soviet Union was that of the stereotypical hard-line "police-boss"; his major accomplishment was a fairly successful campaign to throttle the wave of liberal dissent in the 1970s and early 1980s. During his tenure as head of the KGB methods for dealing with opponents of the Soviet regime were "refined": dissent was severely repressed and dissidents frequently confined to psychiatric hospitals, sent to prison, or forced to emigrate to the West. The parallels drawn by Novodvorskaia involve the promising reforms of the 1860s and 1870s that were prepared by a group of distinguished persons who gained the support of earnest liberals; however, further reforms came to naught following the assassination of Alexander II. All these twists and turns bring to centerstage what the journalist has identified as her key point: in Soviet Russia during the 1960s, the attitude toward foreign and domestic policy recalled attitudes in tsarist Russia, approximately one hundred years earlier.

Novodvorskaia's stylization, like the direct quotation, is unforced: there is no sign of painful labor or of long research about it. This stylization brings to mind a homogeneous Soviet discourse, "a single discursive space to be shared by all,"[14] and meanings, imposing on everyone. The order and content of the allusions is therefore not random, although it might appear so at first. The phrase has a clear function, and that is to create intertextuality between Novodvorskaia's text and Soviet historical discourse, which is part of the Soviet discursive canon. Yet stylization has some value and meaning of its own; the metamorphosed quotation or allusion must be forceful and pointed in its new setting, just as the ordinary quotation or allusion was. Hence, the stylization must be felt to have thrown a new light upon the original and must reveal unexpected capacities within it.

The final example in this chapter, again taken from Novodvorskaia's article, demonstrates another striking insertion of allusions into the journalistic narrative:

> Даже лучшая в нашей злополучной истории судебная реформа Александра II, даровавшего суды присяжных еще не остывшей от рабства стране, внушив светлые надежды образованному сословию и дав Плевако и Александрову причаститься к славе Цицерона, не отменила ни горестного комментария Катюши Масловой "Не виноватая я!", ни

военных столыпинских судов (в силу взаимного одичания левых экстремистов и отчаявшейся власти), ни смертных приговоров русским офицерам, отказавшимся вешать и расстреливать польских повстанцев 1863 года.

[Even Alexander II's judicial reform, the best in our ill-fated history, which granted jury trials to a country that had not yet cooled down from slavery, which just instilled bright aspirations in the educated class and gave a chance for Plevako and Aleksandrov to get a taste of Cicero's fame. The reform didn't cancel either Katiusha Maslova's grief-stricken comment "I am innocent" or Stolypin's military tribunals (by virtual of mutual savagery by both the leftist extremists and the desperate authorities), or death sentences for Russian officers who refused to carry out orders to hang and shoot Polish rebels in 1863.]

The unpacking of these historical parallels, in which the author's intuition, speculation, and critical reflection are all to play an important role, would in turn lead to answers at what Novodvorskaia hints. On close inspection of this passage, the current political situation, as it is viewed by the journalist, is highlighted by recurring leitmotif pertaining to Alexander II's image. His regime implemented judicial reforms; it established courts with Western-style juries. But the regime instructed judges to decide each case on its merits and not to apply the law independent of state authority. The passage also contains another literary reference—an allusion to the novel *Resurrection* by Leo Tolstoy. The plot of this work hinges on a prolonged crisis of conscience for Prince Nekhliudov, who as a young man seduced a young servant girl, Katiusha Maslova. Subsequently, ten years later, he finds himself serving on a jury that is trying Maslova on a charge of murder. The girl's words in court are a celebrated verbal pattern, which the journalist uses with a didactic purpose. Maslova appears to be a very modern and universal character. When she protests her innocence, Nekhliudov realizes he is responsible for everything that has happened to her. Yet another reference is historical and also related to the article's topic. In Russian history, Petr Stolypin is famous as Nicholas II's interior minister and prime pinister (1906–1911) who suppressed the revolution of 1905 and instituted a series of major internal reforms. To deal with the revolution, Stolypin established military courts to try individuals accused of political crimes; between September 1906 and May 1907, these courts sentenced to death 1,200 suspected opponents of the government. Second, he placed entire provinces under martial law and banned the publication of over one thousand newspapers. On the one hand, it would seem that Stolypin's Terror for Terrorists policy was to a great extent successful in calming the situation in Russia. On the other hand, it is also possible that restrictions on the Russian people's freedoms only strengthened their anti-government attitudes and prepared the ground for the events of 1917. As Novodvorskaia borrows from widely literary and historical subtexts, she underscores the motif of the dubiousness of judicial reforms in contemporary Russia. The punch line about the viability of judicial reforms is that there is no real motivation for lauding changes as the dawning of the rule of law. As mentioned above, in applying "non-direct speaking" (Bakhtin 1981: 313), a journalist reduces personal responsibility for what he is saying and distances himself from the contents of his words. It is as if s/he warned readers that what s/he is writing about is meant be taken in a non-serious way. Another important narrative convention successfully utilized in current media discourse is "multivoicedness" (translation of Bakhtin's term "многоголосие"). While the journalist's narration sounds like a discourse of the Other, the shift to emotive abstract idealization becomes apparent. The parallels with dramatic performance are striking.

Reflecting on why and how authors have used classical allusions, one aspect appears obvious: it seems that the motivation for allusions is the employment of lies in the differing discursive norms of the media outlets. As stated previously, the distorted quotations may quite often get rid of markers enabling the identification of the quoted persons. In most cases the reporter included only impersonal introductions, such as "I actually don't remember the source," "people say," "some have referred these words to someone," or "as is (generally) known," which reinforces the generality of the saying. Norman Fairclough, considering the "hidden power" of media discourse, labels these techniques as "high objectivity" and "low agency."[15] This avoidance could stem from the assumption that the audience shares allusions, and a missing part could be easily recovered due to the way they are infinitely recycled. For the reader, the quoted person remained unnamed and, in a sense, nonexistent in the participation of events, but serves as an authoritative Other.

While it is acceptable to play with these classical allusions in a humorous fashion in the independent media, this does not seem possible in the press, because of their highly ideologized status. The canonical position of classical allusions in the Soviet discourse has been observed. Classical allusions were ideologically loaded symbols that embodied a particular message and set of meanings set down in authoritative discourse and embedded in the consciousness of the Soviet citizen. The centrality of these symbols in Soviet discourse means that they may not be satirized in the official sphere of cultural production. Allusions that are commonplace for Soviet readership had strongly linked descriptive and evaluative meaning.

When cultural references are put in a new context, they endorse heterodox interpretation, demonstrate differences in creating intertextual links, erase the ideological reference, and invite "evaluative conversion"[16] allowed to be interpreted in create manifold can take on a very explicit social significance.

Thus the first thing that comes to my mind is that this could also be possible with classical allusions in media, namely that these classical allusions are the clue to the social issues. I concluded, however, that this approach proved fruitless.

The irony lies in the juxtaposition of what the journalist and the ironist make explicit. What makes the ironist different from the journalist is an exchange of perspectives: the journalist may remain officially neutral, while the ironist is interactionally adversarial. Indeed, the same is true for any instance of irony in media discourse.

NOTES

1. Oleg Roldugin, www.tatler.ru/nashi_lyudi/reytingi_25/11466_top8_sputnits_rossiyskih_politikov.php.
2. The last verse of Alexander Pushkin's "Ia pamiatnik sebe vozdvig . . ." reads:

Веленью Божию, о муза, будь послушна,
Обиды не страшась, не требуя венца,
Хвалу и клевету приемли равнодушно
И не оспаривай глупца.

[O Muse, be obedient to the command of God,
Do not be fearful of abuse, do not demand a crown,
Accept both praise and slander with indifference,
And don't dispute with fools.]

3. "Ne pora li valit' iz Rossii," *Sobesednik*, http://sobesednik.ru/incident/ne-pora-li-valit-iz-rossii.
4. Beleet parus odinokii
v tumane moria golubom
Chto ishchet on v strane dalekoi?
Chto kinul on v kraiu rodnom?

[White sail gleams alone
In the blue mist of sea . . .
What does it seek in a distant country?
What has it left in native land?]

5. V. Shenderovich, "Ob alternativnoi sluzhbe," *Itogi*, February 18, 2002, www.liveinternet.ru/users/alan_alexander_meyer/post8368950/comments#comment32804382.
6. Nikolai Gogol, "Mertvye dushi," in *Izbrannye sochinenia v dvukh tomakh*, vol. 2 (Moscow: Khudozhestvennaia literatura, 1984).
7. T. Fileva, "Komu—'Tatory,' komu—'Liatory,' a komu i natsproekt," http://www.orel-news.ru/index.php?main=showorelnews&id=6773.
8. In Moscow, over an electrical store on Myasnitskaia Street hung a sign: KOMUTATORY AKKOMULATORY, which is to say COMMUTATORS AND ACCUMULATORS, but a simple man seeing it, spelled out slowly KOMU TATORY A KOMU LATORY, which is to say WHAT ARE TARTARS FOR ONE MAN ARE LARTERS FOR ANOTHER, on which his comment was: "Just look at that, deceiving the common folk again!" B. Pilnyak, *Naked Year*, trans. Alec Brown (New York: Payton and Clarke, 1928). This is a perfect example of Pilnyak's typical "musical" prose to represent the chaos of Russian provincial life during the "naked" year, 1919. It has implicit sympathy and a comic portrayal of peasantry and the ordinary people affected by the Bolshevik Revolution. Thematically, Pilnyak has focused on the impact of culture on civilization, and the repercussions of political policies on citizens.

9. V. Dragunski, "Obshchestvo zelenykh naslazhdenii i drugie obshchestva," *Novoe Vremia*, nos. 1–2 (2003): 8–10.

10. George Gibian, "How Russian Proverbs Present the Russian National Character," in *Russianness: Studies on a Nation's Identity in Honor of Rufus Mathewson*, ed. Robert L. Belknap (Ann Arbor, MI: Ardis, 1990), 38–43.

11. A. Pomerantz, "Agreeing and Disagreeing with Assessments: Some Features of Preferred/Dispreferred Turn Shapes," in *Structures of Social Action: Studies in Conversation Analysis*, ed. J. Atkinson and J. Heritage (Cambridge: Cambridge University Press, 1984), 57–101.

12. The concept of a kindly tzar who is not aware of the brutalities to which his people are subjected brings to memory a traditional belief of the Russian people that their well-being depended on the personal qualities of their ruler rather than the quality of their political system.

13. V. Novodvorskaia, "Oblavnoe pravosudie," *Novoe Vremya,* no. 48 (2000), http://ds.ru/nt/2000/nt0048.htm.

14. Jan Plamper, "Abolishing Ambiguity: Soviet Censorship Practices in the 1930s," *Russian Review* 60, no. 4 (2001): 526–44.

15. Norman Fairclough, *Language and Power* (Harlow, UK: Longman, 1996), 57–60.

16. Mikhail Epstein, "Relativistic Patterns in Totalitarian Thinking: An Inquiry into the Language of Soviet Ideology," Kennan Institute for Advanced Russian Studies Occasional Paper, 243 (Washington: Woodrow Wilson International Center for Scholars, 1991), 15.

Chapter Nine

Allusions to Russian Classics in the Ukrainian Media

This chapter demonstrates that similar to their colleagues in Russia, Ukrainian journalists use and overuse allusions to classical literature to create and communicate new meaning in the journalistic narrative. With regard to allusions to classical literature in media, I question prevailing assumptions about the value of allusions, discussing the particular allusions and weighing in on whether each one "works" or seems tacked on for the sake of the embellishment. From that point of view my comparison with the Ukrainian press seems to be very revealing. Actually, I found more similarities in the employment of classical Russian allusions and references in the media of both countries than I expected.

Being interested in current media language, I recently conducted extensive Google searches of digital versions of Ukrainian print media. Using the categorizations from the studies in communication, my analysis speaks about the "common frames."[1] It is possible to assume that the common frames also reflect on the political views, the organization, or the cultural position of the particular media team.

In the discussion that follows I focus on allusive headlines and their framing effects. As I proposed in chapter 2, the aptness and salience of allusions are assessed from the perspective of the hypothetical reader, where I as analyst reconstruct the rhetorical and discursive techniques employed in media texts to establish journalists' persuasive intention and readers' interpretive result. Headlines, as research subjects, were chosen as discourse indicators of the media rhetoric used and mapping frames. To identify the frame I combine the results of discourse analysis with content analysis. Discourse analysis resulted in description of allusions according to their semantical, lexico-grammatical, and structural properties. Semantically, the identified allusions were subdivided into representation of literary allusions and historical exemplars. The chosen news stories concentrate on the description of "impressive" problems, tackling the search for their roots and development.

In his careful recent media analyses Volodymyr Kulyk[2] shows that mass media in Ukraine reflect the perils of the period of transition from communism to democracy and from state-owned to free market economy, typical of many East European countries and former Soviet Union republics. As I explained in chapter 2, for the purpose of my study I focus on the framing devices of the news stories containing the allusions to Russian classics. I observe allusions in the headlines, exemplars (i.e., historical examples from which lessons are drawn) in the body of the articles, and choices about language. A considerable share of articles were drawn from the rubrics "Politics and Authority" and "Topic of the Day" of the prestigious analytical weekly magazine *Dzerkalo Tyznia* (*Mirror of the Week*) and the daily newspaper *Den'* (The Day), respectively. The robustly independent sociologist Natalya Ryabinska points out that these outlets are far from classic quality newspapers, such as the U.S. *Washington Post*. However, they are profoundly different from the majority of Ukrainian nationally printed outlets that have a pronounced tabloid character.[3] First, it is obvious that these broadsheets publish a large number of articles devoted to political, economical, and social issues, and offer political analysis, exclusive interviews, and opinions. As Ryabinska observes, "Ukrainian news stories concentrated on impressive problems description, search of problems roots, explanation of problems history and development."[4] These two publications are rather influential in Ukraine, especially among educated people and the political establishment. These publications are often quoted and referred to by other mass media, including local media in different regions. Both are privately owned. It should be noticed that *Den'* uses more direct quotations from the government press releases, which indicates the presence of a stronger censorship (or rather, the unwillingness of the journalists to get engaged seriously in political debates that would have ramifications for their lives), while the weekly magazine is very critical of President Yanukovych and Party of Regions.[5]

My first example is the headline "Діти підземелля" (Children of Underground),[6] which is an explicit reference to the book title, and alludes to Vladimir Korolenko's story; the book title is detached from its classical text and turned into a cultural sign. The article is dealing with the political situation in Ukraine. The reporter discusses the low level of national consciousness among Ukrainians, the article itself says nothing derogatory about them. This is done by the headline. In the newspaper context the quotation preserves the essential features of the source ("children," "underground") and the underlying presupposition that the referent has existed in conditions of cruelty and abject poverty. However, the article's headline is suggestive and suffices to hint at possible parallels between children in Korolenko's story, suffering from neglect and deprivation, and the Ukrainians. Such an attention switch contributes to an exaggerated effect of rhetoric irony. Although the tale's characters are not mentioned in the article, the extended "allusion to the well-known tale constitutes a narrative thread"[7] and contains an ironic hint to the classical text. This allusion obtains its communicative associative power through its pragmatic and semantic interpretation of a title as a metaphor. This is not just the attention-grabbing headline. The expression is ironically colored; however, intertextual irony works only when the reader, possessing sufficient textual knowledge, is fully aware of intertextual connections of the two texts.

Let us take another, rather different example. The following headline "Все змішалося в домі українському" (Everything was in confusion in the Ukrainian house)[8] is an implicit reference to the second sentence of *Anna Karenina*: "Everything was in confusion in the Oblonskys' house." The question of happiness is central to the novel, but Tolstoy does not tell us what would make anyone happy. A journalist, apparently, distorted a line to give it a humorously ironic tone that contrasts with a tone of an original quote. For those who recognize the reference to the beginning of Tolstoy's novel, it alludes to the vital metaphor of a "marriage that is doomed to fail." Using such a distorted phrase, the journalist creates a particular picture of the public life. Allusions not only revive the meaning of Tolstoy's words, but also emphasize pertinent connotations presented in the alluding texts. So the headline suggests that the social situation in "the Ukrainian house" can turn into something that is unstoppable and threatening. Such a pronouncement, with the appearance of thoughtfully dispensed wisdom, holds the promise of a journalist who will illuminate all that follows. But this headline can be more accurately described as an observation, rather than an explanation or an interpretation. As the article progresses, this distinction becomes increasingly evident. Thus the journalist states something about state affairs, but, as to the question of what happens, we get nothing but vague implication. By articulating a cultural theme in a socially situated narrative, the journalist uses the persuasive power of the theme, suggesting that the information is presented from the point of view of the Other. This discursive practice exhibits the journalists' inclination to distance themselves from the text, and to create an effect of generalized, known-to-all experience. This is especially true for allusions from classics.

Contextual mismatch creates irony in the headline that reads "Отселе принуждать мы будем к миру"[9] (From here we shall coerce to make peace). The headline immediately evokes an allusion to a line from Pushkin's *Bronze Horseman* where Peter the Great threatens the Swedes: "Отсель грозить мы будем шведу" (From here we shall threaten the Swedes). However, the made-up quote draws on a forced "act of coercion to peace" rather than an act of aggression. This method of recasting a classical text in a modern, informal wording is popular in Russian journalism, too. Contextual inappropriateness is based on incongruity, as Attardo notes, between the presuppositions of the utterance and the presuppositions of the context in which the utterance is produced.[10] As a result, a "context-bound" (Attardo) classical allusion incorporated in a headline activates the ironic tone if the reader is familiar with the context of the source text, or it would not much matter if an intertextual link does not catch the readers' attention. On a linguistic level, this is not a casual reference; but a transformed allusion, with paronomasia.[11] This pun involves words that are an imperfect rhyme, and could be recognized in a specific context. Words have an indirect correlation to a specific context of Pushkin's poem. Pushkin's "From here we will threaten the Swede" is a symbolic way of showing off Russian military power. At that point the Swedes were a great power and Russia's main enemies.

The allusion is still recognizable for its similarity with phonetic shape and rhyming effect to the pretext. On the surface, the point of using pun is based on a desire to imitate a style of the Other with mockery and derision. Yet a closer look reveals that this wordplay is also involving a juxtaposition of voices—that is, this interplay operates on an ideological as well as linguistic level. There is something more to analyze in the above article, as in the leading paragraph where the Russian tsar Alexander III is quoted as saying that "Russia has only two friends, its army and its navy." Presumably, the journalist, by articulating this quote, reconfigures the historical theme in a socially situated context, but the voice of the reporter and the Other are blended together, making it difficult to differentiate between them.

This headline is also an interesting case of the use of Russian in a headline given to an article written in Ukrainian. Although most attention is directed toward the two languages and the bilingual ethnic identity, the theme of the code-mixing type of language, *surzhyk,* and its local linguistic variations is also a field of contestation. Scholars employ such terms as "ethnicity," "nation," and "identity," but most of the definitions of these terms are not agreed-upon outlines of the theoretical framework for several sub-fields of sociolinguistics—language maintenance and language shift, language and ethnic identity, language and nationalism.[12] Whereas identifying with a particular group through a certain language is one thing, language usage is another matter. The majority of those who live in Ukraine and use mostly Russian on a daily basis define themselves as ethnic Ukrainians. Accordingly, many of those for whom Ukrainian is a native language choose to speak Russian in Russian-dominated settings. Thus the language in Ukraine is not a marker of ethnic identity. With regard to language relations on the regional level, the dividing line is traditionally drawn between a mainly Ukrainian-speaking western Ukraine and the predominantly Russian-speaking eastern and southern parts of the country.[13]

Ukraine separated from the Soviet Union but Ukrainians are still not separated completely from the Russian mentality. Laada Bilaniuk has analyzed the phenomenon of TV programs and interviews in which a question is asked in Ukrainian and answered, "quite self-unconsciously and without provoking any comment," in Russian.[14] She was struck by "the prevalence of a practice I call 'non-accommodating bilingualism': speaking one's preferred language, Ukrainian or Russian, when this is not the language spoken by one's interlocutor, thereby maintaining a conversation in two languages."[15] In her conclusion she admits that "non-accommodating bilingualism facilitates the growing presence of Ukrainian in domains where it was previously unacceptable and marginalized."[16]

As far as tabloidization is concerned, such a performance is, in my opinion, a mirror of a certain linguistic ideology in Ukraine. The latest decade has brought up the topic of a complex and nuanced model of relations between Russian and Ukrainian languages in Ukraine.[17] In most Ukrainian media journalists mix a good deal of Russian with Ukrainian. This may be rightly considered a form of realism since it merely reflects the linguistic practices of the time. I believe, however, that while its realistic function may be small, its symbolic function is great. In this regard, at first glance the quotes I analyzed seem conventional enough. Yet a closer look reveals that the use or non-use of the Russian language by various journalists, while it never violates the principle of social realism, has a much deeper significance. In the analysis of the deliberate use of Russian, the amount of Russian spoken by each major Ukrainian journalist is an important index to the degree of his or her corruption and fits in perfectly with what is now generally recognized as the moral and symbolic disengagement of the media in the issue of securing the national language.[18] If we examine the relevant empirical research done by Kulyk (2010), the evidence seems to suggest, at least for most Ukrainian media, that media have the special role and persuasive power to control ideological reproduction among the population at large. Since media largely control actual public discourse and partly the social representation, the measure of media language is also a measure of their power. While this linguistic coexistence may seem peaceful, of course, it is also a political flashpoint.

In respect to allusive headlines that contain historical exemplars from which lessons are drawn, Ukrainian newspapers quite often present national issues and events through the frame of past historical events. Consider the following example. The headline of the article "'Війна і мир' у Севастополі: в пошуках минулого, яке щезає" (War and Peace: Searching for the past that disappears),[19] contains an allusion to Leo Tolstoy's novel. The newspaper article is concerned with the coverage of the international art festival held in Sevastopol. The journalist reports on negligence in coverage of the major Ukrainian festival and complains on the disastrous advertising campaign. The commentator evaluates the propriety and efficiency of this venue and explains what this event meant for an average citizen. It is important to note that the references to the agents responsible for advertising in this article are rather superficial and do not bring understanding of who in Ukraine was responsible for advertising, and which particular decisions were made. The body of the article consists predominantly of quotes from speeches and personal interviews; meanwhile the factual reporting is scarce. The headline has several layers of interpretation since it alludes to literary and historical references. First, it is a reference to Tolstoy's novel, but it also reminds some readers of his earlier book, *The Sevastopol Sketches,* which details the major siege during the Crimean War. And that is not all: the headline alludes to the current "war" between Russia and Ukraine on Crimea. Thus a wordplay is obvious to some, and hidden from many is the historical significance of the place where the art festival is held, but it requires more interpretative work on the part of the reader. Although the journalist's judgmental stance is quite clear, we cannot be sure what the journalist's orientation toward this piece of information is. Does he use this phrase in a straightforward referential way? Does he use the phrase instead in a mocking or ironic way, and thus place himself against those who use the phrase merely referentially? Does he take this at face value? These questions describe a rudimentary dialogue opened by this one allusive headline. In other words, a journalist is not represented in the utterance, but it is something one could dub in semantic relationship between the allusive headline and the greater context of the phrase. The allusive headline lacks clarity and comprehensiveness. More importantly, as we try to understand this headline dialogically with respect to the journalist's stance, we cannot be sure what the journalist's attitude toward this piece of information is. One could imagine that this phrase is associated with a journalist who evidently reflects the Ukrainian national outlook as superior to those of other nations. In other words, we cannot fully understand the content a journalist communicates without taking into account various aspects of the interactional event in which it occurs.

Typically Ukrainian newspapers avoid clear headlines or headings and while skimming headlines readers remain uninformed what those articles cover, albeit those headlines demonstrate a great deal of aphoristic potential. Moreover, in contrast to the classical references, which can be easily identified for and through their endless repetition, some quoted assorted sayings may leave the reader in the dark, as they are not accessible to the broad audience. However, in the Ukrainian media these assorted sayings are often quoted or alluded to without giving a reference to the source. It seems that the more aphoristic the saying, the more political folk wisdom it contains. My next example is indicative of the headlines that are not complete aphorisms but possess the aphoristic propositional meaning. The typical example is the following headline, "Останній прихисток" (Last refuge),[20] which is a part of an aphorism. In the opening paragraph the journalist comments on the origin of this saying. It is said to be originally drawn from Samuel Johnson's dictum, "Patriotism is the last refuge of a scoundrel," but is also attributed to Leo Tolstoy; thus the authorship is not clear. The article deals with the conflict of the Ukrainian leaders' patriotism, and consists predominantly of the quotations of philosophers and statesmen from Montesquieu to Makhno. The journalist creates a scholastic discussion between those whom he cites. The context of the headline with the allusion and the context of the article are opposed as farce and philosophical with the emergent disparaging tone of the headline, which is incongruous with the seriousness of the following text.

I have taken the coverage of important domains in various sociocultural contexts in Ukrainian media to find out that they read similar to their analogous Russian media stories and editorials. It appears that headlines with allusions very rarely, if ever, present the factual information to the readers, but more often give a type of evaluation of the facts framed. The data showed that avoidance of direct references or any attribution of author in the texts is common. Ultimately, prominent events are addressed on a general and highly philosophical level. The political information thus appears to be frequently transmitted through a semantic field that is prominent in the domain of the literature references used in the article.

This is merely a rough sketch of the media stories with classical allusions in the Ukrainian media, but there is enough evidence that shows that what is true for the employment of classical allusions in the Russian media is also true for the Ukrainian market-oriented media. This might suggest that there is strong continuity in the media style between the Soviet and post-Soviet periods. The parallelism in applying classical allusions in Ukraine and Russia, both post-Soviet countries, is remarkable in virtually all forms of media discourse. In that respect, Russian media discourse does not stand alone, but, interestingly, though perhaps unsurprisingly, this allusion works when the reader and the journalist belong to the same interpretive community and share the same cultural background. The cultural background of the reader should be sufficient enough to appreciate such allusions without a laborious explanation of the hints given by journalists. While none of the top exponents of Soviet journalism remain in major Ukrainian publications today, post-Soviet journalism has been affected by the Soviet press models, and the opinionated partisan mode of journalism is very much viable. Given the historically strong emphasis of Soviet reporting on propaganda, and the empty medium of broadcasting ideology, and observing that the profession of the honest journalist is one of the most dangerous professions in the post-Soviet space, we can assume that post-Soviet media is still not independent from control and censorship and is tied to larger elite structures. All this suggests that Ukrainian as well as Russian media hardly have much leverage to choose, in comparison to its Western counterparts due to specific cultural and political circumstances. In addition, another explanation should be taken into account. Based on my observations, the motives for using these allusions and references are mixed. I found that the punning headline is an art form in Russian and Ukrainian newspapers, and I suspect that sub-editors, on the one hand, compete to outdo each other. On the other hand, the main function of allusions in headlines and in the texts is to cover rather than to reveal details of the news stories. Then the question arises: if the way that the media organizes and packages information is a lens to observe reality, then do the Russian and Ukrainian media organize and package information, or do they create it? But here we largely move out of the discourse analysis and practical stylistics perspective and enter the field of political science. An awareness of this issue keeps this study from simple classification and easy conclusions.

The allusions discussed in this chapter were selected with the aim of showing how journalists demonstrate their communicative intention of framing: by hinting to the readers what is coming and directing their expectations in a certain way. Allusiveness of journalistic discourse is part of cultural reproduction, with the journalist's role as both a guardian of culture and a facilitator of culture. For instance, what most media users in Ukraine know and think about Russia will largely be due to the mass media, rather than to personal experiences and opinions, unless they have alternative personal or social knowledge and opinions that allow them to counter-read the dominant media discourses. The Ukrainian case underscores the same pattern in the journalistic practice of using Russian classical allusion as we see in Russian media discourse. Likewise, in any particular instance where the usage of the words of the Other[21] is observed, it is important to acknowledge what kind of attitude the journalist assumes when he or she repeats the statements of the other speaker. The journalist's particular approach allows him or her to imbue someone else's words with new values, and to accent them in his or her own way—with expressions of irony, mockery, ridicule, doubt, or indignation.

NOTES

1. Studies in news framing differentiate between *common* and *issue-specific* frames. The latter are employed exclusively for certain themes and issues. See the discussion on issue-specific frames in W. A. Gamson and A. Modigliani, "Media Discourse and Public Opinion on Nuclear Power: A Constructivist Approach," *American Journal of Sociology* 1 (1989): 1–37. Common frames, according to frame analysts, are those that can be identified in relation to different topics. They occur widely in different types of news, news issues, and media outlets.
2. See the discussion in Volodymyr Kulyk, *Dyskurs ukrains'kykh medii: identychnosti, ideolohii, vladni stosunky* [The Ukrainian media discourse: Ideologies, identities, power relations] (Kiev: Krytyka, 2010).
3. Natalya Ryabinska, "News Framing in Post-Communist Press: Engagement and Control or Disengagement and Powerlessness?," *Global Media Journal* (Polish ed.) 1, no. 3 (2007): 19.
4. Ibid.

5. For more on media in post-communist Ukraine, see Natalya Ryabinska, "The Media Market and Media Ownership in Post-Communist Ukraine," *Problems of Post-Communism* 58, no. 6 (November–December 2011): 3–20.

6. Sergei Rakhmanin, "Dity pidzemellya," *Dzerkalo tyzhnia,* August 21–27, 2010.

7. Sandra L. Beckett, *Recycling Red Riding Hood* (Florence, KY: Routledge, 2002), 15.

8. Yulia Mostova, "Vse zmishalosya v domi ukrainskomu," *Dzerkalo tyzhnia,* July 1–7, 2006.

9. Sergei Rakhmanin, "Otsele prinuzhdat' my budem k miru," *Den',* August 16, 2008.

10. S. Attardo, *Humorous Texts: A Semantic and Pragmatic Analysis* (Berlin, NY: Mouton de Gruyter, 2001), 11.

11. This is a literary device meaning punning: the use of a word in a different sense or the use of words similar in sound to achieve a specific effect, such as humor or a dual meaning.

12. See the discussion on the linguistic landscape in T. Kuzio, *Ukraine: State and Nation Building* (London and New York: Routledge, 1998); D. Arel, "Language Politics in Independent Ukraine: Towards One or Two State Languages?," *Nationalities Papers* 23, no. 2 (2002): 597–622; J. A. Fishman, *Reversing Language Shift* (Clevedon, UK: Multilingual Matters, 1991); Joshua A. Fishman, ed., *Can Threatened Languages Be Saved?* (Clevedon, UK: Multilingual Matters, 2001).

13. Margrethe Søvik, "Language Practices and the Language Situation in Kharkiv: Examining the Concept of Legitimate Language in Relation to Identification and Utility," *International Journal of the Sociology of Language* 201 (2010): 5–28.

14. Bilaniuk Laada, "Language in the Balance: The Politics of Non-Accommodation on Bilingual Ukrainian-Russian Television Shows," *International Journal of the Sociology of Language* 201 (201): 105.

15. Ibid.

16. Ibid.

17. The Council of Europe's Committee of Experts, considering in 2008 Ukraine's Initial Report for the *European Charter for Regional or Minority Languages* (Languages Charter), reported that 77.8 percent of census respondents state they are ethnically Ukrainian, while 17.3 percent say they are Russian (Council of Europe, *European Charter for Regional or Minority Languages: Report of the Committee of Experts on the Application of the Charter by Ukraine,* adopted on November 27, 2008, released on July 7, 2010.) But this does not reflect the real numbers of Ukrainian and Russian speakers.

18. On discussion of bilingualism in Ukraine, see Volodymyr Kulyk, "Language in Times of Transition: An Introduction," *International Journal of the Sociology of Language* 201 (2010): 1–4; Volodymyr Kulyk, "Ideologies of Language Use in Post-Soviet Ukrainian Media," *International Journal of the Sociology of Language* 201 (2010): 79–104.

19. Serhiy Makhun, "'Viyna I myr' u Sevastopoli: V poshukakh mynulogo yake shchezaye," *Dzerkalo Tyzhnia,* July 10–16, 2010.

20. Serhiy Rakhmanin, "Ostanniy Prykhystok," *Dzerkalo Tyzhnia,* September 4–10, 2010.

21. S. Malykhina, "Chuzhaia rech' v organizatsii ideologizirovannogo diskursa. Visnyk Kharkivskogo derzhavnogo universitetu.V.448. Mif i mifopoetika u traditsiynykh suchasnukh formakh kulturno-movnoi svidomosti" (Kharkiv, Ukraine, 1999), 322–26.

Chapter Ten

Transgressive Language: Stiob and Stylization

In this chapter I discuss several aspects of the category of comic, a phenomenon of transgressive language as it relates to stiob and stylization. In many senses, the ironic discourse demonstrates the features of the "carnivalization" fitting with Bakhtin's special sense of this term. The strong preferences for informality, high tolerance of swear words, and sarcastic and sardonic comments correlate with Bakhtin's treatment of the concept of comic in popular carnival culture. This particular type of text construction can be extended by linking it with a legacy of the traditional Russian buffoons (*skomorokhi*), known for their allusive jests and pointed witticisms (in terms of Likhachev and Panchenko)[1], with the tradition of Gogol, who catalogued the *poshlost* that underlies human existence with "unseen tears through visible laughter," with acknowledgment that what the author laughs at is something ugly but pitiful. In such types of discourse, instead of creating tension, the narrator directs the viewers' attention to the production designed by mockery. At the same time, the folk attitude toward laughter in Russia has been traditionally ambivalent, owing to the tension between "smekh i grekh [laughter and sin],"[2] invoking the claim that humor inherently involves aggression and hostility. From this perspective, this discourse demonstrates the speech figures reflecting the typical Soviet attitude to "laughter as a weapon," which is grounded in the theoretical observations that laughter that was called upon to fight the enemy, means the satirist treats something or someone with scorn. Anatoly Lunacharskii, the commissar of education in the first Soviet government, set out his idea of a laughter as a major weapon of class warfare in the battle of the Soviets with a dying old order. Lunacharskii argues that the concept of victorious laughter has its roots in traditional notions of the contest between summer and winter in the seasonal cycles of the year, the generational battle between impetuous young lovers and repressive aging parents, and the clash between freedom and ritual bondage. Finally, to some extent carnival always parodies the ritual of the Other.

However, in some types of carnavalistic discourse Kharms's elaboration of absurdity has a special relevance. Kharms's prosaic absurdity is meant to reflect the alienation of man in society, the decomposition of language and subsequent failure of communication. Symptomatically, Kharms emphasizes, "I am interested in life only in terms of its absurd manifestation."[3] This crucial concept of laughter was as important to the Soviet state as the legacy of buffoons or fools for Christ had been to pre-modern religious authorities in Russia. It is remarkable that the Russian notion of comic absurdity differs significantly from the much more optimistic Western conception. The Bergsonian concept of the comic "as something like a momentary anesthesia of the heart"[4] is complementary to the Freudian view on laughing as a "safety valve" and offers an effective explanation of the humor's effect of psychological relief through which people can purge themselves of otherwise dangerous anxieties, fears, and hostilities.[5]

Subsequent Soviet works on humor typically espoused the "humor as a weapon" thesis, or grounded theoretical observations in pre-Soviet culture.[6] It seems that Bykov/Efremov performance reflects both the satirical and "heretical" (in terms of Bourdieu) strain in Russian folklore that was also, in part, the legacy of buffoons or tricksters (I discuss this in chapter 11). In contemporary tradition this genre is called *stiob*.

As stated previously, there is a strong continuity in the media style between the Soviet and post-Soviet periods. Then, when official and unofficial symbols and meanings lost their cultural appeal and became equally irrelevant and obsolete, the discourse of new youth subculture based on withdrawal from the official sphere launched as a massive phenomenon. It was based on the aesthetics of the absurd, known in slang since the mid-1970s as stiob. This ironic treatment of ideological symbols differed from sarcasm or derision. As Yurchak puts it, "It required a certain overidentification with the ideological symbols exposed to such treatment, often to the point that it was almost impossible to tell whether the symbols were supported or subverted by subtle ridicule."[7] For members of this generation, stiob-based discourse not only remained entirely unofficial, but also articulates the critical stance to any discourse, be it mainstream of official ideology, the discourse of anti-communist criticism, market reforms, or Western feminism.

In the early 1990s, when stiob first appeared, as it were, in public, there seemed to be a clear ideological component, and the techniques of stiob were used to create an atmosphere of pseudo-transgressivity, in which the practitioners appeared to be indulging in subversive acts, while in fact conforming to the prevailing sentiment (as in the comedy of Igor Ugolnikov in his Oba-na days). By the mid-1990s the ideological component had mostly disappeared, as is illustrated by the use of Soviet slogans and imagery in the 1995 election campaign.

I suspect that the motives for using stiob as a form of humor in the project *Citizen Poet* is difficult to pinpoint. I remember in the 1990s, Dmitry Bykov, who has established his star status with opinionated journalism in the notorious TV show *Sharks of Quills* (Akuly Pera), was often criticized for showing off his knowledge of classics and employing them in wickedly ironic discourse. However at that time, this may have been because readers were unfamiliar with this particular mode of writing, while it was becoming familiar to journalists, who were at the same time freed from the requirement to be serious and to avoid irony. Since stiob, at least in my interpretation, depends on the existence of hierarchies to subvert, it has been difficult to maintain stiob culture in an environment where the existence of clear political and cultural hierarchies is problematic. The repeated examination of recent media materials suggests that the peculiar ironical discourse with its colorful language media is again in retreat in Russia. Aleksei Yurchak and Dominic Boyer summed up the problem facing the contemporary media, defining it as the "hypernormalization" of political and social discourse. This feature of the official media allows stiob to flourish in both Russian and Western alternative media outlets.[8]

In his book *Everything Was Forever until It Was No More*,[9] and in earlier work, Yurchak defines "stiob" as an ironic aesthetic of a very particular kind that thrived in late-Soviet socialism. Stiob "differed from sarcasm, cynicism, derision or any of the more familiar genres of absurd humor" in that it "required such a degree of *overidentification* with the object, person, or idea at which [it] was directed that it was often impossible to tell whether it was a form of sincere support, subtle ridicule, or a peculiar mixture of the two."[10]

What does seem to have survived is the use of techniques and approaches that are derived from stiob, but that now serve, in my view, as an indicator not so much of an ideology, but as a sort of cultural orientation. Since this orientation is based on irony and irreverence, it tends to be associated with people who are in opposition to or at least skeptical toward the authorities, but there are some journalists, such as Vitaly Tretyakov and Mikhail Leontiev,[11] who have put their talents at the service of the powers that be. Sometimes the results are catastrophic, as in Leontiev's short-lived attempt to revive the *Kukly*[12] format; at other times, however, their texts can have a disturbing ambiguity, where they either be taken at face value or be interpreted ironically, almost as self-parodies.

Bakhtin famously emphasized the liberating aspects of laughter, claiming that "violence does not know laughter" and laughter is an essential ingredient of a society's parting with the past.[13] This idea proves itself instrumental with regard to the ironic worldview at the point when language moved away from the authoritative discourse that had dominated the Soviet public domain, to the post-Soviet language liberalization. Since irony and humor tended to be the predominant mode of public discourse in the public sphere, it seemed like sub-editors competed to outdo each other in the art of "punning headlines," and journalists took events that were not funny in any obvious way and reported on them by employing an aphoristic writing style. The media has started to use more ironic catchphrases from radio and television programs, including the so-called social advertising of the 1990s. I have also observed that in the period emerging out of Mikhail Gorbachev's glasnost, when irony and humor tend to be the predominant mode of discourse, the Russian media moved closer to the Western model.

To some extent, these catchphrases or contemporary jokes can be viewed as alternatives to political anecdotes. Since the political anecdote has become obsolete, new kind of jokes and puns turn out to be told among co-workers and classmates. The most popular "Russian radio"–style jokes exposed specifics in social situations. "Russian radio"–style jokes became the main tool of communication. The selection of linguistic practices dealt with the expression of group membership for the young generation and an enjoyment of wordplay for the older generation. Primarily, this style meant being part of the underground, rather than of official culture. The demands of membership to this youth culture is important to its members as part of their sociopolitical identity. A transgressive practice is ideologically transformed into an index of social stratification, with comedy often drawing on vernacular speech as a signifier of low status. On the other hand, vernacular speech styles may have ambivalent and contested meanings to be represented in ways that challenge the stereotypes. Even more, as the context of official media is serious and restricted, some vernaculars are positioned as markers of subcultural, street-smart styles, offering producers and audiences a comic relief. This humor is the source not only of entertainment but also of information about new generation attitudes toward social issues. The main focus is placed on evidences relating to young people's experiences and their life expectations.

The appearance of jiggles like "Машина мужчину красит" (The car maketh the man) may be actually taken for a sign of growing affluence, but also indirectly alluding to a poor variety of goods in the previous years. Or another one: "У него своя философия: 'Дурака надуть—себя порадовать'" (He has his own philosophy: "Screw every sucker and enjoy it"). Interactionally, such witticisms can be viewed as skewed responses to forgoing talk. They presuppose the audience's close attention to the local context as well as require listeners to be able to take a joke.

As Bhartrhari said: "Treading the path of the unreal one attains reality."[14] It is in this way that the outstanding philosopher of the sixth-century India touched upon the very essence of language. A reasonable interpretation of his words seems to be the following: language keeps us incessantly alert to *alternatives* of contrasting, indeed incompatible, states of affairs. In fact, as language users and practitioners in the era of the new language culture, we are constantly facing not just what is real, but also what is incompatible with reality: the unreal being wordplay, anecdotes, alternative interpretations of abbreviations, and so forth. However, the cases of deliberately playing with nonsense bring the authors to "paths toward absurdity." This promises the viewers nothing, or to quote Gogol, when "all is deceit, all is not that which it seems to be."

A sophisticated way of "indirect saying" as parodic double-voiced discourse may be utilized to represent hidden or open polemic. Using other varieties, such as stylization or *skaz*,[15] a journalist can take someone else's discourse, infuse it with his own intentions, while still retaining the original (someone else's) intention. The author's thought and someone else's discourse may complement one another or exhibit telling parallels. In practice, the boundaries between those forms are very often violated.

Stylization is a concept closely associated with the literary and cultural criticism of Mikhail Bakhtin (1981, 1986). For Bakhtin, stylization is a subversive form of the multi-voiced utterance. In most of his later writings, however, he seems to offer a broader account of the notion of "stylization." In specific communicative contexts and at specific linguistic levels stylization seems to be a promising performance device for cultural reproduction. By exploiting cultural content and engaging creatively in cultural signification, a journalist may achieve the effect of stylization. By indicating the topic in its original frame, s/he may create implicit thematic halos that will intrigue readers and that will force the latter to reconsider the text's source. Rather than merely a hidden dialogue consisting of harmless exchange, hidden polemical discourse does not necessarily include the other's thought, "but it only reflected in it, determining its tone and its meaning."[16] I argue that the journalist exhibits double-voiced discourse, whereby he confronts the cited author, using subversive hidden polemic that anticipates, appropriates, and relexifies the utterances of his interlocutors for his own ideological purpose.

Stylization is the knowing deployment of culturally familiar styles and identities that deviate from those predictably associated with the current speaking context. In recent discussions, it has been increasingly argued that stylization, to be recognizable, needs to be viewed as dissonant from the authorized style and must fit an audience's cultural background.[17] Every reconstruction of a virtual style should be compared to the actual one. The link between the "author's" usage and the "alien" prototype can take the form of literal identification or figurative conceptualization. Thus, recognition is a main element in the effect of stylization. Readers will miss much if they do not know the original or if the origin of the phrase is not available to be observed.

I would suggest that stylization should be seen as a structural connection between data, interpretation, and consequences. The latter should be compatible with the journalist's intention. No doubt, however, some stylizations are performed purely for play or for semiotic mystification, and possess no recoverable motivations or implications. Stylization as one of the strategies in ideological media discourse may be summarized as follows:

- Stylization is a reflexive and metacommunicative practice that attends and invites attention to a journalist's own position while s/he attempts to share his/her own understanding of the events under discussion;
- Since stylization's effects emphasize dissonant social meanings, stylized utterances are often emphatic and involve hyperbolic implementation of their targeted styles and genres;
- Stylization is a creative technique and therefore requires aptitude and learning as well as a cultured audience able to read the semiotic value of projected styles and genres;
- Stylization should be analyzed as a strategy with complex implications for discursive practice of the media;
- Stylization is an exemplary case of "indirect saying." Using stylization, journalists make their texts "persuasive," that is, they "show," "reveal," "illustrate," "affirm," "prove" the truths of their views.

The data I have analyzed reveal different ways in which journalists employ the styles of the Other in their own discourse. Articles by Viktor Shenderovich and Valeria Novodvorskaia, who are both political satirists and popular public activists, and whose discourse is highly individual and pointed, offer representative examples of tools pertaining to stylization.[18]

Shenderovich's efforts to get the audience to pay attention to pervasive moral issues confront him with a dilemma concerning which presentational manner is best suited for such a purpose: radical criticism, or indirect yet transparent judgmental commentaries. His article "Безальтернативная Родина, кто ж тебя выдумал?" (Motherland without alternatives, who thought you up?)[19] is a good example of his writing. Here I only consider the case where there is a relationship between "one's own" and "other's" opinions. The way Shenderovich discusses the possible abolition of military service is a kind of performance where he serves as a puppeteer, and where his voice seems to be complemented by several other voices, including Duma deputy Viktor Alksnis, Duma vice-speaker Liubov' Sliska, and so on. Shenderovich has painstakingly scripted the discussion, selecting and shaping what others have said. We may consider this passage:

> Дешевый тест на пацифизм предложил на минувшей неделе один полковник. Он сказал: "Надо дать пацифисту пощёчину и посмотреть, подставит ли он вторую щёку."

> [Last week a certain colonel offered a cheap test for pacifism: "One should slap the pacifist's face, then see whether he turns the other cheek."] (*Ezhenedelnyi zhurnal* 2002)

A few paragraphs below the journalist resumes:

> Пока депутат Государственной думы предлагает бить призывников по лицу для проверки убеждений, первый вице-спикер того же органа, Любовь Слиска, от частной необходимости рукоприкладства в процессе призыва недавно вырулила на крупные государственные обобщения. "Российская Федерация,—сказала она,—не может отстаивать свои интересы, опираясь исключительно на приоритет прав личности над правами народов."
>
> [While a depute of the State Duma offered to slap conscripts' faces in order to check their principles, the first Vice-Speaker Liubov' Sliska moved from the individual argument why physical violence is needed during conscription, to sweeping generalizations on the state level. "It is impossible for the Russian Federation," she said, "to defend its interests by relying solely on the priority of individual rights over the rights of peoples."] (*Ezhenedel'nyi Zhurnal*, February 19, 2002).

In analyzing these two extracts, I have focused on the issue of "authenticity" of the other person's words. In fact, given the complete absence of proper punctuation to distinguish direct speech from its reported context, the very status of reported speech as characters' voices is tenuous. Only pronominal distinctions (we-you), imperatives, and the wildly random attributive "s/he said" stand as some kind of cue for when the characters are supposedly speaking. As a result, the boundaries between the author and characters are highly contestable, a situation that leads to substantial fluidity between two important contexts: what the characters actually said and what the author says they said.

It is obvious that in order to shape the story in a particular way Shenderovich provides quotations and specific commentaries regarding their content and plays with speakers' utterances. Stylization opens up the opportunity for a pattern of reporting that orients readers' perceptions. In my opinion, the social meaning constructed through the stylization undermines and downgrades the official view. The most obvious manifestation of "authentic speech" is the traditional quest for the vernacular, revealed in such expressions as "вырулила на крупные государственные обобщения" and "на самый худой конец" in the above-cited extracts. In the official authorized discourse of politicians, we expect to find circumspection, factual accuracy, seriousness, objectivity, a certain abstraction, and sanitized accounts of motives, coherence, rationality, and so forth. What I call stylization in the present data involves Shenderovich discursively subverting these principles.

The language of the politicians cited in this article displays many common lexical features—localisms, unique colloquialisms, and distorted vocabulary.

As far as its lexical makeup is concerned, Shenderovich's reported speech is shaped through colloquialisms and substandard language. Shenderovich also uses colloquial syntax:

> В чём этот самый долг состоит, не спрашивайте. А то начну рассказывать. [Don't ask me what one's duty involves, or else I'll start telling you.]; Дай ответ. Не даёт ответа—ни Слиска, ни кто иной из наших алкснисов. [Give an answer. No one does so—neither Sliska, nor any other of our "Alksnises."]
>
> Что же это за интересы такие? [What are these special interests after all?] И что это за загадочные права народов? [And what are these mysterious rights of peoples?] И из кого состоят эти народы? [And of whom do these peoples consist?] (*Ezhenedelnyi zhurnal*, February 19, 2002).

Shenderovich's re-creation of distorted speech is not only further evidence of his originality, but also first and foremost the creation of a code that serves as a powerful emphasis of group membership. This code may either index attributes of the lower social class stereotypically associated with those who are in power, or identify the addressee, who is rendered as one of "them," but not one of "us." The author has coined his own distortions, and thus closely emulates the language of his characters. The unofficial elements of language were and still are conceived as a breach of the literary verbal norm. These elements are presented with precise intentions: to transfer the contents of the article to another sphere that is beyond the limits of conventional language. What Bakhtin claims to be profanities can be established for all the strata of unofficial elements in language: "Such speech forms, liberated from norms, hierarchies, and prohibitions of established idiom, become themselves a peculiar argot and create a special collectivity, a group of people initiated in familiar intercourse, who are frank and free in expressing themselves verbally."[20]

The journalist's language, particularly when it is associated with the colloquial speech of the Other, is dotted with vulgarisms and jargonisms, such as "салага" (rookie), "черпаки" (newbies), "деды" (literally: grandfathers, that is, soldiers in their last year of service), "косили по-тихому" (dodged work without drawing attention to themselves), "дать в рыло не из-за дистрофии, а по убеждениям" (to punch someone in the face not because of dystrophy but of convictions); unexpected glosses, such as "хана" (the end), "эхма" (untranslatable emotional utterance); and fractured syntax. We may consider this example: "Типа санитаром в больнице посачковать, вместо чтоб приносить Родине пользу" (As if one would be goofing off in a hospital, instead of being useful to the Motherland) (*Ezhenedelnyi zhurnal*, February 19, 2002). Determining authenticity of the speech seems a central concern of the journalist. This use of a vernacular or distorted linguistic forms is more than just the choice of effective rhetoric. Likewise, departing from the base language of media discourse, the journalist mobilizes the distortion as a symbol to bolster the notion of identity, which is juxtaposed to the author's own identity.

What is deemed purely ornamental in the context of journalistic writing may signify something about ideology. It is taken for granted that journalists in various degrees are engaged in the composition of ideological discourse. While the facts may be the same, rhetorical patterns may be different. Thus, despite the similarity of the "facts," something may either go unreported or be papered over. Depending on the meaning ascribed to the "facts," certain details can effectively change and the whole interpretation may acquire a different value. All these differences are of a functional nature. They have no inherent value except when perceived in a specific discursive context.

Numerous elements of Shenderovich's narrative are polemically directed at negating something. Making someone else's utterance "strange" is a typical way of challenging and undermining an opponent's position on an issue. This polemical device may be constructive when it is employed to defend a positive assumption. The situation in the Russian media today is that artistic polemical constructions turn into an effective way to impress readers.

Another way to impress readers is to offer a generalization that is often referred to as a moral. We may consider the example where Shenderovich strengthens his argument with a proverb. He starts with a generalization about war casualties: "Пуля, как известно, дура" (It's well known that bullet is a fool) (*Ezhenedel'nyi Zhurnal,* February 19, 2002). He then continues with his own aphorism, "а призывник—негодяй" (a conscript is a scoundrel) (Ibid.), which sounds as a fixed-phrase saying and, at the same time, a strong argument with the emotions and spice of traditional wisdom that is difficult to challenge. The journalist parodies proverbial content, articulates a parallel that encapsulates a thought about human nature, which implies a right as opposed to a wrong "picture." In this authorized discourse, where a proverb is added to the author's aphorism, it is unclear just what levels of ownership, authorship, and endorsement are being implied. There is a specific indication that stylized utterances dissociate from their author and from pragmatic implications of what is said.

In terms of speech style, Shenderovich's delivery is playful and verbally emphatic, as, for example, in this paragraph:

> Итак, России не нужны санитары и пацифисты. Ей не нужны учителя, инженеры, физики и лирики . . . Вообще люди—не нужны!
>
> [So, Russia has no need for hospital attendants and pacifists. It has no need of teachers, engineers, physicists and lyric poets . . . Russia has no need for people overall.] (*Ezhenedelnyi zhurnal*, February 19, 2002).

His argument is cadenced by an insertion marking the important point for the reader: "so." This marker implies "let us say again; let us repeat what is completely obvious." Then, the voices of others become an object of deformation and authorial commentaries. When it comes to conclusions, Shenderovich convincingly depicts images of reality in order to impart meaning to quotations he presents in his text:

> А нужны ей генералы и полковники, в крайнем случае—военкомы, на самый худой конец—призывники, которых можно довести до скотского состояния и оставить на краю света с автоматом Калашникова в ожидании счастливого часа, когда кто-нибудь из них перестреляет сослуживцев и убежит в сторону ближайшего сельпо, чтобы поесть.
>
> [What it does need is generals and colonels, or, as a last resort, commanders and, if worse comes to worst, conscripts. The last of these can be driven to despair and left at the end of the earth with an AK-47, hoping for a lucky break, when one of them shoots his fellow-soldiers and escapes towards the nearest country grocery store to get some food.] (*Itogi,* February 19, 2002)

The surreal quality of the reported reality and manifested fictional elements make it unclear what is the precise target of stylization. The author's ironical manner is likely to strike readers with the cruelty of the reality being depicted.

Unusual journalists write unusual texts. Valeria Novodvorskaia has a reputation as a critical and provocative journalist. In her articles, she typically uses stylization and *skaz*[21] as part of a process of cultural reproduction. She sprinkles authorial irony in her writing to such a degree that her articles frequently not only amuse, but also annoy and irritate readers, many of whom tend to reject her manner. As one such reader, I must acknowledge the difficulties caused by her masks, evasions, and hyperboles; still, I appreciate the originality and humor of her writing. As shown below, her polemics often involve skeptical and pessimistic statements. No matter what she writes about, Novodvorskaia cannot let it go by without a smirk on the side. There are ironic intrusions and, most important, fictional and factual components are well integrated and delivered within an authorial frame.

In the following example, a cultural myth from the period of the Cold War recounting by political analyst Denis Dragunsky is introduced in the form of *skaz*:

> Там за большим столом сидели товарищи в серых костюмах с оловянными глазами. А у самого главного товарища глаза были как весь советский стратегический запас олова.
>
> [There were comrades in gray suits sitting at a big table their eyes as if made out of tin. And the chief comrade's eyes were like the entire Soviet strategic tin reserve.][22]

First, the rhythm of this passage violates the telegraphic media style. Second, there is the illogical reference to the time, place, and action the agents are doing. A reader cannot establish where they actually are sitting and why they are sitting there, because the journalist has failed to provide an accurate and by extension realistic portrait of the agents. So, diffusion and incongruity are at the heart of the matter. In this example, *skaz* offers the journalist a way to be responsive to a pervasive issue without being straightforwardly radical. Since the piece has been "constructed" according to the tradition of the genre, readers are not expected to ask where exactly the journalist's real face is, what she is driving at, and what is her "clear vision."

Under the Soviet regime a wide range of negative ideas, events, or actions was kept out of public discourse. To communicate information about the nearly universal criminality and corruption that are typical of periods of great economical difficulty and sharp shortages of food and other goods, journalists applied the narrative technique of *skaz*. In Soviet media, the author used to serve as a narrator who was supposed to rewrite stories so that they would be ideologically and discursively more palatable for a Soviet audience. At present, when using *skaz*, a journalist emphasizes not so much an "appropriate" version of a given situation as multiple interpretations of events.

In *skaz* there may appear many faces (masks). In the following example, politician Boris Nemtsov is himself rendering political affairs as gossip, creating the effect of *skaz*:

> Политтехнологи гурьбой заходили в кабинет и говорили: Немцов, сдай ты этого Чубайса, его страна ненавидит, всех облезлых кошек, как Ельцин говорил, "чубайсами" называют. Я отвечал: не дождётесь.
>
> [The political operatives used to come to my office in crowds saying, "Nemtsov, give up Chubais. The country hates him. Every shabby cat in the street, as Yeltsin used to say, is called Chubais." "It's not going to happen," I would answer them.][23]

In this excerpt, *skaz* can be defined as sociological in origin, since it represents "speech from the streets," with such expressions as "сдай ты этого Чубайса" and "облезлые кошки"; with typical substandard language, as, for example, "не дождётесь"; and with details of a narrated event, such as "гурьбой заходили в кабинет." Therefore, *skaz* serves as a vehicle that gives Nemtsov's voice its individuality and exclusiveness by comparison to the voices of other politicians quoted in the media.

Another relevant observation is that Nemtsov's words are not an actual recording of speech but a created effect, because his discourse creates a verbal parody. Since parody admits a recognized degree of hyperbole and humor, *skaz* creates the illusion of a specific mask that is easily distinguishable for the character's point of view. That may be specially illustrated by reference to verbal parody, which is obviously one of the particular kinds of stylization. In the above passage parody may lose much of its effect if the original is unfamiliar.[24] Within Nemtsov's narrative, as presented by Novodvorskaia, we may distinguish some other participating voices, such as those of Boris Yeltsin himself and of nameless political operatives. The political operatives' and Yeltsin's utterances function merely as an object of representation. What is more, I believe that political need dictates the means to distinguish the journalist's point of view from what Nemtsov implies. The cacophony, indeed, creates the effect of *skaz* rather that offering a realistic vision of the situation, and results in substantial fluidity between two important contexts: what the character actually says and what is the reporter's evaluative context.

My next example is a striking instance of this symbolically strategic transgression. I will demonstrate how functionally restricted, nonetheless relevant form is implied to reveal the journalist's claim. Transgressive language may be directed not only at official mythology, but also at the recently sacred symbols and set of values. In the passage cited below the suffix in the names while indicating smallness of size, also captures linguistic evocation of derision:

> Свобода печати в неграмотной крестьянской России имела смысл лишь для образованной публики—массы разве что немножко повесилились, читая в желтой прессе пошлые расскази-к-и про "Николаш-к-у, его жену Саш-к-у и старца Гриш-к-у.
>
> [Freedom of press in illiterate rural Russia if has any sense only to educated audience, folk might perhaps had very little fun of reading smutty tales in yellow press "on Nicolas, his wife Alex and elder Gregory."] (*Ezhenedelnyi zhurnal*, February 19, 2002).

Names with the suffix -k- are often referred to as diminutives; however, in this particular case they are not really diminutives and are used to caricature a social type. It must be emphasized that the force of the suffix -к- in the words used in the above passage can be represented as follows: the journalist quotes someone else who was showing his or her familiarity with the tsar by calling him "Николаш-*к-а*" and did not think of him as someone special. This practice of coining depreciative forms by the addition of suffixes suits perfectly the modern cult of informality, and it makes perfect sense to juxtapose pre-Revolutionary anti-intellectualism and familiarity toward everybody and the current situation where one refers to everything as trivial concepts.

Also of interest in the cited excerpt is the linguistic phenomenon of "referential expression." As Olga Yokoyama (1994)[25] claims, this phenomenon can be interpreted as a culturally significant fact, but it also illustrates differences in attitude to objective facts of reality. Russian possesses numerous options for the first name. There is a phenomenon of shortening this name to produce a more intimate version. However, on the other hand, the effect of producing a shorter first name can be applied in a context where formality and politeness are being violated deliberately. The example given above is evidence of how diminutives are used to introduce "pejorative" meaning. Cultural tradition requires the addition of titles to the names of royalty (e.g., Tsar Nicholas II). Violation of this norm, that is, recognizable shortening of the full formal title as well as distinguished "expressive derivation," assumes the presence of attitudinal meaning, which can be interpreted as skepticism and derision. The institution of the Russian monarchy as the highest authority had its own peculiarities: the tsar was alleged to be the direct representative of God. Because of this, forms of address developed over centuries demanded expressions of the greatest possible respect toward the figure of the monarch. Moreover, historically, any kind of disrespect toward the crown was considered an expression of blasphemy toward God, that is, a sin or morally unscrupulous behavior.

One of the salient features of the alternative discourse is the experiment with language, narrative, and genre conventions. Alternative discourse of the opposition[26] used the format of oral folklore and carnival tradition. To illustrate this, I want to point out that the most popular Internet sensations in the period after the 2011 Duma election in Russia was a music video called "Our Nuthouse Votes for Putin," in which a supposed mental patient asks where all the country's oil and gas revenues have gone. Entries included "146 percent," a reference to the laughably wrong vote total that state-run television showed for one Russian region. One joke that made the rounds after December's disputed parliamentary vote goes: "The wives of United Russia party members don't fake orgasms. They falsify them." Remarkably, if a transgressive speech pattern is represented in media reports, it will be contained within reported voices—that is, as the speech of the Other rather than in the reporter's own voice.

Short forms such as slogans, anecdotes, the newspaper report, poetic couplet, guitar song, street poster, and short movies were accessible and mobile while appealing to the masses. The unrestrained language play in the alternative discourse of opposition derived from official public discourse and its textual interplay, which, in creating a highly eclectic and stylized language, provides a critical reading of official culture and invites it to the dialogue. The whole situation leads us to seek the roots of alternative discourse in the Bakhtinian culture of the carnival.

My next example is drawn from the alternative discourse performed by the feminist punk band Pussy Riot.[27] Pussy Riot's provocative performance in the Cathedral of Christ the Saviour in Moscow in February 2012 can be interpreted in many contexts, including current Russian politics, church-state relations, the worldwide Occupy movement, political dissidence. and Russian alternative culture. Media and scholarship still have not reached a consensus about either the true identity and nature of these women, or the role they played in the Russian culture. They were named "mad women," "punk artists," "truth-seekers," "tricksters," "libertines," "buffoons," "holy fools," "feminists." I attempt to interpret the myth created around Pussy Riot by arguing that, as a sign within a complex semiotic system, they were all of these personas at the same time and "materialized" as a culture-specific sign depending on the "reader." I also argue that the ongoing confusion was caused, originally, by the blurred "contours" of the two primary signs—holy fool and feminist: both of them are undergoing a certain revival. I will thus erase the dichotomy of their presumed "victimization" and their presumed "profaneness," and address their discourse, which heavily depends on the intended audience's familiarity with the texts they alluded to. For the stylization they chose one hymn particularly venerated by Eastern Orthodox believers with a tune sung by the believers during pilgrimages, or a prayers for the family members. Falsely reported as a "punk prayer to the Virgin Mary," the lyrics they recited were in fact a grotesquely and objectively disrespectful performance. It was not a prayer of any sort, but a kind of a vulgar parody of the beliefs and rituals of believers. They mocked an Orthodox prayer service by making parodical prostrations and singing the Orthodox equivalent of "Ave Maria" mixed with a song containing foul language and the verbal violent statement addressing the chief hierarch of the church and faithful ("sran' Gospodnia"), referring to the non-existence of heavenly freedom ("prizrak svobody na nebesakh"), the mocking of parishioners' deference for the clergy ("Vse prikhozhane polzut na poklony"), and asking "Our Lady, chase Putin out."

The example drawn from Pussy Riot lyrics demonstrates the need to apply various forms of linguistic transsgressivity to deliver the critical reaction to the official normative "speak." Thus an analysis of voices and stylization may show how the dominance of "heretic" language persists even within highly heteroglossic media discourse. However, transgressive linguistic patterns can also reveal where any exceptions and challenges to the dominant pattern lie. The nexus of transgression, stylization, and stiob may give the voice of the Other legitimacy in the media, but it also confines it to niches and excludes it from wider official uses.

NOTES

1. D. S. Likhachev, "Smekh kak mirovozzrenie," *Istoricheskaia poetika russkoi literatury: Smekh kak mirovozzrenie i drugie raboty* (St. Petersburg: Aleteiia, 1997), 342–403. Nikolai Gogol, "Mertvye dushi," in *Izbrannye sochinenia v dvukh tomakh*, vol. 1 (Moscow: Khudozhestvennaia literatura, 1984), chap. 7.

2. Anatoly Lunacharskii, "We Are Going to Laugh," *Vestmk Teatra* 58 (1920): 23–28.

3. Kharms, *Gorlo bredit britvoiu: Sluchai, rasskazy, dnevnikovye zapisi* (Riga: Glagol, 1991), 134.
4. Henri Bergson, "Laughter," in *Comedy* (New York: Doubleday, 1956), 63.
5. Sigmund Freud, *Jokes and Their Relation to the Unconscious*, trans. James Strachey (New York: W. W. Norton, 1960).
6. Vladimir Propp's *Problemy komizma i smekha* and Dmitrii Likhachev's "Smekh kak mirovozzrenie."
7. Aleksei Yuarchak, "Gagarin and the Rave Kids: Transforming Power, Identity, and Aesthetics," in *Post-Soviet Nightlife in Consuming Russia: Popular Culture, Sex, and Society Since Gorbachev*, ed. Adele Barker (Durham, NC: Duke University Press, 1999), 76–109.
8. Aleksei Yurchak and Dominic Boyer, "American Stiob: Or What Late-Socialist Aesthetics of Parody Can Teach Us about Contemporary Political Culture in the West," *Cultural Anthropology* 25, no. 2 (2010). Visual materials for this article and an interview are available at www.culanth.org/?q=node/322.
9. Aleksei Yurchak, *Everything Was Forever until It Was No More* (Princeton, NJ: Princeton University Press, 2006).
10. Ibid., 250; see also Yurchak, "Gagarin and the Rave Kids," 84.
11. Mikhail Leontiev is a pro-Kremlin journalist and polytologist. He is known for his program *Odnako* (However, or Still), irregularly appearing on air with commentaries on certain political occasions. Leontiev made several scandalous accusations both in his own show and in various interviews; for example, in 2001 he accused Viktor Yushchenko's wife, Kateryna Yushchenko, of influencing her husband's political decisions with U.S. ideas, hinting that she is an agent of American government in Ukraine. In 2006, the Ukrainian government banned Leontiev from visiting the country for five years, referring to his "insulting statements" denying the existence of Ukrainian national identity.

Vitaly Tretyakov is editor-in-chief of *Politichesky Class* magazine of the Moscow State Institute of International Relations, Russian Ministry of Foreign Affairs; and a member of the Valdai Discussion Club. He supports the idea of reviving the Ministry for Ethnic Affairs with the Russian question as a fundamental issue in developing strategies and policies in the sphere of interethnic relations. He considers that to deal with the nationalist "illness" in the Kremlin, Russia should rely on the experience of the Russian Empire and particularly from the Soviet Union, which, in his opinion, offers many positive examples and some negative ones.

12. *Kukly* (Puppets) was the most popular weekly television show on channel NTV during 1994–2000. Modeled on British show *Spitting Image*, this political satire featured the actual politicians as lifelike puppets, usually operated by two actors and showed them in various contexts evoking the real politicians' behavior, so that any Russian who saw the program knew precisely what was meant. *Kukly* modeled on senior government officials tweaked the authorities on the issues that were handled gingerly in the mainstream Russian press. *Kukly*'s most memorial political jabs often drew on Russian classics to satirize the Russian political elite. In 2002 NTV was forced to close this show down claiming that the highest officials in government were portrayed in an insulting manner.
13. M. Bakhtin, *Speech Genres and Other Late Essays*, ed. C. Emerson and M. Holquist, trans. V. McGee (Austin: University of Texas Press, 1986), 134.
14. Esa Itkonen, *Universal History of Linguistics* (Amsterdam: Benjamins, 1991), 80.
15. Close examination of the narrative structure of *skaz* in the Russian literary tradition can be found in Hugh McLean, "On the Style of a Leskovian Skaz," *Harvard Slavic Studies*, vol. 2, ed. Horace G. Lunt et al. (Cambridge, MA: Harvard University Press, 1954), 298–99; Jeremy Hicks, *Mikhail Zoshchenko and the Poetics of Skaz* (Nottingham, UK: Astra Press, 2000); Cathy Popkin, *The Pragmatics of Insignificance: Chekov, Zoshchenko, Gogol* (Stanford, CA: Stanford University Press, 1993); Olga Mesropova, "Between Literary and Subliterary Paradigms: 'Skaz' and Contemporary Russian 'Estrada' Comedy," *Canadian Slavonic Papers* 46, nos. 3–4 (2004): 417–33.
16. Mikhail Bakhtin, *Problems of Dostoevsky's Poetics*, ed. and trans. Caryl Emerson (Minneapolis: University of Minnesota Press, 1999), 196.
17. R. Bauman, "Transformations of the Word in the Production of Mexican Festival Drama," in *Natural Histories of Discourse*, ed. M. Seiverstein and G. Urban (Chicago and London:

University of Chicago Press, 1996), 301–27. See also Urban, "Entextualization, Replication and Power," in *Natural Histories of Discourse*, ed. M. Seiverstein and G. Urban (Chicago and London: University of Chicago Press, 1996), 21–44.

18. The following passage is adapted from Svitlana Malykhina, "Irony," in "Linguistic Aspects of Contemporary Russian Print Media" (M.A. diss., University at Albany–State University of New York, Russian Literature and Culture, May 2004).

19. Viktor Shenderovich, "Bezalternativnaia Rodina: Kto zh tebia vydumal," *Itogi,* February 19, 2002.

20. Bakhtin 1986, 87.

21. The following examples and analyses were adapted from Svitlana Malykhina, "*Skaz* and Stylization," in "Linguistic Aspects of Contemporary Russian Print Media" (M.A. diss., University at Albany–State University of New York, Russian Literature and Culture, May 2004).

22. Denis Dragunsku, "Obshchestvo zelenykh naslazhdenii," http://clear-text.livejournal.com/92113.html.

23. www.izvestia.ru/politic/article32130.

24. Anatoly Chubais was the mastermind of Russia's privatization of state property during the early 1990s. Privatization itself was carried out "respecting the criminal code," while exploiting loopholes and human weaknesses. A new class of well-connected insiders, the so-called oligarchs, snapped up state assets at prices that often were ridiculously low. Meanwhile, ordinary Russians received the so-called privatization vouchers, which Chubais promised would someday be worth as much as a car. Mistrusting these promises, some people swapped their vouchers for a bottle of vodka, while others invested them in a well-advertised money fund that soon collapsed, leaving the unfortunate investors without enough cash for even a single tire. The widespread corruption and shady deals of the era of privatization have prompted some sociologists to describe the Russian establishment as a "government of thieves." Later in 1998, when Chubais was Russia's chief loan negotiator, Russia was successful in winning billions in loans from the International Monetary Fund. Yet these billions in loans melted away when in August 1998 the government defaulted on its short-term debt (GKOs) and devalued the ruble. As a result of this crisis much of the banking system became insolvent, depriving millions of Russians of their savings.

25. O. Yokoyama, "Iconic Manifestation of Interlocutor Distance in Russian," *Journal of Pragmatics* 22 (1994): 83–102.

26. Protesters believed that Russia's future depends entirely on the level of protest and that the opposition managed to influence Putin's domestic policy. The opposition remained united but not under the wing of some political organization, but united in the sense of coordinated action. Participants in the rallies on Bolotnaya Square, Academician Sakharov Prospekt, and other places in Moscow and other cities signed the united opposition program of political reforms. It consists of several points, the most important of which are abolition of political censorship, including on TV, and the release of political prisoners. Although the authorities announced that the elections of governors will be introduced as well as political plurality, not a single item of this program has been implemented. Obviously, the law on political parties that entered in force was aimed at preserving Putin's power. The goal of the law is the fragmentation of political forces and the division of the political landscape.

27. Most of the reporters started their story with the fact that on February 21 women in cartoonish, bright-colored outfits in masks entered Moscow's largest cathedral to perform a song asking for the Virgin Mary to "chastise of Putin." Secular liberals embraced them as the authentic voice of upwelling of dissent since the disputed parliamentary elections in December, although ostensibly the political comments were spliced into the video later. The Pussy Riot criminal trial captivated and scandalized the public, attracting protests from the Western celebrities and revealing tensions in modern Russian society. Three members of the feminist punk collective Pussy Riot were sentenced to two years in prison after being convicted of hooliganism and inciting religious hatred by a Moscow district court. For more on this, see A. Epshtein, "Arest uchastnits gruppy 'Pussy Riot' kak katalizator khudozhestvenno-grazhdanskogo aktivizma" (www.nlobooks.ru/node/2585); A. Epshtein, "Mobilizovannaia Bogoroditsa: Pank-moleben gruppy 'Pussy Riot' v Khrame Khrista Spasitelia" (www.nlobooks.ru/node/2285); Elena

Gapova, "Delo 'Pussy Riot': Feministskii potest v kontekste klassovoi bor'by (Neprikosnovennyi zapas)" (www.nlobooks.ru/node/2794).

Chapter Eleven

Citizen Poet Project

As I pointed out earlier in the book, the concept of the heterodox discourse[1] and repressed practices lying beneath the surface and competing with the dominant orthodox discourse has become a part of contemporary journalistic rhetoric. What Bourdieu's model offers[2] for the Russian context is theoretical predictions that heretic oral tradition comes to fore displaying stylistic complexity, the semantic density of symbolic and allegorical allusions, expressiveness of the speech, including overplay with curses, swearing, crude, and vulgar language that replace official and bookish written language.

For the purpose of this book Bourdieu's writings provide a possible explanatory framework for the presence and nature of alternative journalism (see the discussion in chapter 4). One point of entry for considering the role of alternative media is to compare the use of classical allusions across different media types. Instead of cataloguing and analyzing alternative news outlets in Russia, this chapter is concerned with one project that offered a constructive contribution to civic society through aggressive scrutiny of political actors and institutions, as well as satirical deconstructions of contemporary issues and events. As the following observations suggest, an open, inclusive understanding of alternative media may increase awareness of the highly diverse ways in which allusions may signal affiliations in public discourse. The following sections attempt to flesh out such an approach.

A typical example would be that of project *Citizen Poet*, where the authors approach the Russian poetic tradition to create a new performative discourse. The selection of original texts is a recursive and reflexive process: associated meanings are established, debated, refined, rediscovered, and exhibited in parody spoofs. This project offers a series of performative parodies to classical nineteenth- and twentieth-century poetry purportedly focused on the relations between poetry, politics, and Russian history. Parodies articulate the poet's relationship to the past cultural heritage, which he both rejects and in a peculiar way celebrates.

I find it significant for my general discussion to note that the project represents a tendency of post-Soviet cultural production to nostalgically borrow familiar narratives, offering an obvious ideological strategy of its interpretation. I focus on the phenomenon of the words of the Other in media discourse and see the need to approach the phenomenon of the Other's words from the pragmatic perspective. The unique discourse of this project, with classic poetry as both cultural reserve and reference points for the circulation of allusions, contains diverse speech genres such as sayings, jaw-dropping quotes, witticisms, repartees, and snatches of anecdotes circulated in the circles of literary intelligentsia and framed to capture the mood, milieu, and personalities of the celebrated social figures. Although the progenitors of *Citizen Poet*—actor Michail Efremov and producer Andrei Vasil'ev—never considered themselves political activists, and deny the commitment to any political activity,[3] they started the media project, which lasted for thirteen months and contains fifty satirical spoofs. It was closed on a symbolic date—March 5—the day after the presidential election in Russia. Most of the clips of current affairs were aired within days after the event or accident occurring in Russian society, with response to the latest development in covering the news that many Russian mass media outlets downplayed or even ignored.

Allegedly, the satirical project *Citizen Poet* received a rebirth under the name *Gospodin Khoroshii* (Mister good). Although the love of sensationalism and commercial success has undoubtedly played a part in the creation and reception of this digital project, it seems that the authors also harbor serious political ambitions to exert a sensational impact on their audience, involving character-driven humor.

As I focus mostly on the text written by Bykov, I would like to give his brief profile. In Russia, Dmitry Bykov (born 1967) is one of the most remarkable figures of modern literary life. A member of the Writers' Union since 1991, he is the outspoken and provocative Moscow-based poet, critic, television presenter, school teacher, radio host, biographer of Boris Pasternak, Bulat Okudzhava, and Vladimir Mayakovsky, and an influential writer whose early fiction falls into the category of "historical fantasies."[4] On the other hand, the genre and the playful echo of the *Citizen Poet* evoke one of Bykov's early quasi-historical novels, *Orthography* (first published in 2003). It seems useful to remind that *Orthography* includes historical characters under their own names, such as Gorky, and others with pseudonyms whose prototypes are easily recognizable, such as the writers Maiakovsky (Korabel'nikov), Khlebnikov (Melnikov), and Khodasevich (who is called Kazarin, the name of the egoist and hypocrite in Lermontov's play *Masquerade*). Meanwhile, it is possible to assume that an author of such a novel as *Justification* (first published in 2001), in which Bykov creates a fantastic version of the time of Stalin's purges, represents the new "generation of thirty-year-olds" and their approach in pondering the theme of Stalin's terror in the atmosphere of the early post-Soviet period. As Rosalind March argues, Bykov demonstrates the tendency of certain writers of the younger generation, who did not experience the Stalin era, not merely to explain Stalinism, but to justify it, expressing regret for the end of the Soviet empire.

Ironically enough, in his early novels *Justification* and *Orthography*, Bykov—in his usual idiosyncratic and provocative manner—is articulating his own conservative critique of the "new Russian revolution" of 1991. Clearly, then, in the early 2000s he was not sympathetic to the liberal intellectuals, and displayed an imperial nostalgia and love of power. However, these views were, more likely, a reflection of the changing climate of opinion in contemporary Russia, or, as he admitted in his interviews, he had written the novels in his struggle against his own "imperial complex."

When Putin's regime annoyed many Russians, Bykov took a sharp turn from the "love of power" by reverting to satire and jokes to cope with concerns over a rollback of democracy. As a columnist for *Novaya Gazeta*, Bykov has always found inspiration in poetry. Not surprisingly, the idea of the joint project *Citizen Poet* reflects his belief that everything that happens in political life has a parallel in literature. The two other authors of the project are TV journalist Andrey Vasilev, and one of Russia's most popular actors, Mikhail Efremov, who takes up a position in front of the camera and delivers a two- to three-minute parody spoof.

On the one hand, it seems that *Citizen Poet* is just another project reflecting on "obsession" with politics available in the Russian segment of the Internet. Apparently, it cannot be regarded as totally original, since it resembles NTV channel's highly popular and successful political satire, *Kukly* (Puppets). (See chapter 10, note 13 for more information on *Kukly*.) The author, the widely known Russian writer, poet, journalist, and political activist Viktor Shenderovich, reinforced the satirical effect by giving his puppets pet names, such as Michael Stavropolsky (Mikhail Gorbachev, who originally came from Stavropol); Tolik Voucher (Anatoly Chubais, the privatization minister), and Zhirik (Zhirinovsky). While investing into the psychology of the characters, he also defines the characters by their purpose. One can also find some similarities with the program *Plavlennyi syrok* (Processed Cheese), a broadcast on the Ekho Moskvy radio channel and a trademark of NTV—a sharp political magazine, summing up the events of the weekly program *Itogo* (Total) and parodying Evgeny Kiselyov's program *Itogi* (Summing Up), both authored by Shenderovich. Shenderovich employed linguistic tools to oppose the official discourse, and used argumentative strategies to construct the oppositional version of identity. The authorities' difficulty in controlling the show stemmed from the ambiguous function of the genre as it was stuck between the official notions of how genre should be used and how it really functions. Those shows aroused the hostility of both Yeltsin and Putin and were taken off the air. I suggest that the need for this genre of TV program was mainly a reaction to the ambivalent feelings provoked by the official media coverage. With biting satire, the program commented on the events of the week, mixing political discourse and popular entertainment.

Citizen Poet also bears some relationship to the satirical tradition of Gogol and his accounts of the trips taken by Pavel Chichikov in *Dead Souls* around Nicholas I's Russia. To complicate matters, *Citizen Poet* heavily relies on the satirical tradition employed by Ilf and Petrov, particularly in terms of exposing ironic folklore, vernacular, and language variability mapping the language landscape of Putin's Russia. As satire is often less concerned with traditional shape and more intended to reflect and comment on contemporary situations, this project's satire is evident in the comedic genre of spoof, which is somewhat difficult to define. Authors are particularly concerned with the image and perception of the Other by employing multivoiced discourse as the rhetorical strategy, making spectators feel inclusive or exclusive depending on shared frames of reference and likemindness.

If scholarship has so far neglected the typological similarities between the Russian post-Soviet media and post-colonial/Western alternative media, the authors of Internet projects not only are acutely aware of the penchant for social engagement and spectacular entry into the world of the pop culture canon they shared with Western authors but also looked upon the latter as a model. The relation between the two traditions was not limited to fascination from afar. Between the late 1980s and the late 2000s it took the form of borrowing the form and stylistics. This borrowing not only anticipated some of the development of the genre but also left a lasting trace on the narrative forms of the alternative projects. Nevertheless, the Russian case reveals that this exchange did not necessarily translate into political engagement, or even, ultimately, more openness. Alternative media succeeded materially even as, in the end, it failed politically. As we search for a Western counterpart of *Citizen Poet*, an entertaining commercial news outlet *The Onion*, which can be called investigative satire, comes to mind. *The Onion* is a satirical parody of a newspaper.[5] The visual format of *The Onion* mirrors a "real" online paper; but fake "news" helps create the ambiguity in meaning necessary for irony. Some stories are quite crude and many contain curses and profanities.

Satirical television shows of the pre-Putin era, however, were powerful enough to affect politicians' approval ratings. Likewise, the Internet project *Citizen Poet*, according to the former owner of Web portal F5 and the supporter of the project Yuri Katsman, enjoys its deserved popularity. The authors of an irregular series of satirical skits expected their videos to be viewed at most by a few thousand people, but their first clip received 250,000 hits. In addition to being broadcast and repeated on the Dozhd channel, the project is available on YouTube, Facebook, and other networking sites. The viral nature of the series is almost unheard of in the realm of recent culture trends. The irregular series was a response to current events. The project has become an online sensation and by February 2012 releases of the show collected over 13 million viewings on YouTube. The show also has fared very well at theaters.[6]

As suggested by the discussion so far, progenitors of *Citizen Poet* exploit the know-how of the Soviet program and Western satirical media by appealing to Russian classics, and stress the role of national imagery in the formation of a new cultural identity. What is original and unique in the Bykov-Efremov-Vasil'ev project is a belief that everything that happens in political life has a parallel in poetry. Bykov's texts follow forms and structure of the classical Russian poetry he parodied, suggesting a trajectory of critical engagement. The real life political figures are playing principal roles, but they do so as mere caricatures. Bykov keeps rhyme, alliteration, assonance, and consonance of the original text in an attempt to retain the effect of authenticity. This project creates an emotional link of continuity with the past, with Russia's imperial past as well as with the Soviet era, particularly with the 1970s. This is the period that Russian citizens in various opinion polls of the last years have described as the most stable and "democratic" in twentieth-century Russian history. To achieve this goal authors are engaged in an exercise aimed at reproducing firmly shared past national mythologies through a range of poetries, in which emotional tones, particularly those leaning toward nationalist rhetoric, clearly outweigh the importance of information accuracy.

A special consideration is given to the particularly "appropriate visual language" to construct a stage set rooted in myth rather than reality. The basic line of remaking the tradition is the following:

- an easily recognizable phrase or styles extracted from their contexts to be reanimated in the new discourse;
- an author and a performer layer their parodies with allusions to the texts of the Others, using idiosyncratic language to give distinctive voices to their characters;
- the nuances and style of someone else's texts are constructed carefully, though within the episodic format;
- different in each episode, actor Efremov bears a remarkable facial resemblance to the original authors of the poems.

Visual context determines production of new verbal texts. The structure of parody allows multidimensional reading and the phenomenon involves the visual perception of parody at different angles. The mechanism of building such of a parody can be compared to the skillful use of "intellectual montage" (Eisenstein) of images, sounds, and shots, cut to highlight one common theme.[7] This leads to a carnivalesque polyphony, similar to that found by Bakhtin in Dostoevsky's novels. By placing a well-known Russian actor within the frame of a well-known literary masterpiece, the project creators enhance the effect of recognition. The resemblance between Efremov and prototypes is reinforced by the additional interpretive details set up meticulously to restore the epoch and environment of the classical masterpiece. From this point of view, the visual pleasure of the spectacle to a large extent comes from one's ability to register formal similarities between the authentic poetry and its contemporary parody.

At first glance, this complex design elicits the active participation of the addressee, as the coordination of this multitasking performance falls on the viewer. However, because of the exaggerated mode of expression, no empathy results from this performance, which is a mockery. Hence, the project creators not merely encourage their viewers to laugh at political figures, but rather humorously invite us to recognize the literary canon. It results in the parodic treatment of a literary tradition, which evokes post-modernist playful referentiality. By blurring the line between an allusion and its new environment, the project makers promote certain abridgment and stereotyping. The routine that is commonly employed in every episode is a complex interplay of stage setup, the performer's make up and costume, and the background projected image of an author being parodied.

Their experiments with visual and verbal images are supremely carnivalistic, while settings are fantastic, with characters moving through a world of extremes. If examined more closely, one can see the surprisingly disoriented spatio-temporal patterns of the clips. Since at issue in the series are matters of good and evil, as well as love and hate, the characters consistently find themselves on the verge of hysteria and collapse. The actors' histrionics appropriately communicate these liminal states. I would add to this that the function of those discursive models made the chronotopic liminality (threshold situations) in this discourse possible by offering an alternative way of talking about it, such as presenting it as something funny.[8]

The most frequently deployed in the series are the liminal mental states of dream, daydream, introspection, imagining, phobia, and so on. In fact, as language users and practitioners in the era of the new language culture, we are constantly facing not just what is real, but also what is incompatible with reality: the unreal wordplay, anecdotes, alternative interpretations of abbreviations, and so forth. Verbal addition, supplements, or distortion of the literary source functions as a tool to change meaning. In other words, this cultural production offers a reproduction with distortion, and the function of parody is not only to negate and mock the tradition but also to adapt it to the contemporary context. As a result, the viewers are exposed to the words of the Others imbued with the journalists' expression of irony, mockery, ridicule, doubt, indignation, and so on.

The linguistic diversity has challenged translators since Bykov to use a spicy mixture of nineteenth-century coinage with iffy language and slang or argot. To use the jargon of the time, the project is meant to be not only topical but also politically effective. Furthermore, authors provide sarcastic swipes and pointed political and social commentary at society's foibles, to which the audience is accustomed, and create new chances for vernacular voices to be heard publicly. More than just the choice of a vernacular variant for rhyme and transgressing language, symbolism is mobilized here to bolster the notion of contemporary identity, which is juxtaposed to the "other" classical identity. To some extent, what is presented in the project *Citizen Poet* seems to be a way of negotiating the gap between what has to be reported and what the spectator knows in a society that is open to no longer pretending the gap does not exist. In the next chapter I offer the discussion of allusions, particularly jocular irony in allusions, and the aim of my further analysis is to describe, contextualize, and interpret contexts with this rhetorical phenomenon.

NOTES

1. Pierre Bourdieu, *Outline of a Theory of Practice* (Cambridge: Cambridge University Press, 1977); Bourdieu, *Language and Symbolic Power* (Harvard: Cambridge University Press 1991), 131–32.

2. Bourdieu, *Outline of a Theory of Practice*, 169.

3. Evgenia Albats, "Citizen and Poet," *Novoe Vremya,* December 26, 2011. http://newtimes.ru/articles/detail/48395/.

4. A profound discussion of his novels is given in a publication by Rosalind Marsh. See discussion in Rosalind Marsh "The 'New Political Novel' by Right-Wing Writers in Post-Soviet Russia," *Forum für osteuropäische Ideen- und Zeitgeschichte* 14, no. 1 (2010): 159–87, http://opus.bath.ac.uk/23134/1/The_New_Political_Novel.pdf.

5. On a particular mode of parody in *The Onion*, see Dominic Boyer and Alexei Yurchak, "American Stiob: Or, What Late-Socialist Aesthetics of Parody Reveal about Contemporary Political Culture in the West," *Cultural Anthropology* 25, no. 2 (2010): 179–221.

6. Links to the episodes can be found at http://ru.wikipedia.org/wiki/%D0%93%D1%80%D0%B0%D0%B6%D0%B4%D0%B0%D0%BD%D0%B8%D0%BD_%D0%BF%D0%BE%D1%8D%D1%82#.D0.A1.D0.BF.D0.B8.D1.81.D0.BE.D0.BA_.D0.B2.D1.8B.D0.BF.D1.83.D1.81.D0.BA.D0.BE.D0.B2.

7. For more about experiments with the organization of visual and verbal images in Pushkin's narrative poems, see Aleksandra Smith's comments on Eisenstein's essay "Montage-Maker," in A. Smith, *Montaging Pushkin: Pushkin and Visions of Modernity in Russian Twentieth-Century Poetry* (Amsterdam/New York: Rodopi, 2006), 330.

8. Anthropologists classify this time as one of liminality, when "the participants in rites of passage are neither in one state nor the other; they are 'betwixt and between' . . . The liminal period epitomizes that which is ambiguous, paradoxical, and anomalous. As a result, things associated with it are often considered unclean, polluting, and dangerous." See the discussion of luminal states in Victor Turner, *The Ritual Process: Structure and Anti-Structure* (Chicago: Aldine, 1969), 95.

Chapter Twelve

Citizen Poet Allusions

The performative discourse created by Dmitry Bykov and Mikhail Efremov presumably rests on the use of the classical allusions permitting the introduction of symbolic subtext. This project is undeniably committed to the goal of mobilizing civil society activists and supporting an alternative social universe in the Russian media landscape. While most of the references would probably require no explanation to a Russian audience, several references, particularly to the Soviet-era popular culture, are less accessible and should be explicated. These ready-to-use familiar phrases and names are subjected to different contextual changes to attain the desired effect. This appears to be a particularly recurring feature of this project. In this chapter, I focus on the linguistic dimension rather than on material medium of parody, and I aim to decipher the discursive means of the parodic discourse.

The following question arose: Should we perceive such digital project as a satire or a mere parody? What does the title of this project bring on? Is it more appropriate to see the title as an oxymoronic juxtaposition of two contradictory social roles—poet and citizen—appearing side-by-side? Or does the title refer back to the nineteenth-century tradition in Nekrasov's civic poetry and to what has become a famous poetic slogan, "It is possible for one not to be a poet, / But one is obliged to be a citizen"? I think the latter is probably the case. The project's title alludes to Nekrasov's tradition, which survived in the Soviet regime, and was represented by Mayakovsky, and later in Evtushenko's poetry. Then it is not by accident that this project includes parodies on Nekrasov, Mayakovsky, and Yevtushenko's verses. Their civic poetry contains optimism for the future and revolutionary zeal. The oratorical expressions and civic pathos of these poets are resound in the episodes "O Zhenskoi Dole" (On woman's lot),[1] "Dvuglavoe" (Doubleheaded),[2] and Ai-padlo.[3]

I suggest taking a look at the episode titles. Sometimes headlines may appear cryptic at first glance, with no apparent symbolic cues. In the analysis that follows, I focus on some examples of these ready-to-use familiar phrases and names to explore the way "the implied reader" (in Iser's terminology) might make sense of the allusions.

The segment that got people talking about this project was a broadcast of the episode "O zhenskoi dole." This easily recognizable set phrase from the famous poem by Nekrasov[4] evokes one of his anthological themes of compassion for the daunting female fate in the time of serfdom and his sincere admiration of woman's dignity and spiritual quality. This allusive headline gives advance notice of the upcoming episode's reference domain. The clip was aired within days after the Russian court employee Natalia Vasilieva[5] publically declared that the second verdict convicting former Russian oil tycoons Mikhail Khodorkovsky and Platon Lebedev had been dictated to her from above.

Another example is a line from Pushkin's *Eugene Onegin* referring to the Italian nationalist revolutionary movement of the nineteenth century that has lost its sense of pathos and has become an ironic reference to the revolution in Egypt and Tunisian events.[6] The episode "Arab Variant,"[7] a parody on Mikhail Lermontov, has been a particular source of amusement, since Efremov appears wearing a dashing Hussar uniform, evidently personifying a veteran of the war of 1812 and repeatedly appealing to Dima, presumably Russian president Dmitry Medvedev—inviting him to consider the historical parallels between two political regimes: of Mubarak and Putin. Dialogical structure of Lermontov's poem is employed to entertain the viewers and presents an unimaginable discussion between a veteran of the war of 1812, who is voicing an opinion of many on the contemporary political situation, and Dima, a political figure, who voiced the position of the Kremlin.

Another of Pushkin's famous headlines, "Demons,"[8] is used as foregrounding, as the authors, by recycling the famous title, call attention to the shift in discourse. In the episode featuring the news that both Putin and Medvedev do not exclude the possibility to run for president in the same elections, Pushkin's rhythm and the repetition of the sounds of his rhyme require only tacit acknowledgment, leaving the audience to analyze potentially enriching connections with the original.

The change in perspective achieved by allusion sounds critical through the ironic overtones in yet another example: the parody on Vladimir Mayakovsky's[9] utopian anthem of 1929, "Here Will Be a Garden-City."[10] This episode has real repercussions to the political anniversary, but it's structurally a farce. It was aired days after Russia marked the twenty-year anniversary of the State Emergency Committee's failed coup in 1991, which attempted to remove perestroika leader Mikhail Gorbachev from power and prevent the collapse of the Soviet Union. The allusive metaphor "город-сад" (garden-city) functions to provide a background reference domain against which to judge main results of perestroika. A parallel is also created between Mayakovsky's futuristic vision of the USSR and Gorbachev's political project.

Another allusion may not be obviously ironic while its comic frame is undeniable. In the imitation of Aleksandr Tvardovsky verse,[11] an allusion to Tvardovsky's[12] characters is retrofitted to comment on Putin's and Medvedev's stage-managed outings. Within the larger framework of a jocular tone, the president and prime pinister are personified as Tvardovsky's new folk heroes, good fellows who wonder how they can "shake things up." The allusion is related to the news about the prime minister and president harvesting corn on a farm, and to the news that Medvedev used the Kremlin video blog to discuss the benefits of playing badminton.

It is obvious that this project's episode titles mostly possess ultimate explanatory power and are revealing of the episode content. However, I came across several titles that contain less visible allusions for "the full-knowing reader" and may receive an opaque allusive reply. It seems to me that among the less transparent and least effective title is "I Was Killed Near Rzhev,"[13] eponymous to Aleksandr Tvardovsky's requiem for the heroes fallen in the World War II. This clip was aired a few days after the murder of former colonel Yuri Budanov[14] and relates to the public ramifications of this murder. A necessary condition, on the part of the reader, for the realization of this allusion is background knowledge of one of the bloodiest battles on the Soviet-German front that occurred in Rhzev,[15] the city that for almost a year was at the front line. While the reader familiar with Russian history may recognize this allusion, the effect of allusion is not revealed to uninformed readers.

In addition to numerous allusions to the titles, references to proper names, or so-called onomastic allusions, are framed in Bykov's parodies (see the discussion on onomastic allusions in chapter 7). By using onomastic allusions the author reinforces the effect of the name, while investing into the character's psychology and defining the character by his purpose.

As one can see, the dialogue in Bykov's spoofs is obvious and open, such as, for example, in the episode related to an open letter that circulated early in 2011, a petition to denounce the pressure placed on Judge Viktor Danilkin by Khodorkovsky's supporters. The episode, "Woe from Wit,"[16] was based on the 1825 play by Alexander Griboedov,[17] and features the old Famusov and his daughter Sofya, who discuss the letter "in defense of medicine," Famusov wrote and insisted on his daughter signing it. In this Bykov parody, Sofya's old boyfriend Chatsky was committed to an asylum after Famusov and Sofya publically declared him insane. Now, with talk of letting Chatsky out, Famusov is concerned about the consequences. The letter was released to the public and signed by fifty-five prominent Russian figures,[18] including TV anchor Tina Kandelaki.[19]

Bykov grotesquely misplaced Griboedov's characters, detached them from their original spatial context, and placed them in the realm of the world Tina Kandelaki inhabits. He skillfully takes advantage of hyperbole, so the real facts acquire fantastic contours, and exposes the identities of those who feel hostility toward Chatsky. By juxtaposing Griboedov's plot to a real-life drama, Bykov reveals the identity of those whose hostility to Khodorkovsky is similar in spirit and nature to that of Chatsky. Not only is there a modification of a basic plot, but also there is a new set of literary code in the foreground.

Bykov and Efremov breathed new life into the old and famous literary names to reinvent classical characters, identifying the emotional triggers of the audience. My next example is drawn from the episode "Otche Nash" (Our Father). Here Kharms's[20] character Ivan Toporyshkin inspires Bykov and Efremov to create an episode related to the decision of a Russian actor and screenwriter as well as a Russian Orthodox priest (though temporarily defrocked from priesthood), Ivan Okhlobystin,[21] to run for presidency. By linking a political trickster, Ivan Okhlobystin, to Kharms's protagonist Ivan Toporyshkin, Bykov introduces the trickster's post-Soviet incarnation. As Mark Lipovetsky[22] claims, tricksters reflect the constant presence of irresolvable contradictions in the Soviet (as well as post-Soviet) social universe and epitomize the realm of cynical culture. His arguments provide a strong framework for the idea that tricksters, be they in mythology, folklore, fiction, or "real" life, are masters of disguise and manipulation; and mediation between the sacred and the profane, as well as between cynical and creative, is indicative of the trickster. The discourse of Okhlobystin, although it has no informational function, serves as a "shortcut to characterization" of a contradictory character that represents not only the cynical and inadequate, but also the creative and playful world. The jargon of Bykov's parody in this spoof is the mixture of the ecclesiastic and secular register and has a symbolic function. The humor is considered to be more grammatical than sociological, but, like so many jokes, it works because it reflects a concealed but easily identifiable social attitude. Of course, the language spoken by Bykov's protagonist is not the real language spoken by Ivan Okhlobystin; however, it is used to index the origin of the character and is presumably associated with a specific target audience.

Not only the famous nineteenth-century classical names are being explored for the present project, but also popular verse and rhyme of Soviet days, including popular children's rhymes. Ironically, while this project has been sponsored by the billionaire owner of the New Jersey Nets, Mikhail Prokhorov, authors have lampooned him in the segment "Diadia Stiopa milliarder" (Billionaire Uncle Styopa),"[23] when he announced plans to form a new liberal party. Mikhalkov's once-popular children's rhyme, "Uncle Styopa policeman,"[24] features the story of the Soviet folk hero who was unusual due to his very large height and unalloyed authenticity. For the uninformed reader, the allusion to Uncle Styopa comprises an ironic commentary on Prokhorov's highly formulaic, almost fake role as a presidential candidate.

While rearrangement and reinterpretation of classical clues—verbal and visual—is the basic principal of parody, at times the plots of episodes challenge the viewer's memory and imagination for detail. At times the plot structure recalls that of the detective genre with the interspersion of clues in the narrative, which the attentive spectator should piece together.

As I mentioned above, while the dialogue with early classical tradition is apparent in Bykov's discourse, the hidden polemics[25] are not so easily recognizable. One of the main features of the hidden polemic, in Bakhtin's view, is "self-deprecating overblown, speech that repudiates itself in advance, speech with a thousand reservations, concessions, loopholes and the like."[26] I argue that devices such as alliteration, assonance and rhythm, alliteration combined with antonymy, and alliteration combined with repetition presented in allusions also reveal the contesting voices within Bykov's discourse.

Another way of punning found in this project is the allusive recycling of biblical expressions, which when reused in a secular context is imbued with a new meaning. In the spoof entitled "Our Father,"[27] which I discussed above, an allusion to the Lord's Prayer "Our Father" is obvious. The title acquires irony within the context of the announcement made by Ivan Okhlobystin on his decision to run for president. In addition to the pun in the episode title, a homographic pun on "Our Father" is created in the text where Ivan Okhlobystin is called "our father," which is actually a term of address for priests and deacons in the Orthodox Church. In his position as a priest, Okhlobystin is also associated with a spiritual father. So figuratively and literally, in signifying precisely the role of the priest in the church, and indicating his profession, this allusion is a pun. While most puns link two contexts, this allusion contains a triple-context pun, and its immediate realization derives from the simultaneous presence of multiple and disparate meanings. The comic effect of this pun comes from the perception of incongruity released in this situation.

Other instances of wordplay in the project require more interpretative work on the part of the audience. From a reader-oriented pragmatic perspective, the allusion functions to alert the reader to the issue raised by the text. The dual function of the allusion, namely, to envelop information in a particular frame and to entertain, is part of a larger trend in contemporary media, which use various elements of popular journalism, in particular the presentation of news in personalized, emotional language with techniques similar to those in advertising. The duality suggested by the allusion creates triggers that target the audience. In this respect, allusion has a rhetorical function intended to remove the reader's neutral attitude to the information. This involves certain presuppositions related to the reader, his or her background knowledge and expectations.

Let me show an allusion that was performed by means of lexical substitution combined with punning on the substituted word. I am talking about Seligerishche,[28] which alludes to the Chukovskys poem "Tarakanishche" (The monster cockroach)[29] and echoes Lake Seliger.[30] Bykov wrote a burlesque remake of a classical poem with dystopian overtones. He starts with a phrase "Once upon a time there lived a crocodile," and every viewer immediately recognizes Chukovsky's rhyming language suited to rote learning and recalls his humorous story about crocodile. So, these allusions result directly from the use of sound consonance. However, as Bykov continues, we hear that the crocodile led gopota. The word "gopota" is not a clever poet's invention, but rather it comes, as so many argo Russian words do, from an acronym: Gosudarstvenoe Obshchezhitie Proletariata, or State Dormitory of the Proletariat, and while it is difficult to translate it literally, it can be rendered in English as the "Russian lower class and youth from the criminal regions of Moscow, who were controlled by the local mafias." The episode, based on Chukovsky's poem was a response to the emblematic case of *Kommersant*'s special correspondent and blogger Oleg Kashin,[31] who suffered a fractured skull after being beaten with iron bars. The title of the episode is referring to the camp at Lake Seliger, which since 2005 has been sponsored by Nashi. To envelope the plot of the episode one should be aware of the further development of the plot. In June Kashin was sued for defamation when he said that he suspected Vasily Yakimenko, head of the Nashi youth movement, was involved in the attack. Thus Bykov focused on this story and once again confronted his audience with the use of iffy slang not only due to its powerfully metaphoric effect, but also for vernacular voices to be heard that result in a dramatic effect of the presence of lay speakers in the mythological realm of the children rhyme.

I am particularly interested in the instances of transgressive language in the alternative discourse to bring out the analysis of the hidden polemics through the forms of indirect language, with new word formation as one of its features. Bykov reflects on the widespread practice in the Russian satirical media of the past few years, the phenomenon of deviation from the perceived normative word formation and drifting into the domain of popular laughter culture. There are mixed motives for this kind of "linguistic creativity."

Examining alternative discourse of the project *Citizen Poet* it is not hard to identify the poetical practice of deviation from the perceived normative word formation in order to create words/concepts pertaining to the "the poetry of everyday language" or, in other words, iffy slang. One can observe the destabilization of word-related stereotypes, in other terms, words seem to have lost their connotations and function as materialized metaphors.

One of the episodes, titled "Citadel," was based on the eponymous film by prominent film director Nikita Mikhalkov. The episode aired on the occasion of film nominations for the 2012 Oscar awards. The nomination caused a lot of controversy, as the film drew mostly negative reviews and flopped at the box office. Bykov based his text on Sergey Esenin's erotic poem "Shagane, You Are My Shagane!" Bykov's parody follows the meter, rhyme, and rhythm of the original poem while suggesting a trajectory of critical engagement, where the original classic example is nothing but a pretext, the formula on which the account on a current event depends, and conjures up the original poem in a humorous way. Bykov uses Esenin's line to make a wordplay. One stanza in Bykov's text ends in the refrain "Citadel, You are my citadel." Yet another stanza ends in the refrain where the word "похабель," derived from "похабный" meaning "bawdy" appears. As obscene as it seems, it also an anagrammatic wordplay, based on similarity between the words "citadel" and "*pokhabel'*." Interestingly, the word "*pokhabel'*" does not exist, so the listner presupposes to replace this invented word with the word "похабщина" rendered in English as crudeness and obscenity. In the next stanza that ends in "Пошехонь ты моя, Пошехонь" Bykov is referring to Mikhail Saltykov-Shchedrin's novel *The Old Times of Poshekhona*, where the name of the area in nineteenth-century Russia is the embodiment of wild tyranny and a symbol of violence and oppression.

For example, a vulgar linguistic metaphor—*derma naest'sia* or *nakhlebat'sia*, which implies a deviation from the perceived norm in order to generate a keen satiric grotesque with application of a salty expression.

The carnavalistic orientation of alternative discourse is manifested in its use of such prefab elements of official public discourse as formulaic phrases, slogans, characters of popular fiction, and quotations from mass literature. This project engenders a new cultural discourse. Cultural producers and web practitioners deploy the ideological potentialities of the traditional styles and genres in an attempt to mold a national community through production and dissemination of critical discourse, which comprises a "cultural politics" and an "aesthetic ideology" to apply the concepts of Michel Denning.[32] His political verses with moralizing messages are examples of a special kind of genre that I would call fairy-talish skaz. I would like to suggest that Bykov—perhaps unwillingly—uses *skaz* (see the discussion on *skaz* in chapter 10) as an alternative narrative. Much has been written on the function of fairy-talish motives and genre itself in the Soviet discourse. In a discussion of the coexistence of mythological and fairy-talish motives in the language that the Soviet power used to communicate with the people, Mark Lipovetsky points out that "fairy-tales actually offer probably the most democratic cultural code, which hardly requires any preparation in order to be understood."[33] The most important value of this genre lies in the fact that it is appealing to an *adult* audience and caters openly moralizing messages. Some examples I discuss in this chapter are not proper quotations or allusions but rather linguistic hybrids that I tend to identify as instances of what in Russian is labeled *skaz*. This term designates a type of writing that imitates the form of an individual oral narrator. It has no equivalent in English. Since *skaz* admits a recognized degree of illogical statements, hyperbole, humor, and the like, it has become a kind of critical panacea employed in political debates. It seems that journalists feel uncomfortable saying or characterizing things directly. Though the journalist's judgmental stance may be quite clear and his or her critical attitude rather transparent, she or he can employ another personage as a cover through which to make accusatory comments. The crucial factor in *skaz*, as Irwin Titunik emphasizes, is not only that "another's speech is manipulated by the author but that the author's speech itself is manipulated as well. At the basis of *skaz* lie a reciprocal relationship, an interpenetration and interaction of both these speech contexts."[34] The link between the "author's" usage and the "alien" prototype can take the form of literal identification or figurative conceptualization.

Skaz allows him to represent more than one viewpoint, because his protagonist often renarrates the speech of others, telling readers what someone said on a specific occasion. The essential of *skaz* is not that an author transmits another's speech correctly, but that the protagonist appropriates the voices of the Other, reworking them for new purpose, and provides a cohesive and consistent hierarchy of voices through which readers can make secure judgments regarding characters, can postulate the intentions of the author, and can come to some conclusion as to the nature of reporting. The author of the text—Dmitry Bykov—deployed culturally familiar styles and identities that are marked as deviated from usually neutral literary voices to generate a keen sarcastic context. Stylization of different voices involves performing first-person personas by phonological and related means, such as salty expressions or taboo language, and implying a deviation from the perceived norm in order to reconsider the cultural and new authentic discourse. Instead of creating tension, the narrator directs the viewers' attention to the production that was designed by mockery.

Their peculiar satirical project, which I label (albeit provisionally) "performative livejournal," reflects an analytic interpretation of the political landscape, value judgment, and semiotic models of social behavior. The series resembles a sequence of journal entries, stressing life as a process, and emphasizing the unfinished character of the described events. Semiotic model of contemporary consciousness meets the fundamental human need to interpret life's experiences and reveals itself in the mechanism of everyday conversation—people idly chatting, bragging, gossiping embedded in Bykov's text. The functional versatility of speech genres demonstrates the presence of the various interpreting voices. Bykov's narrators present themselves as all knowing, possessing a particular kind of non-objective omniscience and typical human unreliability of judgment characteristic of a neighborhood gossip. Gossip becomes a vehicle for reporting about current events by identifying the vicissitudes of an individual's life to the bigger picture of national upheavals and the spreading of unsubstantiated rumor to the writing of history.

In turning to the Internet audience, web practitioners produce statements of their philosophical and aesthetic credo in forms most suitable for their genre, including stiob, burlesque, and buffoonery. This discourse intrigues us as a living political history with classic literature as both reservoir and reference points for the circulation of the words of the Other. It seems that the authors of this project echoed mass-mediated discourse around the current events relying on a verbal criticism and rebuke. The social circulation of phrases and discourse styles extracted from the literary text and then recycled and reanimated in contemporary discourse, outside of their context, is essential for the production of shared meaning because it creates a sort of "public accessibility."[35]

NOTES

1. See www.youtube.com/watch?v=FwhULXuNxdQ.
2. See www.youtube.com/watch?v=7lwVrE47_b0.
3. See www.youtube.com/watch?v=qR3XnyNwatg&feature=related.
4. Nikolai Nekrasov (1821–1878) was a prominent Russian poet and editor-in-chief of the journal *The Contemporary* (founded by Pushkin in 1836). Throughout his work the fate of women is a constant concern. He learned love of poetry and awareness of the plight of the peasant from his mother. The radically oriented "thick" journal became the most respected of the time, publishing Dostoevsky, Tolstoy, Turgenev, and Chernyshevsky, among others. He is the author of "Riding to the Hounds," a satiric idyll that is critical of the violence of the hunter. His most important poem, "Who Is Happy in Russia," functions as an encyclopedia of peasant life and stands out among his lesser later works, written in a stylized folk verse style.
5. Under Russian law, it is for the judge alone to write his verdict, without any interference by other members of the judiciary. An aide to the Russian judge who convicted Mikhail Khodorkovsky at his second trial last year, Natalia Vasilieva, has said he did not write his own verdict. Judge Viktor Danilkin resented having to take orders from above during the trial of the former tycoon, Natalya Vasilyeva told Russian media. However, the judge denied her allegations, describing them as slander. According to Vasilyeva, Judge Danilkin was indignant at having to take orders and was anxious and irritable because of it.
6. Tunisian unrest was a series of ongoing protests in the streets of Tunisia in December 2010–January 2011. The Egyptian Revolution of 2011 took place following a popular uprising that began on January 25, 2011. It was a diverse movement of demonstrations, marches, plaza occupations, riots, non-violent civil resistance, acts of civil disobedience, and labor strikes. Millions of protesters from a variety of socioeconomic and religious backgrounds demanded the overthrow of the regime of Egyptian president Hosni Mubarak. Part of the Arab Spring, the Egyptian revolution, along with Tunisian events, has influenced demonstrations in other Arab countries including Yemen, Bahrain, Jordan, Syria, and Libya.
7. See www.youtube.com/watch?v=UoSbhVHu73Q&list=PL82BB4FB05D0A2170.
8. See www.youtube.com/watch?v=2qYeBIlKbjE.
9. The cult and mythology built around Mayakovsky after his suicide in 1930 emerged from the Stalin regime's need for a cult figure with the roots in the revolutionary period. Mayakovsky's image was firmly linked with the avant-garde experience of the 1920s, and the Mayakovsky legend was crafted for the purposes of Soviet cultural and political policy after

1935. This legend required fundamental distortions of his poetic project and biography to correspond to the needs of Soviet imperial patriotism, expressed in literary terms in the doctrines of Socialist Realism. In caricatured form, Mayakovsky became a feature not merely of intellectual life but of ordinary life and popular culture. During the glasnost era the Mayakovsky museum was recreated in 1989, at a time when a new interest in the poet, though mostly negative, was at its peak, Mayakovsky was mostly blamed for the artistic utopianism of the Russian avant-garde for Stalin's terror. In post-Soviet Russia he would take on new contemporary relevance, although there is still insufficient research on one of the founders of avant-garde art, nonconformist and psychedelic.

10. See www.youtube.com/watch?v=8BBdhgu2KKM&list=PLdkRu6lsGvYCBVTtaKaR1kNiM_wyiViH_.

11. See at www.youtube.com/watch?v=Tg0kZcECa9c.

12. Tvardovsky's *Vasili Tyorkin* was perhaps the most popular work of literature among Soviet soldiers during the Great Patriotic War. It was surprisingly non-politicized, down-to-earth, and intentionally devoid of any picturesque heroism. It was printed chapter by chapter and immediately sent to the front in newspapers and magazines as well as read over the radio by Dmitry Orlov. Tvardovsky was awarded his second Stalin Prize for *Vasili Tyorkin.* Appearing in installments between 1942 and 1945, it presented a new folk hero who was everything a Soviet soldier could ever hope to be—clever, witty, inventive, thoughtful, resourceful, dependable, courageous, loveable, fun-loving, and calm under fire. Under his liberal editorship (1958–1970), *Novyi Mir* was the first to publish Solzhenitsyn's novels *One Day in the Life of Ivan Denisovich* and *Cancer Ward.*

13. See www.youtube.com/watch?v=MjqvIYnlNjs&list=PL82BB4FB05D0A2170.

14. Russian colonel Yuri Budanov, a former tank commander in the war in Chechnya, was jailed for ten years in 2003 for the kidnapping and killing three years earlier of Elza Kungayeva, eighteen in 2000, but was controversially released on parole in 2009. He was the most notorious of a handful of officers to face justice for the wars in the Muslim region in southern Russia, where two wars raged in the 1990s and early 2000s after separatists clashed with federal forces. In 2011 he was gunned down in Moscow.

15. "Rzhev Battles" is a general term for a series of World War II offensives known for its huge losses. This part of the Great Patriotic War was poorly covered by Soviet military historiography and what coverage exists occurred only after the dissolution of the Soviet Union, when historians gained access to relevant documents. Exact dates of particular battles, their names, outcomes, significance, and even losses have not been fully clarified.

16. See www.youtube.com/watch?v=g9-u3CGSvgc.

17. Alexander Griboedov (1795–1829) was a person of outstanding ability. He entered Moscow University at the age of eleven, and by sixteen he had successfully completed the literary, law, and natural science and mathematical faculties, learned French, German, English, and Italian, and was preparing to defend his doctorate. The Napoleonic invasion of 1812 interrupted these peaceful scholarly endeavors, and he never returned to them. Anxious to leave St. Petersburg, Griboedov commenced his diplomatic career in 1818 as first secretary of the Russian embassy in Persia. The young diplomat quickly learned Arabic and Persian and acquired remarkable erudition in the area of Middle Eastern cultures. On January 30, 1829, an enraged mob, urged on by fanatic mullahs and with the tacit encouragement of the government, invaded the Russian embassy and slaughtered all the Russian representatives (only one survived by chance). Griboedov perished in that bloody episode as he bravely and calmly fought to the end. *Woe from Wit* is Griboedov's greatest literary achievement. The play was published in 1833, but with cuts; the full text became available only in 1861. One of the most brilliant classics of the Russian stage, the comedy's greatest appeal lies in the naturalness and pithiness of its dialogue and the sparkling liveliness of its. Within the confines of a single setting—the Famusov home—and a twenty-four-hour time frame, *Woe from Wit* presents an unflattering picture of contemporary Moscow society dominated by political and cultural conservatives afraid of change and stubbornly resistant to it. Returning to this society is an angry young man named Chatsky, who quickly recognizes his estrangement from it and the hopelessness of any reconciliation. He becomes outspokenly critical of everything around him and is ultimately compelled to run away.

18. "Letter 55" is an appeal directed against the information to undermine confidence and trust in the judicial system in Russia. Among those fifty-five public representatives who signed the letter, there were a few doctors, guardians, members of the party United Russia, and people sympathetic to the Kremlin power. The letter in defense of the judicial system of the pressure came to light shortly after the speech spokesman Hamovnichesky court Natalia Vassilieva said that the second sentence in the "Yukos case" was not written by Judge Victor Danilkin, and in the Moscow City Court. Many perceived this letter as an attack on Natalia Vasilieva and others for casting aspersions on Russian jurisprudence in the wake of the Khodorkovsky trial and the Vasilieva interview

19. Tina Kandelaki is an extremely popular Russian journalist, public figure, TV presenter, and producer, who not especially hides her friendship with statesman Vladislav Surkov. In 2008–2009 she hosted one of the most popular talk shows, *Unreal Politics*, which was aired on NTV. The show started as an experimental online project, and in time *Unreal Politics* turned into a Russian TV show with celebrity guests from politics, business, and entertainment. In 2011 Tina signed "Letter 55," which condemned the pressure put on the judicial system during the trials against the heads of the Yukos Oil Company.

20. Daniil Kharms (pen-name of Daniil Ivanovich Iuvachev) is a poet and black humorist, creator of Russia's literature of absurd, eccentric, and often grotesque stories. In most of his stories the plots seem perverse and arbitrary. He was one of the founders of Oberiu (Association of Real Art), a group that was active between 1927 and 1930. His great poetic versatility and absurdist playfulness is still regarded as fresh and compelling. He obtained relatively little attention for his hilarious stories and verses cast in an appropriate style with striking imagery and grotesque during his lifetime. As an absurdist author he captured the surreal, illogical life of the society where widespread theft, bribery, and corruption conflict with the declared ideals of socialism. Between 1928 and 1930 in the public house ZIL appeared about twenty poems and short stories written by Kharms, including "Ivan Ivanovich Samovar," "Ivan Toporyshkin," and so on. By the 1930s Kharms was unable to publish his poetry as there was no tolerance in the USSR for avant-garde, provocative works, and he made a living as a writer of children's literature. His works were passed from hand to hand after his disappearance in 1941. He died in a prison asylum in 1942. Unsurprisingly, in official Soviet reference, his works are put down as works for children, and he remained largely unknown or misunderstood for the usual ideological reasons. After perestroika he became known as an innovative author, appreciated by many and internationally recognized.

21. Ivan Okhlobystin, a Russian actor and screenwriter and also a Russian Orthodox priest, announced that he would run for the presidency. The news came as a big surprise for both members of a secular society and the clergy. The Russian Orthodox Church and the Central Election Commission got involved in hot debates on whether a priest can join a presidential race, while the country's prominent politicians shared their views on Okhlobystin's candidacy.

22. Mark Lipovetsky, *Charms of the Cynical Reason* (Brighton, MA: Academic Studies Press, 2011).

23. See www.youtube.com/watch?v=fNEEQzAioV8.

24. Sergei Mikhalkov is known as the leading Soviet children's author, and as a poet who managed to create three revisions on national anthems of the Soviet Union and Russian Federation. Starting in 1933 the young poet was constantly present in the most reputable Soviet papers and magazines. But a real boost to his career happened when he published the love poem "Svetlana," which was read by Stalin, liked by the dictator, and mistakenly taken by him as a dedication to his daughter, Svetlana Stalina. Soon after that Mikhalkov was offered all kinds of support in his creative work. "Uncle Styopa" is Mikhalkov's trademark and the character known by literally everyone in the Soviet Union.

25. This notion of "hidden polemics" as part of a process of cultural reproduction is examined in S. Malykhina, "Rechevye strategii v polemicheskikh zhanrakh sovremennogo nauchnogo diskursa. Visnyk Kharkivskogo derzhavnogo universitetu.V.411. Spadshchyna D. M. Ovsianyko-Kulikovskogo ta suchasna filologiia" (Kharkiv, Ukraine, 1998), 412–19.

26. Mikhail Bakhtin, *Problems of Dostoevsky's Poetics*, ed. and trans. Caryl Emerson (Minneapolis: University of Minnesota Press, 1999), 196.

27. See www.youtube.com/watch?v=QZfFGqmRyvU&feature=related.

28. See www.youtube.com/watch?v=9M4o-iRkGF4.

29. Widely read children's poet Kornei Chukovsky excelled in mordant satire of the Soviet regime veiled by a naive facade. His "Tarakanishche" depicts a red mustachioed insect terrorizing the animal kingdom. Perhaps the only reason Chukovsky was not shot outright was because the caricature was too brazen. Just recognizing Josef Stalin in the self-important cockroach would have spelled a death sentence for his accusers as well.

30. Seliger is a place, built on the model of Soviet summer camps like Artek, which were both rewards for Party loyalty and sites of communist indoctrination. It is run by Nashi, an organization created in 2005, after pro-Western color revolutions swept former Soviet republics and terrified the Kremlin, to provide political training for Russian youth. The camp, like other Nashi projects, is funded by the state, and Russian businesses cover the rest.

31. Oleg Kashin, an anti-Kremlin journalist, had been writing about, among other subjects, nationalism and the ideology of the pro-Putin youth movement, as well as Nashi.

32. Michael Denning, *The Cultural Front: The Laboring of American Culture in the Twentieth Century* (London: Verso, 1997) .

33. Mark Lipovetsky, "Skazkovlast': Tarakanishche Stalina," *NPO*, no. 45 (2000), www.chukfamily.ru/Kornei/Biblio/lipovetskiy.htm.

34. I. R. Titunik, "The Problem of Skaz (Critique and Theory)," in *Papers in Slavic Philology* 5, no. 1 (1977): 290.

35. Greg Urban, *A Discourse-Centered Approach to Culture: Native South American Myths and Rituals* (Austin: University of Texas Press, 1991), 10, 27, 191.

Conclusion

As stated previously, there is a strong continuity in the media style between the Soviet and post-Soviet periods. The question of how to understand allusion is linked to two aspects mentioned above: first, the status and the subject matter of allusion, and second, the rhetorical means of their representation. The possible cognitive aspect of allusion has often been ignored, not without reason, it seems, since it has proven to be rather problematic to describe and analyze.

The Russian media, like the American one, and like media elsewhere, are full of allusions. I am trying to find specifics that, due to the cultural and political circumstances in Russia, demonstrate the particular mode of writing practice.

First, I would like to mention that the cultural space or status occupied by this sort of linguistic device in the Western media discourse as opposed to the Russian press is not necessarily the same, and in this respect the question of readership and attitude toward the printed word becomes key. Of course, it is not enough to point to this difference. The problem comes when we try to determine what is so different between the ways Russian and Western journalists tell the news stories. One possible difference in the usage of allusions in the Russian media is different standards of journalism. Communication studies compare the opinion-driven journalism led by political attitudes or ideological stances in the modern-day Russia and the Western model of fact-based journalism. In my data I have singled out these types of examples to demonstrate yet another feature of news reporting: the practice of addressing issues at a highly philosophical level, using abundant literary tropes as rhetorical devices. This characteristic of news stories can be dated back to the eighteenth century, when literature and journalism in Russia arose together.

In my study I examined plenty of headlines that have highly aphoristic potential. First, the aphorism as such does not exist as a distinct category or genre in Anglophone culture. You do not, for example, have published collections of aphorisms in the way that you do in Russia. Although, Anglophone media, like the media elsewhere, are full of assorted sayings (real or apocryphal), *obiter dicta,* or catchphrases and the like, many of which can be described as aphoristic in nature, more catchphrases probably come from popular culture (radio and TV shows) and children's literature. In the Western media no matter how much political folk-wisdom these sayings may contain, in general, it is believed that any wit, wisdom, or humor these sayings contain is lost through endless repetition. Indeed, I think the whole point of these sayings is that they are capable of infinite recycling. This is perhaps why they appear more often than sayings taken from sources conventionally perceived as witty. One of the devices that is particularly characteristic of the Russian press and rare in the American media is the widespread use of circumlocution and puns in headlines. Indeed, and the punning headline is an art form in American newspapers, although not in the quality media. I suspect that most Western editors would remove them instantly, for the latter are more tied to a particular context and therefore more resistant to being reused elsewhere.

Another difference between Russian and Western public discourse is the rhetorical practice and modes of their respective philosophical influences. Russian journalism demonstrates the practice of addressing issues in news reporting at a highly philosophical level, using abundant literary tropes as rhetorical devices. This characteristic of news stories dates back to the eighteenth century, when literature and journalism in Russia sprang up together. If such is the case, substantive difference can be explained by the attitude to the traditions of the Russian philosophy of language. In the Russian culture the word is understood not only as the symbol used in communication, but also (and primarily) as the carrier of ideas and creative energy. The central position of the word is reflected in the works of Trubetskoi, Bakhtin, as well as works of Lossky, Losev, Florensky, Potebnia.[1] The ontological value of the word has been recognized and repeatedly mentioned in Russian literature (by Pushkin, Gogol, Mandelshtam, Akhmatova, just to name a few). It is important to acknowledge that the two types of journalism—Russian and Western—speak in different voices that adopt observational or inferential stances, dwell in different domains, and are directed to different audiences. Of course, the distinction in the domain of ideological differences is apparent, but also is the separation in linguistic domain, namely the semantic discrepancy between Russian and Western humanities.

Historically, Russian journalism was an integral part of the overall literary process. In the nineteenth century, those whom we now refer to as journalists were writers, authors of fiction, poems, satire, literary criticism, and also acted as press observers. Nikolai Polevoy, Nikolai Nekrasov, Alexander Herzen, Mikhail Saltykov-Shchedrin, Fedor Dostoevsky are a few such figures who confound, who repeatedly aligned themselves with the journalistic (publitsistica) tradition and were often highly critical of society and government. The differentiation of writers and journalists really occurred only in the twentieth century with the development of the mass information market and growth of audiences. Having analyzed "Soviet public culture" (first and foremost the Soviet press), Jeffrey Brooks posed a question how it could happen that a highly educated people that had reached such heights in science and culture became so stupefied by propaganda. Unable to believe that all this can be attributed to "lies" and "censorship," Brooks concludes that the "full answer lies in the function of the press in creating a stylized, ritualistic, and intentionally consistent public culture that became its own reality and supplanted other forms of public reflection and explanation."[2]

There is another important, but usually neglected feature of post-Soviet journalism that is the crucial control of the newspaper text by journalists. While none of the top exponents of Soviet journalism remain in major Russian publications today, we still can see some trends of post-Soviet media. Appealing to ideas the reader is already familiar with, journalists provide implicit and interpretive messages, which lend meaning, coherence, and ready explanations for complex issues. Therefore, the use of allusions as part of culture that greatly circulate in public picked up by the news media for strategic purpose may also be a way of negotiating the gap between what has to be reported and can be banned by the censorship and what the reader knows and it is no longer possible to pretend that the gap does not exist.

Thus, in my analysis I explore the role and functions of allusions that come to be compelling means of argumentation in the contemporary Russian media. Allusive references are always evocative and suggestive. Journalists' particular strategies and textual choices can only be understood in establishing ritualistic function of allusion. In my view, the aspects of ritual listed in Victor Turner's analyses of the capacity of ritual to create what he calls *communitas*, and defines as a force that breaks down the boundaries that separate people.[3] Also highly relevant to the ritualistic function of allusion are its two main characteristics: repetition and authority. The constant reference to a familiar line, repetition of and variations on well-known text, clearly contribute to a sense of community. The authority of the writer's name is, without doubt, of crucial importance. The linking of common idea with a reference to authoritative values is certainly relevant also to the ritualistic function of allusion. A journalist is one who tries to establish a sense of community centered on particular values recognized by the readers.

Allusions in the headlines and the bodies of articles appear to be a particularly recurring feature of contemporary media. The use of allusions in objective mainstream journalism in a culture where for decades readers, in their search for identity, were urged to look to the classics, is not surprising. In many respects, the use of allusions in current Russian media resembles the previous stages of the development of Western media. One possible area of difference, however, is the source of these allusions. Most of the catchphrases in Western media come from popular culture, including children's literature, rather than from the classics. Another interesting observation, which John Dunn offered to me, is that most of catchphrases of the 1960s are now largely forgotten. In the West, it is believed that generally any wit, wisdom, or humor these catchphrases and folk sayings contain is lost through endless repetition. In Russia, on the contrary, it is believed that modern philosophers share the same philosophy, the same values, and the same worldviews, and thus through the poetic veil of classical ideas and plots we can see that of contemporary ones, as if Russian classics might offer magical ways out of the complex problems of society. Thus the aesthetic paradigm of the Russian classical tradition is exceptionally conducive for mythologizing and retranslation in the public discourse. Classical allusions, therefore, draw from sources conventionally perceived as witty, which supports the belief that contemporary ideas have a philosophical lineage that goes beyond twentieth-century history and back to Russian thinkers of the mid-nineteenth century, or even to the earlier myths. While there is a clear parallel, one makes an unwarranted leap in claiming that the values and worldviews of mid-nineteenth-century Russia and contemporary Russia are the same.

This way of communication is an opportunity for complicit transaction: the journalist shows off his wide range of reference while the reader gets the pleasure of recognizing the source. It should be noted, however, that the allusions in contemporary discourse may mystify readers in the way their Soviet precursors never did. First to bring allusions to mainstream media was gutty media, and its block was typically aimed toward younger audiences. The intention of journalists communicating in this fashion was to promote the classics from a typical school curriculum, ensuring the allusions are for mass readers, and marketed them as such.

In many respects, the concept of the reader is the starting point for my discussion of allusion. In an interesting study on "the state reader" Evgeny Dobrenko convincingly proves that the Soviet reader's reception was shaped by the Soviet aesthetics imposed on the average literature consumer.[4] In addition, Petr Vail' and Aleksandr Genis have outlined the model of the "nostalgically idealized reader" whom the authors constructed.[5] On top of that, Katriona Kelly detailed a wide-ranging account of a variety of literary genres in pre-revolutionary Russia, as well as in the USSR, and post-communist Russia stimulates an interest to explore the role of the reader in the diverse types of the cultural production.[6]

However different these approaches are, nonetheless they provide a relevant framework for my study. I apply Iser's[7] concepts of the implied reader, focused first on the ability to interpret the cultural and historical context, and then make relevant the changes happening in identity formation. The analysis of allusions shows how knowledge of the Russian cultural context facilitates recognition of allusions in media of both types: official and alternative. While the reader familiar with the Russian cultural context may recognize the allusions, the effect of allusion is not revealed to uninformed readers.

Where the typical literary allusion seeks the fantasy world provided by it, the allusion in media deals with a very different situation. In other words, to truly understand the purpose of the allusion the reader may need to restore the whole inferential chain by using the background knowledge and presupposition data, which, in essence, is the skill of reading between the lines. The media text sometimes allows omitting of the allusion to preserve the "general" information without giving much concern to what is alluded. The journalist can talk about the abstract or the political in a form that is both enigmatically poetic and simply personal, yet it results in having the reader choose which level of interpretation is the best to pursue. Allowing for a range of reader receptions, allusions are never neutral or informative. In media discourse, these properties of allusions are eventually rejected in favor of the polemical or ironic. It appears that journalists employ different rhetorical strategies, including irony for different audiences, elevating rhetoric above politics and thus placing the publicist above newsmaker.

Significantly, one of allusion's most important features as a figure of speech is amplification, which, to a certain extent, is used to increase the rhetorical effect of a journalistic text. But this characteristic should not lead us to regard the allusion as being deprived of content or meaning and helping to embellish or smooth out a journalistic narrative. Generally, *amplificatio* is regarded by Aristotle primarily as a form of argumentation, not as mere ornament. Within the journalistic context, rhetorical amplification must be understood here not solely as a stylistic device, but as an essential constituent of making an allusion visible and meaningful to the reader. It is not my intention to imply any direct link between rhetorical theory of Aristotle and contemporary media discourse; however, the persuasive aspect of media is evident from a functional point of view and has been studied extensively. I would argue that once an allusion becomes an invaluable reference point in the context, it is meant to evoke a response in the readers. This response is more closely linked to the subject matter of an article. After all, a good allusion makes a forceful association, strong connections that reinterpret an event or an issue emphasized by a journalist. It is quite clear, however, that allusion that focuses instead on the rhetorical effect, and has itself an amplificatory aim with no or little connection with the context, remains irrelevant. For such allusions I propose a distinction. In some articles an allusion is used in a certain mode that has sought to minimize the connection with a context, downplay the question of journalist accountability, and hence, displace the whole point of allusiveness to somewhat peripheral to the overall context. Using an allusion the journalist must either engage and affiliate with the ideas reconstituted by allusion, or disavow and resort to what I called "allusive fetishism." "Allusive fetishism" begins with intactness, or expungement of the traces of origin. Allusive fetishism posits a framing device that simulates the new understanding, but releases the journalist from the burden of affiliation. Allusive fetishism is a political, moralizing strategy of framing, one that exculpates the narrator, and reader, from complicity. As a strategy it transforms the modernist event into a traditional one, available to representation in conventional terms.

Much of my argument demonstrates the fluidity of allusions before, during, and after their contextualization, suggesting that the audience does gain agency in shaping meaning of allusion within the media discourse. Due to the ambiguous nature of allusions, I follow the well-established tradition to describe and analyze them (Lennon, Allan H. Pasco, Josef Michael Pucci, Oleg Lekmanov) rather than classify them. I specifically focus on the allusions in the headlines and in the body of the articles and analyze allusions in official and alternative discourses. Even though I have limited my subject to one aspect of an allusion's integration into the media text, it embraces an enormous corpus. The combination of basic factors within allusion—knowledge of scripts and clichés, the ability to restore the inferential chain incorporated in allusion—enables readers to perceive an allusion more adequately.

Allusions in texts disrupt the linearity of the text and call attention to the appearance of the Other in the body of the article. Allusions allow the journalist to enliven a text by introducing an elaboration or a note of irony, though they also offer a way to use certain political or folk wisdom in a more aphoristic way. It appears that classical dogmas have long since become common currency, but names of classical writers are hardly ever mentioned. While allusive discourse depends upon the popular quotes, I have noted the tendency to underlie mostly the general ideas by means of the allusions and stretch out the detailed narrative of the media texts with limited connections to the social reality. It is a rare case when a journalist or editor copies discourse of the Other; most of the time we observe the transition in style and in tone from the alluded source to that of a journalist's own style. Thus, in any particular instance where the usage of the words of the Other is observed, it is significant what attitude a journalist assumes while s/he repeats the statements of the Other, investing it with new values and accenting them in his/her own way—with expressions of irony, mockery, ridicule, doubt, or indignation. It appears that deployment of allusions in both official and alternative discourse depends on a specific model and this model is highly subjective.

The post-Soviet public and media discourses are populated by ironic allusions or mere glancing references to the classical characters that seem to embody specific meaningful similarities to the facts of the contemporary life. Instead, allusions with built-in deprecatory biases tend to "unsettle all doxa, all accepted beliefs and ideologies."[8] Since journalists in state-sanctioned Russian newspapers can hardly be allowed to be pluralistic and competitive, they have found alternative ways to show readers the disparities between official mythology and the facts of everyday life. Nevertheless, the allusions as the Other's apt verbal expressions and ironic play with society's contradictions mostly remain indifferent to the context of political discourse.

This is especially the case for headlines, where pressure for brevity motivates the use of an allusion, which quickly creates a larger cognitive framework. Both official and alternative media are full of allusive headlines. However, for the example of allusive headlines, it is clear that allusions are not quite obvious in the headlines themselves. As we try to understand this headline dialogically with respect to a speaker's position, we can look to the socio-moral positioning, which is essential to the meaning. Although a journalist's judgmental stance is quite clear, we cannot be sure what a journalistic orientation toward this piece of information is. Does he use this phrase in a straightforward way? Does he use the phrase instead in a mocking or ironic way, and thus place himself against those who use the phrase merely referentially? Does he sarcastically mimic someone's dismissive attitude? These questions describe a rudimentary dialogue opened by this one phrase. In other words, we cannot fully understand the content a journalist communicates without taking into account various aspects of the interactional event in which it occurs. What is projected by the headline is apparently subverted. Yet it is only in its sequential context that the headline can be seen as an alternative story. Analysis of the material shows that such interpolated references may shape profoundly a journalist's tongue-in-cheek approach. A mixture of expressions that are part the journalist's own and part someone else's characterizes this alternative world proposed by the author's standpoint. Thus the headline functions as an editorial addition that may be read with amusement and through which readers may access the author's point of view.

No doubt, most media sources in Russia can be sharply criticized for very bland coverage of serious problems or for using surreal stories to hide or exclude problematic issues. But public discourse full of sarcastic jokes and pop references exhibit ironic tendencies and provoke the mode of journalism where indirect speaking prevails. If a public discourse does not directly exhibit ironic tendencies, and official media is relatively irony-free, alternative media has undoubtedly helped certain ironic sensibility to flourish, while irony signals a combative stance against authority. Ironical mode of liberal journalism is certainly a provisional answer to the seriousness of the official, state-run news reporting. The culture of ironic criticism undermines the spirit of not only individuals in public roles but also those who read about them, who become afraid to believe in anyone or anything because the next story may tell them why they should not do so. It is appropriate to ask: Is it possible to identify irony as a concept, or is it more reasonable to discuss specific instances, where a journalist has used another's discourse to convey aspirations that are hostile to it? A hidden or obvious irony in any concrete instance radically changes the semantics of the discourse of the Other.

Alongside its referential meaning appears the journalist's intentional orientation toward someone else's words. So, the resemblance to a specific model in applying allusions in media discourse is more of a diversionary, misleading game rather than a parodic replication. I still do not solve the dilemma: either a journalist consciously selects an allusion to integrate into his or her own discourse, or he or she is unconscious of the ambiguity in the allusion that becomes part of the reading experience. The readers who are not familiar with the original verses or lines do not grab hold of the possible interpretation and remain blind to their hidden meanings of classical lines in the contemporary media text. While it seems that allusion addresses real issues, in terms of their rhetorical effect in the journalistic writing, they are a "value-free, decorative"[9] tool rather than a call to evaluate a problem. This goes a long way in explaining the fluid nature of allusions since they are constantly redefined and presented in various contexts, either as weird or committed, as dull or creative.

Certainly, allusions themselves exist as a distinct category in post-Soviet media. Evidently, the classical allusion is a vehicle for critical commentary and proprietary attitude toward the discourse exhibited by journalists. The key problem here is related to the idea of authenticity, the way that traditions are used and manipulated by various groups and persons seeking authority and symbolic control of a particular audience. Allusions continually being remade or renegotiated in communicative praxis allow for facilitation in the creation of a community identity.

The discussion of cultural identity is quite pertinent in my book as it demonstrates a rather fundamental function of allusion—to form a community. One of the new aspects of cultural identity for the Russian reader is religious identity. The extent of attraction of religion for Russians seems to be related either to the mystical knowledge, or to the social value of the Eastern Orthodox Church, or to spiritual experience. Whichever aspect of the religious identity is intended, it finds a manifestation in media discourse through allusions.

I explored the inclusion of religious, more often biblical, allusion in secular media discourse. Apparently, many politicians and journalists are religious and articulate their religious convictions openly in the public discourse they produce. I observed different types of reference to overall content or to meta-language in biblical sources with a wide variety of overtones: from ironic treatments of allusions as moralism, to moralism of allusions offered straight. What is intriguing is that biblical allusions appear not only in Orthodox media (e.g., *Neskuchnyi Sad*) or in communist media (e.g., *Zavtra*), but also in the state-run secular outlets, which, in general, are not suited for a pluralistic society. There are different ways to interpret these observations. These results can be viewed as an important confirmation of religious renaissance (Eastern Orthodoxy, to be precise) or a fetishization of Church authority in the public sphere. Allusions to biblical sources appearing mostly in headlines are viewed as journalists' drive for summarizing information of the article, which may have a disturbing effect on readers. The reader who is unskillful in discerning the context of the alluded phrase, and thereby determining the meaning generated by the allusion, can be led to confusion.

Via discussion of allusions I focus on the dynamics of new cultural and linguistic elements that discursively manifest authors' alignments with some and separation from others. Namely, the current re-reading of classics is taking place amidst debates over political affiliations, religious identities, and choices for new language needed to communicate with the younger generation in matters concerning the nation's future. In the process of immediate and essential creation of self and other, both groups rely on a common set of allusions known as "cultural tools," but each group deploys them differently, and self-consciously so. Allusions have an important function: they help to identify and support the cultural self by distancing and criticizing the Other. So while recycling the distinct quotations, literary reminiscences, and allusions from classical literature media construct a tolerant reader's reception of the Russian pre-revolutionary past, the legacy of the Soviet period, and the vision of Westernized and business-oriented future. It may seem that media create a platform for addressing the past constructively, in an almost therapeutic sense, and making a conventional inventory in shaping "key scenarios" (Ortner's concept) of collective perception. However, intertextual by the nature texts of media no longer give the readers a clue to a media subject's membership within overlapping cultural and political spheres that reflect on the consequences the fragmentation and disintegration of the society/reality.

Coming to terms with the past is taking place as a new rhetoric emerges. It may come as a shock to realize that in contemporary Russian media discourse communist symbols are widespread, and language reveals different styles reflected in old ideologies. It appears that contemporary media style has much in common with Soviet media language. A subjective mode of treating the event, permeated with the remnants of Soviet signifiers, can potentially become a functional model of working through the past, because it is ironic. My argument is not that this feature is unique, as Russian media has a rich tradition of mixing discourses, but the mass media communication in Russia today, along with its linguistic behavior, demands closer scrutiny as it reflects both an impoverishment as well as an elaboration of Russian as a communicative tool.

In this change of guards the current authors assume an important role not only as readers of the classical traditional discourse, but also as active agents in glossing over versions of the past for their own political purpose and for construction of national integrity according to the social context.

Alluding to classics leads to the reinforcement, redistribution, or leveling of social division. In this process of remembering and evaluating the past, various social groups build their identities on some analogy to, as well as contrast with, alluding prototypes. In line with critical discourse analysis, I explore the use of allusions in terms of discursive strategies of solidarity and distance, merit and blame. It is fascinating to see how allies and antagonists use these classical allusions, and how the old texts are implicated in the current political arguments.

The allusions in the headlines and in the text of Russian mass media articles are considerably more flexible in their range and more subtle in their outcomes than hitherto recognized. This flexibility stems from the inherent qualities of allusion, which in its many tantalizing dimensions, is a kind of linguistic distancing mechanism from an all-too-obvious reality. The findings in this book show how allusions allow for detachment, enabling a journalist to deal with a sensitive and potentially insoluble problem. What can be said with certainty is that the current media language has been taking shape under the influence of postmodern literature that was highly infused with allusions and quotations. At the same time, in search of subtle manipulative language and elaborate persuasive tactics, journalists find allusions as a brief, identifiable tool of verbal reminiscence of an earlier literary work. Finally, allusions, particularly those used in print media, always function as a clue to membership. Consciously or subconsciously, one of the primary means by which readers place a journalist's identity within overlapping cultural and political spheres in an often ambiguous media discourse is by looking at their allusions.

Historically, irony has appeared when political restrictions on expressing oppositional points of view frame the journalistic coverage of the current state of affairs. By making innuendoes and writing indirectly, journalists pass along to the readers the responsibility for drawing conclusions and making sense of the allusive subtext of the articles. Moreover, readers have to draw links between the distinct quotations, literary reminiscences, and tags of popular songs and the politicians' eloquent rhetoric and multifaceted metaphors. Furthermore, journalists' allusions challenge readers and require a high level of literary competence and political sophistication. There is, however, one aspect of allusiveness in media discourse that can almost unambiguously be considered a manipulative tactic. A reader of this type of journalism, apart from being a consumer, is supposed to be able to reach judgments referring to current political affairs and to assume a "sophisticated" or "intellectual" role. The allusion is among those rhetorical devices that are responsible for "packaging" information and having a potential in shaping a persuasive argumentation, especially when they are seen in headlines, and kickers (small headlines over the main headlines), subheads, leads (the beginnings of news stories), pull quotes (quotes that are blown up in size for emphasis), and concluding statements or paragraphs of articles. The allusions in the headlines and in the text of Russian mass media articles are considerably more flexible in their range and more subtle in their outcomes than hitherto recognized. This flexibility stems from their inherent qualities of linguistic distancing mechanisms. To a certain extent, the current media language has been taking shape under the influence of postmodern methods of reflecting the reality. Though in Russian post-modernism references to and re-cycling of the allusions and quotations allow public thinkers to build up an explosive overproduction of meaning in an utterance. However, intertextual by the nature texts of media no longer give the readers a clue to a media subject's membership within overlapping cultural and political spheres that reflect on the consequences the fragmentation and disintegration of the society.

The very fact of multifaceted and ambiguous use of classical allusions in media displays their relevance not only as incisive comments on the political agenda or a sign of utilitarian interest in bringing the classics back to the readership. One of the functions of the allusions in media discourse is to create myths (in the Barthian sense) that construct a notion of continuity and bridge the gap between the past and present Russia. We are, therefore, faced with a great semiological system—a purposeful mixture of a past, a memory, and a comparative order of facts, ideas, and decisions.[10]

The most influential journalists invested into creating the cultural community based on the symbols of the past that acquire new expanding meanings. So while recycling allusions from classical literature media practitioners construct a tolerant readers' reception of the Russian pre-revolutionary past, the legacy of the Soviet period and the vision of Westernized and business-oriented future. This means that media tend to create a platform for addressing the past constructively, in an almost therapeutic sense, and reiterated allusions are conventional inventory in shaping "key scenarios" (Ortner's concept)[11] of collective perception. There is, however, one aspect of allusiveness in media discourse that unambiguously can be considered a manipulative tactic. The use of classical allusions in the journalistic texts creates a fictional mode of treating the events. As a result, the important part of the media discourse is fictionalizing the social reality, and it does so by ironically deconstructing the past. Today there is no shortage of alternative media as well as sources of non-government information, but with the readership generally indifferent and apathetic in a fragmented digital landscape, media remain ineffective in the quest to form the community and preserve cultural identity.

NOTES

1. This point is noted in Thomas Seifrid, *The Word Made Self* (Ithaca, NY: Cornell University Press, 2005).

2. J. Brooks, *Thank You, Comrade Stalin! Soviet Public Culture from Revolution to Cold War* (Princeton, NJ: Princeton University Press, 2001), 246–47.

3. Victor Turner, *The Feasts of Symbols* (Ithaca, NY: Cornell University Press, 1967).

4. Evgeny Dobrenko, *The Making of the State Reader: Social and Aesthetic Contexts of the Reception of Soviet Literature* (Stanford, CA: Stanford University Press, 1997).

5. Petr Vail' and Aleksands Genis, "Rodnaia rech': Uroki iziashchnoi slovesnosti," in *Sobraniie sochinenii v dvukh tomakh*, vol. 1 (Yekaterinburg: U-Faktoriia, 2003), 7–8.

6. Catriona Kelly, *Children's World: Growing Up in Russia, 1890–1991* (New Haven, CT: Yale University Press, 2008), 7; Kelly, *Refining Russia: Advice Literature, Polite Culture, and Gender from Catherine to Yeltsin* (Oxford: Oxford University Press, 2001).

7. W. Iser, *The Act of Reading: A Theory of Aesthetic Response* (Baltimore: Johns Hopkins University Press, 1978).

8. Linda Hutcheon, *The Politics of Postmodernism* (New York: Routledge, 1989).

9. Ibid., 94.

10. Roland Barthes, *La Chambre claire, Note sur la photographie* (Paris: Seuil, 1980).

11. Sherry B. Ortner, "On Key Symbols," in *Reader in Comparative Religion: An Anthropological Approach,* ed. W. A. Lessa, E. Z. Vogt, and J. M. Watanabe (New York: Harper and Row, 1979), 92–98. Ortner identifies as key symbols such things as symbolic forms of expressions and clear-cut modes of action appropriate to correct and successful living in the culture that are dramatized for all to see.

Bibliography

Albats, Evgenia. "Citizen and Poet." *New Times,* December 26, 2011. http://newtimes.ru/articles/detail/48395/.

Anderson, Benedict. *Imagined Communities: Reflections on the Origin and Spread of Nationalism.* Rev. and expanded ed. London: Verso, 1991.

Arel, D. "Language Politics in Independent Ukraine: Towards One or Two State Languages?" *Nationalities Papers* 23, no. 2 (2002).

Attardo, S. *Humorous Texts: A Semantic and Pragmatic Analysis.* Berlin, NY: Mouton de Gruyter, 2001.

Averintsev, S. S. "Bakhtin i russkoe otnoshenie k smekhu." In *Ot mifa k literature: Sbornik v chest' semidesiatipiatiletiia Eleazara Moiseevicha Meletinskogo*, compiled by S. Iu. Nekliudov and E. S. Novik. Moscow: Rossiiskii universitet, 1993.

Bakhtin, Mikhail. *The Bakhtin Reader: Selected Writings of Bakhtin, Medvedev and Voloshinov.* Edited by Pam Morris. London: Arnold, 2001.

———. *The Dialogic Imagination.* Translated by C. Emerson and M. Holquist. Austin: University of Texas Press, 1981.

———. *Problems of Dostoevsky's Poetics.* Edited and translated by Caryl Emerson. Minneapolis: University of Minnesota Press, 1999.

———. *Speech Genres and Other Late Essays.* Edited by C. Emerson and M. Holquist. Translated by V. McGee. Austin: University of Texas Press, 1986.

Balmforth, Tom. "Russians Turning Away from State TV to Internet for News." *Telegraph,* June 12, 2012.

Baranov, A. N., and Yu. N. Karaulov. *Russkaia politicheskaia metafora (materialy k slovaru).* Moscow: Pomovskii i partner, 1991.

Barthes, Roland. *La Chambre Claire, Note sur la photographie.* Paris: Seuil, 1980.

Bauman, R. "Transformations of the Word in the Production of Mexican Festival Drama." In *Natural Histories of Discourse*, edited by M. Seiverstein and G. Urban. London: University of Chicago Press, 1996.

Beckett, Sandra L. *Recycling Red Riding Hood.* Florence, KY: Routledge, 2002.

Belyaev, Demyan. "'Heterodox Religiousness' in Today's Russia: Results of an Empirical Study." *Social Compass* 58 (2011). http://scp.sagepub.com/content/58/3/353.

Berdiaev, Nikolai A. *The Russian Revolution.* Ann Arbor: University of Michigan Press, 1971 [1931].

Bergson, Henri. "Laughter." In *Comedy.* New York: Doubleday, 1956.

Bethea, David M. *The Pushkin Handbook.* Madison: University of Wisconsin Press, 2005.

Beumers, B., S. Hutcheson, and N. Ryulova. *The Post-Soviet Russian Media: Change and Conflicting Messages.* New York: Routledge, 2008.

Beumers, Birgit, Stephen Hutchings, and Natalia Rulyova. *Globalisation, Freedom and the Media after Communism: The Past as Future*. London: Routledge, 2012.

———. *Post-Soviet Russian Media Conflicting Signals Exemplifies Such Treatment*. New York: Routledge, 2008.

Bourdieu, Pierre. *Language and Symbolic Power*. Cambridge, MA: Harvard University Press, 1991.

———. *Outline of a Theory of Practice*. Cambridge: Cambridge University Press, 1977.

———. "Structures, Habitus, Practices." In *The Logic of Practice*. Stanford, CA: Stanford University Press.

Boyer, Dominic, and Alexei Yurchak. "American Stiob: Or, What Late-Socialist Aesthetics of Parody Reveal about Contemporary Political Culture in the West." *Cultural Anthropology* 25, no. 2 (2010): 179–221.

Boym, Svetlana. *Common Places: Mythologies of Everyday Life*. Cambridge, MA: Harvard University Press, 1994.

———. *Death in Quotation Marks: The Cultural Myth of the Modern Poet*. Cambridge, MA: Harvard University Press, 1991.

Brooks, Jeffrey. "Official Xenophobia and Popular Cosmopolitanism in Early Soviet Russia." *American Historical Review* 97, no. 5 (December 1992).

———. "Socialist Realism in *Pravda*: Read All about It!" *Slavic Review* 53, no. 4 (Winter 1994).

———. *Thank You, Comrade Stalin! Soviet Public Culture from Revolution to Cold War*. Princeton, NJ: Princeton University Press, 2001.

Callaghan, K., and F. Schnell. "Assessing the Democratic Debate: How the News Media Frame Elite Policy Discourse." *Political Communication* 18 (2001): 183–212.

Chekrygin, O. "Otdaite den'gi detiam, chtoby oni rodilis'." *Novaya Gazeta*, January 30, 2003. http://2003.novayagazeta.ru/nomer/2003/39n/n39n-s01.shtml.

Condee, Nancy. "Tales Told by Nationalists." In *Soviet and Post-Soviet Identities*. Cambridge: Cambridge University Press, 2012.

DeBlasio, Alyssa. *Between Philosophies: The Emergence of a New Intellectual Paradigm in Russia*. PhD diss., University of Pittsburgh, 2010.

———. "Writing the History of Russian Philosophy." *Studies in East European Thought* 63 (2011): 203–26.

Denning, Michael. *The Cultural Front: The Laboring of American Culture in the Twentieth Century*. London: Verso, 1997.

Diliguenski, Guerman, and Sergei Chugrov. "'The West' in Russian Mentality." Office for Information and Press, Brussels and Institute of World Economy and International Relations, Moscow, 2000. www.nato.int/acad/fellow/98-00/diliguenski.pdf.

Dobrenko, Evgeny. *The Making of the State Reader: Social and Aesthetic Contexts of the Reception of Soviet Literature*. Stanford, CA: Stanford University Press, 1997.

———. *Metafora vlasti: Literatura stalinskoi epokhi v istoricheskom osveshchenii*. Munich: Otto Sagner, 1993.

———. "Total'naia lingvistika: Vlast' grammatiki i grammatika vlasti." *Russian Literature* 63 (2008): 533–621.

Dragunski, V. "Obshchestvo zelenykh naslazhdenii i drugie obshchestva." *Novoe Vremia*, nos. 1–2 (2003).

Dubin, B., and N. Zorkaia, *Chtenie v Rossii—2008: Tendentsii i problemy*. Moscow: Mezhregionalnyi tsentr bibliotechnogo sotrudnichestva, 2008.

Dulicenko, A., and W. Lehfeldt. *Russkii iazyk kontsa XX stoletiia*. Munich: Otto Sagner, 1994.

Earle, Jonathan. "Journalists Toe Fine Line with Opposition Politics." *St. Petersburg Times*, March 28, 2012. www.sptimes.ru/story/35373.

Epstein, Mikhail. *Relativistic Patterns in Totalitarian Thinking: An Inquiry into the Language of Soviet Ideology*. Kennan Institute for Advanced Russian Studies Occasional Paper, 243. Washington, DC: Woodrow Wilson International Center for Scholars, 1991.

Etling, B., K. Alexanyan, J. Kelly, R. Faris, J. Palfrey, and U. Gasser. *Public Discourse in the Russian Blogosphere: Mapping RuNet Politics and Mobilization*. Cambridge, MA: Berkman

Center for Internet and Society, Harvard University, 2010. http://cyber.law.harvard.edu/sites/cyber.law.harvard.edu/files/Public_Discourse_in_the_Russian_Blogosphere_2010.pdf.

Evans, Richard. *In Defense of History*. New York: W. W. Norton, 1999.

Fairclough, Norman. "Conversationalization of Public Discourse and the Authority of the Consumer." In *The Authority of the Consumer*, edited by Russel Keat, Nigel Whiteley, and Nicholas Aberchombie, 253–68. New York: Routledge, 1994.

———. *Critical Discourse Analysis: The Critical Study of Language*. New York: Longman, 1995.

———. *Discourse and Social Change*. Cambridge, UK, and Cambridge, MA: Polity Press, 1992.

———. *Language and Globalization*. London and New York: Routledge, 2006.

———. *Language and Power*. London: Longman, 1998.

Fairclough, Norman, and Ruth Wodac. "Critical Discourse Analysis." In *Discourse as Social Interaction,* edited by T. van Dijk, 258–84. London: Sage, 1997.

Fateyeva, N. A. *Kontrapunkt intertekstualnosti, ili intertekst v mire tekstov*. Moscow: AGAR, 2000.

Fegan, Geraldine. *Believing in Russia: Religious Policy after Communism*. London: Routledge, 2013.

Ferm, Ludmila. "Osobennosti razvitiia russkoi leksiki v noveishii period (na materiale gazet)." Uppsala, Acta Universitatis Upsaliensis. *Studia Slavica Upsaliensia* 33 (1994).

Ferree, Myra Marx, et al. *Shaping Abortion Discourse Democracy and the Public Sphere in Germany and the United States*. Cambridge: Cambridge University Press, 2002.

Fileva, T. "Komu—'Tatory,' komu—'Liatory,' a komu i natsproekt." www.orel-news.ru/index.php?main=showorelnews&id=6773.

Fish, S. "Literature in the Reader." In *Reader Response Criticism*, edited by Jane P. Tompkins. Baltimore: Johns Hopkins University Press, 1980.

Fishman, J. A. "Reversing Language Shift." In *Can Threatened Languages Be Saved?*, edited by Joshua A. Fishman. Clevedon, UK: Multilingual Matters, 2001.

Fitzpatrick, Sheila. *The Cultural Front: Power and Culture in Revolutionary Russia*. Ithaca, NY: Cornell University Press, 1992.

———. "The World of Ostap Bender: Soviet Confidence Men in the Stalin Period." *Slavic Review* 61, no. 3 (Autumn 2002): 535–57.

Fossato, Floriana. "The Russina Media: From Popularity to Distrust." *Current History* 100 (2001).

Foucault, Michel. *The Archaeology of Knowledge and the Discourse on Language*. New York: Pantheon, 1972.

Freud, Sigmund. *Jokes and Their Relation to the Unconscious*. Translated by James Strachey. New York: W. W. Norton, 1960.

Friedlander, Saul, ed. *Probing the Limits of Representation Nazism and the Final Solution*. Cambridge, MA: Harvard University Press, 1992.

Gamson, W. A., and A. Modigliani. "Media Discourse and Public Opinion on Nuclear Power: A Constructivist Approach." *American Journal of Sociology* 1 (1989): 1–37.

Ganapolsky Matvey Ianvar'—dostat' chernil I plakat'. Moskovskii Komsomolets, no. 25840 (January 12, 2012). www.mk.ru/politics/article/2012/01/11/659680-yanvar-dostat-chernil-i-plakat.html.

Geldern, James van. "Cultural and Social Geography in the Mass Culture of the 1930s." In *New Directions in Soviet History*, edited by Stephen White. New York: Cambridge University Press, 1992.

Gibian, George. "How Russian Proverbs Present the Russian National Character." In *Russianness: Studies on a Nation's Identity in Honor of Rufus Mathewson*, edited by Robert L. Belknap, 38–43. Ann Arbor, MI: Ardis, 1990.

Goffman, E. *Framing Analysis: An Essay on the Organization of Experience*. New York: Harper & Row, 1974.

Gogol, Nikolai. "Mertvye dushi." In *Izbrannye sochinenia v dvukh tomakh*, vol. 2. Moscow: Khudozhestvennaia literatura, 1984.

Golomstock, Igor. *Totalitarian Art in the Soviet Union, the Third Reich, Fascist Italy and the People's Republic of China*. New York: HarperCollins, 1990.

Golts, A. "Smerdyakovshchina, Ezhenedelnyi Zhurnal." *Ezhenedelnyi zhurnal*, June 9, 2012. www.ej.ru/?a=note&id=11850.

Gorham, Michael. "Language the Economies of Mat." In *Post-Soviet Russia: Culture and Identity*, 237–54. Cambridge: Cambridge University Press, 2012.

Grice, H. P. "Logic and Conversation." In *Syntax and Semantics: Speech Acts*, edited by P. Cole and J. Morgan, 3:41–58. New York: Academic Press, 1975.

Gross, P. *Entangled Evolutions: The Media and Democratization in Eastern Europe*. Washington, DC: Woodrow Wilson Center Press/Johns Hopkins University Press, 2002.

Habermas, J. *The Structural Transformation of the Public Sphere: An Inquiry into a Category of Bourgeois Society*. Cambridge, MA: MIT Press, 1991.

Haiman, John. *Talk Is Cheap: Sarcasm, Alienation, and the Evolution of Language*. Oxford: Oxford University Press, 1998.

Halbwachs, Maurice. *On Collective Memory*. Translated and edited by Lewis Coser. Chicago: University of Chicago Press, 1992.

Hall, S. "Cultural Studies and Its Theoretical Legacies." In *Cultural Studies*, edited by L. Grossberg, C. Nelson, and P. Treichler, 277–94. New York: Routledge, 1923.

———. "Culture, the Media and the 'Ideological Effect.'" In *Mass Communication and Society*, edited by J. Curran, M. Gurevitch, and J. Woollacott, 315–48. London: Edward Arnold, 1977.

Hoggart, R. *The Uses of Literacy*. Piscataway, NJ: Transaction Publishers, 1998.

Hutcheon, Linda. *The Politics of Postmodernism*. New York: Routledge, 1989.

Idov, Michael. "New Decembrists." *New York Magazine*, January 2012. http://nymag.com/news/features/russian-revolutionaries-2012-1/.

Ilyin, Ivan A. *Sobranie sochinenii v 10 tomakh*. Edited by Iuri Lisitsa. Moscow: Russkaia Kniga, 1993–1999.

Ioffe, Julia. "What Is Russia Today?" *Columbia Journalism Review*, September/October 2010.

Iser, W. *The Act of Reading: A Theory of Aesthetic Response*. Baltimore: Johns Hopkins University Press, 1978.

Itkonen, Esa. *Universal History of Linguistics*. Amsterdam: Benjamins, 1991.

Iyengar, S., and D. R. Kinder. *News That Matters*. Chicago: University of Chicago Press, 1987.

Kaftan, L. "Ia tebia porodil, ia tebia i pristroiu." *Komsomolskaia Pravda*, June 5, 2003. Accessed June 5 2003. http://komsomolka.com/daily/23046/4188/.

Kahneman, D., and A. Tversky. "Choices, Values, and Frames." *American Psychologist* 39 (1984).

Kakorina, E. V. *Transformatsiia leksicheskoi semantiki i sochetaemosti (na materiale iazyka gazet): Russkii iazyk kontsa XX stoletiia (1985–1995)*. Moscow: Iazyki russkoi kul'tury, 1996.

Kelly, Catriona. *Children's World: Growing Up in Russia, 1890–1991*. New Haven, CT: Yale University Press, 2008.

———. *Refining Russia: Advice Literature, Polite Culture, and Gender from Catherine to Yeltsin*. Oxford: Oxford University Press, 2001.

Kharms, D. *Gorlo bredit britvoiu: Sluchai, rasskazy, dnevnikovye zapisi*. Riga: Glagol, 1991.

Khodnev, Sergei. "Kak nam obustroit' Rossiu." *Kommersant*, April 15, 2005.

Kierkegaard, S. *The Concept of Irony*. Translated by M. Lee. Princeton, NJ: Princeton University Press, 1965.

Kiriya, Ilya. "The Culture of Subversion and Russian Media Landscape." *International Journal of Communication* 6 (2012): 446–66. http://ijoc.org/ojs/index.php/ijoc/article/viewFile/1196/713.

Kishkovsky, Sophia. "In Russian Chill, Waiting Hours for Touch of the Holy." *New York Times*, November 23, 2011.

Klemperer, Victor. *The Language of the Third Reich: A Philologist's Notebook*. Translated by Martin Brady. London: Continuum, 2002.

Klimtsev, V. "Svoi liudi sochtutsia." *Trudovaia Rossia* 3 (2006).

Klugman, Jeffrey. *The New Soviet Elite: How They Think and What They Want*. New York: Praeger, 1989.

Koltsova, Olessia. "News Production in Contemporary Russia." *European Journal of Communication* 16, no. 3 (September 2001): 315–335.

———. *News Production and Power in Post-Soviet Russia*. London and New York: Routledge Curzon, 2006.

Kon, Igor. "Moral Culture: Public Morality and Private Responsibility." http://cdclv.unlv.edu//archives/nc1/kon_moral.html.

Kormina, J. "Pilgrims, Priest and Local Religion in Contemporary Russia: Contested Religious Discourses." *Folklore* 28 (2004): 31–33. www.folklore.ee/Folklore/vol28/pilgrims.pdf.

Kostomarov, V. G. *Iazykovyi vkus epokhi: Iz nabliudenii nad rechevoi praktikoi mass-media*. Moscow: Pedagogika, 1994.

Kristeva, Julia. *Desire in Language: A Semiotic Approach to Literature and Art*. New York: Columbia University Press, 1980.

Kulyk, Volodymyr. *Dyskurs ukrains'kykh medii: Identychnosti, ideolohii, vladni stosunky*. Kiev: Krytyka. 2010.

———. "Ideologies of Language Use in Post-Soviet Ukrainian Media." *International Journal of the Sociology of Language* 201 (2010).

———. "Language in Times of Transition: An Introduction." *International Journal of the Sociology of Language* 201 (2010).

Kuzio, T. *Ukraine: State and Nation Building*. London and New York: Routledge, 1998.

Laada, Bilaniuk. "Language in the Balance: The Politics of Non-accommodation on Bilingual Ukrainian-Russian Television Shows." *International Journal of the Sociology of Language* 201 (2010).

Lakoff, G., and M. Johnson. *Metaphors We Live By*. Chicago: Chicago University Press, 1980.

Lekmanov, Oleg. "Russkie modernisty—'soavtory' zagolovkov moskovskikh gazet (1985–1995)." *Novoe Literaturnoe Obozrenie* 71 (2005). http://magazines.russ.ru/nlo/2005/71/lek35-pr.html.

Lennon, Paul. *Allusions in the Press: An Applied Linguistic Study*. New York: Mouton de Gruyter, 2004.

Leontiev, M. "Byt' derzhavoi voobshce ili ne byt'." *Trud*, November 3, 2006.

Leppihalme, Ritva. *Culture Bumps: An Empirical Approach to the Translation of Allusions*. Clevedon, UK: Multilingual Matters, 1997.

Lessa, William Armand, Evon Z. Vogt, and John M. Watanabe, eds. *Reader in Comparative Religion: An Anthropological Approach*. 4th ed. New York: Harper and Row, 1979.

Levi-Strauss, Claude. *The Savage Mind*. Chicago: University of Chicago Press, 1966.

Likhachev, D. S. "Smekh kak mirovozzrenie." In *Istoricheskaia poetika russkoi literatury: Smekh kak mirovozzrenie i drugie raboty*, 342–403. St. Petersburg: Aleteiia, 1997.

Lipovetsky, Mark. *Charms of the Cynical Reason*. Brighton, MA: Academic Studies Press, 2011.

———. *Russian Postmodernist Fiction: Dialogue with Chaos*. Armonk, NY: M. E. Sharpe, 1999.

———. "Skazkovlast': Tarakanishche." *Novoe Literaturnoe Obozrenie* 45 (2000). www.chukfamily.ru/Kornei/Biblio/lipovetskiy.htm.

Livshits, A. "Golovokruzhenie ot uspekha." *Izvestia*, April 9, 2008. http://izvestia.ru/news/335298.

Loseff, Lev. *On the Beneficence of Censorship: Aesopian Language in Modern Russian Literature*. Translated by Jane Bobko. Munich: Otto Sagner, 1984.

Lotman, Yu. M. *Universe of the Mind: A Semiotic Theory of Culture*. Translated by A. Shukman. London and New York: Tausis, 1992.

Lotman, Yuri. *Izbrannye stat' i v trekh tomakh. Tom I: Stat' i po semiotike itopologii kul'tury*. Tallinn: Aleksandra, 1992.

Makhun, Serhiy. "'Viyna i myr' u Sevastopoli: V poshukakh mynulogo yake shchezaye." *Dzerkalo Tyzhnia*, July 16, 2010.

Malykhina, S. "Chuzhaia rech' v organizatsii ideologizirovannogo diskursa. Visnyk Kharkivskogo derzhavnogo universitetu.V. 448. Mif I mifopoetika u traditsiynykh suchasnukh formakh kulturno-movnoi svidomosti." Kharkiv, Ukraine, 1999.

———. "Linguistic Aspects of Contemporary Russian Print Media." M.A. diss., University at Albany–State University of New York, Russian Literature and Culture, May 2004.

———. "Rechevye strategii v polemicheskikh zhanrakh sovremennogo nauchnogo diskursa. Visnyk Kharkivskogo derzhavnogo universitetu.V.411. Spadshchyna D. M. Ovsianyko-Kulikovskogo ta suchasna filologiia." Kharkiv, Ukraine, 1998.

Marsh, Rosalind, "The 'New Political Novel' by Right-Wing Writers in Post-Soviet Russia." *Forum für osteuropäische Ideen- und Zeitgeschichte* 14, no. 1 (2011): 159–87. http://opus.bath.ac.uk/23134/1/The_New_Political_Novel.pdf.

Mikhail, Antonov, and Vladimir Pozner. "Segodnia pyshnym tsvetom rastsvela samotsenzura." www.sensusnovus.ru/interview/2012/01/06/12390.html.

Morley, D. "The Nationwide Audience: A Critical Postscript." *Screen Educ.* 39 (1981): 3–14.

Morley, D., and C. Brunsdon. *The Nationwide Television Studies.* London: Routledge, 1999.

Mostova, Yulia. "Vse zmishalosya v domi ukrainskomu." *Dzerkalo Tyzhnia,* July 1–7, 2006.

Muecke, Douglas Colin. "The Communication of Verbal Irony." *Journal of Literary Semantics* 2 (1973): 35–42.

Negt, O. *L'espace public oppositionnel.* Paris: Payot, 2007

Nekhamkin, Sergey. "Bogdanov i Shvondery." *Izvestia*, January 25, 2006.

Neuman, Russell, Marion Just, and Ann Crigler. *Common Knowledge: News and the Construction of Political Meaning.* Chicago: University of Chicago Press, 1992.

Nevinnaia, A. "Pensionerom mozhesh ty ne byt'." *Rossiiskaia Gazeta*, no. 3629 (2004).

Nikolaeva, I. "Vykhozhu odin ya na dorogu: A zachem?" *Trud*, no. 234 (2004).

Novodvorskaia, V. "Oblavnoe pravosudie." *Novoe Vremya* 48 (2000). http://ds.ru/nt/2000/nt0048.htm.

Oates, Sarah. "The Neo-Soviet Model of the Media." *Europe-Asia Studies* 59, no. 8 (2007).

Olick, Jeffrey K. *The Politics of Regret: On Collective Memory and Historical Responsibility.* London: Routledge, 2007 .

Ortner, Sherry B. "On Key Symbols." In *Soviet and Post-Soviet Russia: Ideology, Consumption and Competition*, 321–40. Cambridge: Cambridge University Press, 2012.

Oushakine, Serguei. "The Terrifying Mimicry of Samizdat." *Public Culture* 13, no. 2 (2001): 191–214.

Pasco, Allan H. *Allusion: A Literary Graft (Theory/Culture).* Toronto: University of Toronto Press, 1994.

Pasti, Svetlana. "Two Generation of Contemporary Russian Journalists." *European Journal of Communication* 20, no. 1 (2005).

Peters, John Durham. "Media as Conversation, Conversation as Media." In *Media and Cultural Theory*, edited by James Curran and David Morley, 115–26. New York: Routledge, 2006.

Pipes, Richard. *Russian Conservatism and Its Critics: A Study in Political Culture.* New Haven, CT: Yale University Press, 2005.

Plamper, Jan. "Abolishing Ambiguity: Soviet Censorship Practices in the 1930s." *Russian Review* 60, no. 4 (2001): 526–44.

Poe, Marshall. "Moscow, the Third Rome: The Origins and Transformations of a Pivotal Moment." *Jahrbücher für Geschichte Osteuropas* 49, no. 3 (2001): 412–29.

Pomerantz, A. "Agreeing and Disagreeing with Assessments: Some Features of Preferred/Dispreferred Turn Shapes." In *Structures of Social Action: Studies in Conversation Analysis*, edited by J. Atkinson and J. Heritage. Cambridge: Cambridge University Press, 1984.

Prokhanov, A. "Chasha sia." *Zavtra*, February 15, 2012.

Propp, Vladimir. *Problemy komizma i smekha.* 2nd ed. St. Petersburg: Aleteiia, 1997.

Pucci, Joseph Michael. *The Full-Knowing Reader: Allusion and the Power of the Reader in the Western Literary Tradition.* New Haven, CT: Yale University Press, 1998.

Putin, Vladimir. "Rossiia: Natsional'nyi vopros." *Nezavisimaya Gazeta*, January 23, 2012. www.ng.ru/politics/2012-01.

Rakhmanin, Serhii. "Dity pidzemellya." *Dzerkalo Tyzhnia*, August 21–27, 2010.

———. "Ostanniy Prykhystok." *Dzerkalo Tyzhnia*, September 4–10, 2010.

———. "Otsele prinuzhdat' my budem k miru." *Den'*, August 16, 2008.

Remnick, David. "Echo in the Dark." *New Yorker*, September 22, 2008. www.newyorker.com/reporting/2008/09/22/080922fa_fact_remnick.

Rorty, Richard. *The Linguistic Turn*. Chicago: University of Chicago Press, 1967.

Roth, Andrew. "Warriors of the Keyboard." *Russia Profile*, December 14, 2011. http://russiaprofile.org/culture_living/50997.html.

Ryabinska, Natalya. "The Media Market and Media Ownership in Post-Communist Ukraine." *Problems of Post-Communism* 58, no. 6 (November/December 2011).

———. "News Framing in Post-Communist Press: Engagement and Control or Disengagement and Powerlessness?" *Global Media Journal* 1, no. 3 (2007).

Ryazanova-Clarke, Lara. "'The Crystallization of Structures': Linguistic Culture in Putin's Russia." In *Landslide of the Norm: Language Culture in Post-Soviet Russia*, edited by Ingunn Lunde, 31–64. Bergen, Norway: Slavica Bergensia, 2006.

Sakwa, Richard. *The Crisis of Russian Democracy: The Dual State, Factionalism and the Medvedev Succession*. Cambridge: Cambridge University Press, 2011.

Schiffrin, Deborah. *Approach to Discourse: Language as Social Interaction*. Hoboken, NJ: Wiley, 1994.

Searle, J. "Metaphor." In *Pragmatics: A Reader*, edited by S. Davies, 519–39. Oxford: Oxford University Press, 1991.

Seifrid, Thomas. *The Word Made Self*. Ithaca, NY: Cornell University Press, 2005.

Seriot, P. "Dereviannyi iazyk, iazyk drugogo i svoi iazyk: Poiski nastoiiashchei rechi v sotsialisticheskoi Evrope 1980-kh godov." *Politicheskaia lingvistika* 5, no. 25 (2008): 160–67. www.philology.ru/linguistics1/serio-08.htm.

Seton-Watson, H. *Nations and States: An Inquiry into the Origins of Nations and the Politics of Nationalism*. Boulder, CO: Westview Press, 1977.

Shenderovich, V. "Ob al'ternativnoi sluzhbe." *Itogi*, February 18, 2002.

Shoemaker, P. J., and S. D. Reese. *Mediating the Message: Theories of Influences on Mass Media Content*. 2nd ed. White Plains, NY: Longman, 1996.

Smith, A. *Montaging Pushkin: Pushkin and Visions of Modernity in Russian Twentieth-Century Poetry*. Amsterdam/New York: Rodopi, 2006.

Søvik, Margrethe. "Language Practices and the Language Situation in Kharkiv: Examining the Concept of Legitimate Language in Relation to Identification and Utility." *International Journal of the Sociology of Language* 201 (2010).

Stepanov, Yuri. *Intertext, Internet, Intersub"ekt: (k osnovaniiam sravnitel'noi konsteptsiologii)*. St. Petersburg: Neva, 1999.

Tankard, J. "The Empirical Approach to the Study of Media Framing." In *Framing Public Life*, edited by S. Reese, O. Gandy, and A. Grant. London: Lawrence Erlbaum, 2001.

Titunik, I. R. "The Problem of Skaz (Critique and Theory)." *Papers in Slavic Philology* 1 (1977): 276–301.

Tsherbina, Tatyana. "Razocharovannaia strana." *Novoe Vremia* 3 (2005).

Tumashkova, M. "Mobil'niki otobrat'—i po etapu." *Novaya Gazeta* 41 (June 4, 2007). www.novayagazeta.ru/arts/35385.html.

Turner, Victor. *The Feasts of Symbols*. Ithaca, NY: Cornell University Press, 1967.

Urban, Greg A. *Discourse-Centered Approach to Culture: Native South American Myths and Rituals*. Austin: University of Texas Press, 1991.

———. "Entextualization, Replication and Power." In *Natural Histories of Discourse*, edited by M. Seiverstein and G. Urban. Chicago and London: University of Chicago Press, 1996.

Vail', Petr, and Aleksandr Genis. "Rodnaia Rech': Uroki iziashchnoi slovesnosti." In *Sobranie sochinenii v dvukh tomak*, vol. 1. Yekaterinburg: U-Faktoriia, 2003.

Van Dijk, Teun A. "Critical Discourse Analysis." In *Handbook of Discourse Analysis*, edited by D. Tannen, D. Schiffrin, and H. Hamilton, 352–71. Oxford: Blackwell, 2001.

———. "Discourse Semantics and Ideology." *Discourse & Society* 6 (1995).

Vasil'eva, L. "Semeinye pary shchastlivee odinochek." *Komsomolskaya Pravda*, no. 71-t/20 (2006).

Verbitskii, Semen, and Aleksei Pimenov. "I etot lyod tronulsa." *Ezhenedelnyi zhurnal*, no. 39 (2002): 22–23.

Voloshinov, V. N. *Marxism i filosofia iazyka*. Leningrad: Priboy, 1930.

———. *Marxism and the Philosophy of Language*. Translated by Ladislav Matejka and I. R. Titunik. New York: Seminar, 1973.

Wheeler, M. *The Art of Allusion in Victorian Fiction*. New York: Barnes and Noble Books, 1979.

Wilson, D., and D. Sperber. "On Verbal Irony." *Lingua* 87 (1992): 53–76.

Wodac, Ruth. "Populist Discourses: The Rhetoric of Exclusion in Written Genres." *Document Design* 4, no. 2 (2003): 132–48.

Wodak, R., et al. *The Discursive Construction of National Identity*. Edinburgh: Edinburgh University Press, 1999.

Yokoyama, O. "Iconic Manifestation of Interlocutor Distance in Russian." *Journal of Pragmatics* 22 (1994).

Yuarchak, Aleksei. "Gagarin and the Rave Kids: Transforming Power, Identity, and Aesthetics." In *Post-Soviet Nightlife in Consuming Russia: Popular Culture, Sex, and Society Since Gorbachev*, edited by Adele Barker, 76–109. Durham, NC: Duke University Press, 1999.

Yurchak, Alexei. *Everything Was Forever until It Was No More*. Princeton, NJ: Princeton University Press, 2006.

Yurchak, Alexei, and Boyer Dominic. "American Stiob: Or What Late-Socialist Aesthetics of Parody Can Teach Us about Contemporary Political Culture in the West." *Cultural Anthropology* 25, no. 2 (2010).

Zamora, Lois Prakinson. *The Usable Past: The Imagination of History in Recent Fiction of the Americas*. Cambridge: Cambridge University Press, 1997.

Zassoursky, I. *Media and Power in Post-Soviet Russia*. Armonk, NY: M. E. Sharpe, 2004.

Zemskaya, Y. A. "Klishe novoiaza i tsitatsiia v iazike postsovetskogo obshchestva." *Voprosy Iazikoznaniia* 3 (1996): 23–31.

Zhosul, E. "Kadry reshauit vse." September 6, 2012. www.pravmir.ru/elena-zhosul-kadry-reshayut-vse-1/.

Zolotov, A. "You Know It When You See It." February 23, 2012. http://en.rian.ru/andrei_zolotov_blog/.

Index

About the Author

Svitlana Malykhina is lecturer in Russian in the Department of Modern Languages, Literatures, and Cultures at University of Massachusetts Boston.